TH[illegible] CARTIER

Jacques Cartier's voyages of 1534, 1535, and 1541 constitute the first record of European impressions of the St Lawrence region of northeastern North America and its peoples. The *Voyages* are rich in details about almost every aspect of the region's environment and the people who inhabited it.

As Ramsay Cook points out in his introduction, Cartier was more than an explorer; he was also Canada's first ethnographer. His accounts provide a wealth of information about the native people of the region and their relations with each other. Indirectly, he also reveals much about himself and about sixteenth-century European attitudes and beliefs. These memoirs recount not only the French experience with the Iroquois, but also the Iroquois' discovery of the French.

In addition to Cartier's *Voyages*, a slightly amended version of H.P. Biggar's 1924 text, the volume includes a series of letters relating to Cartier and the Sieur de Roberval, who was in command of Cartier on the last voyage. Many of these letters appear here for the first time in English.

Ramsay Cook's introduction, 'Donnacona Discovers Europe,' rereads the documents in the light of recent scholarship as well as from contemporary perspectives in order to understand better the viewpoints of Cartier and the native people with whom he came into contact.

RAMSAY COOK is professor of history at York University and general editor of the *Dictionary of Canadian Biography*. Among his numerous other books is *The Regenerators: Social Criticism in Late Victorian English Canada*, for which he was awarded the Governor General's Award.

Though there are many portraits of Jacques Cartier, none is contemporary. This one is taken from M. de Clugny's *Costumes français depuis Clovis à nos jours* (Paris 1836).

The Voyages of Jacques Cartier

With an introduction by Ramsay Cook

UNIVERSITY OF TORONTO PRESS
Toronto Buffalo London

Toronto Buffalo London
Printed in Canada

ISBN 0-8020-5015-8 (cloth)
ISBN 0-8020-6000-5 (paper)

Printed on acid-free paper

The Voyages of Jacques Cartier and *A Collection of Documents relating to Jacques Cartier and the Sieur de Roberval* were first published as part of the Publications of the Public Archives of Canada in 1924 and in 1930, respectively.

Canadian Cataloguing in Publication Data
Main entry under title:

The Voyages of Jacques Cartier

ISBN 0-8020-5015-8 (bound)
ISBN 0-8020-6000-5 (pbk.)

1. America – Discovery and exploration – French.
2. New France – Discovery and exploration.
3. Indians of North America – Canada.
4. Indians of North America – Languages.
I. Cook, Ramsay, 1931–

FC301.C3C66 1993 971.01'13 C92-095268-2
E133.C3C66 1993

All illustrations reproduced in this book were originally from H.P. Biggar's *Voyages of Jacques Cartier* except for the photographs of the walled town of St Malo and Cartier's manor house at Limoëlou, which were taken by Ramsay Cook.

Publication of this edition has been assisted by the Canada Council and the Ontario Arts Council under their block grant programs.

Contents

Preface

Henry Percival Biggar was an accomplished historian of the earliest period of European exploration and trade in the St Lawrence region. He was born in Carrying Place, Ontario, on 9 August 1872 and educated at the University of Toronto (BA 1894) and at Oxford University (B.Litt. 1899, D.Litt. 1927). Queen's University granted him an LLD in 1924. After Oxford, Biggar joined the staff of the recently established Public Archives of Canada, and in 1905 he was appointed chief archivist for Canada in Europe, a post he held until his death in 1938. His task was to search out and copy documents relating to the early history of Canada, a responsibility that required expert historical knowledge and a firm command of early modern French and English. Biggar's major book, *The Early Trading Companies of New France*, appeared in 1901. Subsequently he edited the *Works of Samuel D. Champlain* in six volumes, published by the Champlain Society between 1922 and 1936, and two collections of documents: *The Precursors of Jacques Cartier* (Ottawa 1911) and *A Collection of Documents relating to Jacques Cartier and the Sieur de Roberval* (Ottawa 1930). *The Voyages of Jacques Cartier* (Ottawa 1924), with its carefully collated texts and informative footnotes, displayed Biggar's talents as an editor and historian to the full.

It is Biggar's translation, with some minor but interesting alterations and corrections, that is published in this new edition. The changes, apart from what appear to be typographical errors and careless proofreading, all relate to usage. Cartier never used the words 'Indian,' 'squaw,' 'chief,' 'tribe,' or 'wigwam.' On those occasions where Biggar used them I have reverted to translations of Cartier's terms: 'sauvaige,' 'homme,' 'gens du pays,' 'femme,' 'peuple,' 'seigneur,' 'maison.' These words better express Cartier's outlook and, in some cases, our own. Since it is Cartier's thought rather than Biggar's that is important here, I believe these small alterations are justified.

Biggar's French version of the *Voyages* has been dropped from this edition, and his notes have been reduced. That seemed a sensible decision since the French version has recently been made available in a splendid new critical edition edited by Michel Bideaux. *Jacques Cartier Relations* (Montréal: Les Presses de l'Université de Montréal 1986) is, appropriately, the first volume in the Bibliothèque du Nouveau Monde. The editor pays deserved homage to Biggar in making very few changes in the edition of 1924. There are also two recent editions in modern French, based on Biggar's edition: Robert Lahaise and Marie Couturier, *Jacques Cartier Voyages en Nouvelle-France* (Montréal: Hurtubise HMH 1977), and Ch. A. Julien, R. Herval, and Th. Beauchesne, *Jacques Cartier Voyages au Canada* (Paris: François Maspero 1981). The standard work on Cartier's geographical discoveries remains W.F. Ganong, *Crucial Maps in the Early Cartography and Placenomenclature of the Atlantic Coast of Canada,* with an introduction by T.E. Layng (Toronto: University of Toronto Press 1964).

Conrad Heidenreich, Olive Dickason, and Joe Brandao all made helpful suggestions about my introduction. John Flinn translated the documents I selected from Biggar's *Collection of Documents relating to Jacques Cartier and the Sieur de Roberval* (except for numbers 8, 12, and 17, which were in English). I wish to thank them all, and also my editors, Gerry Hallowell, Laura Macleod, and Rosemary Shipton.

RAMSAY COOK

Donnacona Discovers Europe: Rereading Jacques Cartier's *Voyages*

> During the year or so that I lived in that country, I took such care in observing all of them, great and small, that even now it seems to me that I have them before my eyes, and I will forever have the idea and image of them in my mind. But their gestures and expressions are so completely different from ours, that it is difficult, I confess, to represent them well by writing or by pictures. To have the pleasure of it, then, you will have to go see and visit them in their own country. 'Yes,' you will say, 'but the plank is very long.' That is true, and so if you do not have a sure foot and a steady eye, and are afraid of stumbling, do not venture down the path.
>
> Jean de Léry, *History of a Voyage to the Land of Brazil, Otherwise Called America* (1578)

> There are, it may be, so many kinds of voices in the world, and none of them *is* without signification.
>
> Therefore if I know not the meaning of the voice, I shall be unto him that speaketh a barbarian. And he that speaketh *shall be* a barbarian unto me.
>
> 1 Corinthians 14: 10–11

I

Jacques Cartier's *Voyages* is the most informative and reliable French description of the northern coast and the St Lawrence region of North America written in the sixteenth century. The report that the Florentine navigator Giovanni Verrazzano composed for the French king, Francis I, describing the 1524 voyage along the coast from the Carolinas to Cape Breton, captures both the changing topography and the different groups of people who lived on the Atlantic seaboard. But it lacks detail and depth. André Thevet, cosmographer to Francis I, wrote two works about 'France antartique' during the second half of the century – though he may never have travelled to the St Lawrence area. His works, *Les Singularitez de la France antartique* (1556) and *La Cosmographie universelle* (1575), relied heavily on Cartier, with whom he was acquainted. He provides some fascinating details not found elsewhere – his description of the snowshoe for example – but his reliability is problematic. If Verrazzano approximated Montaigne's 'plain simple fellow' who did not 'construct false theories,' then Thevet exemplified the 'men of intelligence' who could not 'refrain from altering the facts a little' in order to substantiate their interpretation.[1]

Cartier's observations are frequently detailed and include an impressive range of information about the geography, natural history, and ethnography from Funk Island to the Amerindian settlement at Hochelaga at the foot of the mountain he named Mount Royal. The *Voyages*, for over 450 years, have provided almost the only documentation for the beginning of European contact with this region. They reveal a man with both the virtues of an honest observer and the assumptions and preoccupations of a shrewd Breton navigator. Since he interpreted what he saw, he 'never presents things just as they are' and, especially in his discussion of his relations with the people who lived along the St Lawrence, he 'could twist and disguise [facts] to conform to [his] point of view.' Like all historical documents, Cartier's *Voyages* can be both informative and misleading.[2]

II

The *Voyages* present three immediate problems: their authenticity, their authorship, and the paucity of information about Cartier himself.

First the question of authenticity. No original manuscript exists

1 Laurence C. Wroth, *The Voyages of Giovanni de Verrazzano, 1524–28* (New Haven and London: Yale University Press 1970); Roger Schlesinger and Arthur P. Stabler, eds., *André Thevet's North America: A Sixteenth-Century View* (Kingston and Montreal: McGill-Queen's University Press 1986). See also Frank Lestringant, *Le Huguenot et le Sauvage* (Paris: Aux Amateurs de Livres 1990).

2 The Montaigne quotations are from 'On Cannibals' in Michel Montaigne, *Essays* (London: Penguin Books 1958), 108.

– or at least none has been found – for the texts of any of the three *Voyages*. The report of the first expedition was initially published in Italian in 1565, in English fifteen years later, and finally in French in 1598. A French manuscript discovered in 1865 is thought to be either the original or a copy of it. The original of the second *Voyage* also appears to be lost, though some scholars believe that at least one of the three extant manuscript versions is Cartier's own. To complicate matters, the second *Voyage*, which was the first to be published and appeared as an anonymous book in French in 1545, differs in some respects from each of the three known manuscript editions. Finally, there is the third *Voyage*: it exists only in English in a version compiled by the famous English publicist of overseas expansion, Richard Hakluyt, in 1600. It is incomplete, and no French version has ever been discovered. How much certainty about early Canadian history can such a fragile tripod support?

The issue of authorship, though somewhat less significant, is also tangled. The absence of original manuscripts makes stylistic analysis difficult, though the first two *Voyages* seem to reveal a common author. Both are probably based on a ship's log – now lost – kept during the voyages most likely by the captain, Cartier, himself. Whether he alone or with the aid of an amanuensis or literary editor (the claim once made that Rabelais played this role seems unsustainable) produced the published versions is impossible to ascertain. Since the second, and most important, of the three accounts appeared during Cartier's lifetime, it seems likely that he at least approved it. His nephew – Cartier apparently had no children – Jacques Noël may have approved publication of the third *Voyage*, though the puzzle about the primacy of the Italian edition of the first and the English-only version of the third remains unsolved and probably always will.[3] The problem is really Cartier himself.

Biographical information – apart from what can be gleaned from the *Voyages* – is extremely sparse. Born in St Malo, Brittany, in the year before Columbus encountered America, Cartier probably went to sea at an early age. There is evidence in the *Voyages* that

3 On the status and authorship of the *Voyages* the most authoritative statement is found in the excellent *Jacques Cartier Relations*, édition critique par Michel Bideaux (Montréal: Les Presses de l'Université de Montréal 1986) 9–72.

he had visited both Brazil and Newfoundland before 1534. When and under what auspices cannot be established. It is a safe speculation that growing up in St Malo, a seaport town that was early engaged in the north Atlantic fishery and in overseas trade, Cartier was familiar with news from the New World. He may, for example, have been aware that in 1508 a sea captain, Thomas Aubert, brought seven Amerindians for display in Rouen, an event sufficiently important to receive extended notice in Eusebe's *Chronicon* published in Paris in 1512.[4] In 1528 Catherine des Granches, who had become Cartier's wife in 1520, acted as godmother for 'Catherine de Brézil,' likely a Brazilian aboriginal brought to St Malo by a returning trading expedition.[5] Obviously, then, when Cartier sailed out of St Malo as a full-fledged navigator and captain in 1534 in his quest for riches and a route to Asia, he was quite aware that 'America' and 'Americans' had already been 'discovered.'

Not much else is known about the first European to navigate and chart the St Lawrence River and attempt the first French settlement in the area. His career as a navigator apparently ended after his unsuccessful third trip to North America. Subsequently, he probably devoted his time to trade as a business partner and to the supervision of his estate, 'Limoilou.' That he was a faithful Roman Catholic and an active citizen of St Malo is evident from some scattered references in surviving documents. He had married well and established himself as a successful *bourgeois.* He died on 1 September 1557, having lived to the age of sixty-six, a long life for the time.[6] Though there are several portraits of the sea captain of St Malo, including the thoughtful romantic who appears in François Riis's 1839 painting, only the two-inch figure of a man in conversation with a few soldiers on Pierre Descellier's faded

4 Gilbert Chinard, *L'exotisme américain dans la littérature française au XVIe siècle* (Genève [1941], Stalker Reprints 1970), 6

5 F. Joüon de Longrais, *Jacques Cartier: Documents nouveaux* (Paris 1888), 15–16. Jody Green, 'New Historicism and Its New World Discoveries,' *Yale Journal of Criticism* 4, 2 (spring 1991): 182. This excellent article has much to say about Amerindians in France and about the active role of Amerindians in the contact period, as does Olive Patricia Dickason, 'The Brazilian Connection: A Look at the Origins of French Techniques for Trading with Amerindians,' *Revue française d'histoire d'outre-mer* 71 (1985): 129–46.

6 Marcel Trudel, 'Jacques Cartier,' *Dictionary of Canadian Biography* (DCB), I (Toronto: University of Toronto Press 1966), 170

1546 map is contemporary.[7] The Jacques Cartier who 'discovered' Canada, or at least the St Lawrence, has to be coaxed or conjured out of the pages of the *Voyages*.

The glimpses that can be captured of Cartier suggest a prosperous French renaissance figure. His overseas adventures typified an important aspect of that period, as did his curiosity about the unfamiliar surroundings and people he came upon during his travels. He willingly questioned the authority of ancient writers on the inhabitability of the four corners of the earth, though he did it by citing an ancient favoured during the Renaissance: 'experimentia est rerum magistra,' Aristotle proclaimed, and Cartier approved (36). Even his decision – if it was his – to publish and distribute the story of his second trip to North America was characteristically modern, for Gutenberg's technology and Columbus's news of America nearly coincided. Cartier was a man of his times in other ways, too. Though fully conscious of rising religious dissent, he remained a loyal Catholic opposed to 'wicked heretics and false law-makers' (37). Nor did his experiences in North America – the discovery of other religions – shake his own faith. Indeed, his attitude confirms Lucien Febvre's contention that 'what the discoveries engendered in their [the sixteenth-century explorers'] messianic souls was an old-fashioned, amazing zeal for proselytizing.'[8] Without being especially chauvinistic about it, Cartier assumed that extending the Catholic culture of Christendom would benefit all mankind, moving east to west 'just like the sun' (37).

These beliefs were as yet little affected by the dogmatism of the Counter-Reformation, and even less by any scientific rationalism. Sixteenth-century French Catholicism retained an element of mysticism that refused to distinguish between the natural and the supernatural, between 'the possible and the impossible.'[9] The medieval belief in monstrous races and wild men, founded on Pliny the Senior's *Natural History*, retained some of its hold. There existed in the woods or the wilderness people who ate strange food,

7 Gustave Lanctot, 'Portraits of Jacques Cartier,' *Canadian Geographical Journal* 10, 3 (1935): 149–53; Fernand Braudel, ed., *Le monde de Jacques Cartier* (Montreal: Libre-Expression 1984)

8 Lucien Febvre, *The Problem of Unbelief in the Sixteenth Century: The Religion of Rabelais* (Cambridge, Mass.: Harvard University Press 1982), 458. Marcel Trudel, in his extensive writings about Cartier, seems always to underestimate the religious dimension of the man and the era.

9 Ibid., 442

including human flesh, spoke barbarous tongues if at all, ran about naked or clothed only in animal skins, and defended themselves with clubs and sticks. Sometimes their heads were submerged in their chests; some had only one foot.[10] Cartier showed no scepticism when told of a place 'where the people, possessing no anus, never eat nor digest, but simply make water through the penis ... [and] ... the land of the Picquenyans and ... another country whose inhabitants have only one leg and other marvels too long to relate' (82). Sixteenth-century Frenchmen, Cartier included, like sixteenth-century North Americans, lived in a world permeated by the supernatural: life, death, disease, the weather, prosperity, starvation, good and ill fortune were all explained by it. But that shared belief left much room for difference about the nature of the supernatural.

Nor should the differences between sixteenth-century France and North America in other areas be exaggerated. While some European technology – seagoing ships and firearms most notably – gave Europeans some advantages, the suitability of native technology to North American conditions cannot be doubted.[11] And in both societies, not just France, 'man could neither rationally comprehend nor actively control the world in which he lived.'[12] Moreover, though clothing, food, housing, and other elements of North American material life often seemed primitive to Europeans, the reality of French life was not much different for most people, since malnutrition was widespread and living conditions rudimentary at best. Town labourers earned low wages while the

10 John Block Friedman, *The Monstrous Races in Medieval Art and Thought* (Cambridge, Mass.: Harvard University Press 1981), 26–36. How did Amerindians know about the 'Plinean Races'? Did Europeans simply translate American stories into familiar European terms as they did with birds and animals? This, the usual explanation, is challenged by Edmundo Magàna, in *Anthropos* 80 (1985): 299–303, who argues that Americans believed in similar monsters. See also François-Marc Gagnon, 'L'anthropologie sans tête – Fondement d'une iconographic de l'Indien,' *Recherches amérindiennes au Québec* 11, 4 (1981): 273–80.

11 Nancy O. Lurie, 'The Indian Cultural Adjustment to European Civilization,' in J.M. Smith, *Seventeenth-Century America* (Chapel Hill: University of North Carolina Press 1959), 33–60; Karen O. Kupperman, *Settling with the Indians: The Meeting of English and Indian Cultures in America 1580–1640* (Totowa, NJ: Rowman and Littlefield 1980), 8–106

12 Robert Mandrou, *Introduction to Modern France 1500–1640: An Essay in Historical Psychology* (London: Edward Arnold 1975), 239

peasantry's meagre standard of life fluctuated with the harvest: 'the commonest meal was bread floating in a thin vegetable soup. Fresh meat was eaten rarely, perhaps a dozen times a year by most families.'[13] The dominant emotion of sixteenth-century French men and women, Robert Mandrou argues, was fear, and there is every reason to think that Cartier and his crew brought that emotion with them to the new world. 'Everything combined,' the French historian writes, 'to produce fear: the material conditions of life, the precarious nature of the food supply, the inadequacies of the environment, and above all the intellectual climate. Approximate knowledge was responsible for its own brand of terror, adding to the fear of wolves the fear of werewolves, or men changed into wolves by the hand of the Devil.'[14]

But if, from a distance, it is the many similarities between the French and the North Americans that is striking, that was not the way sixteenth-century men and women saw it. Jacques Cartier, a practical navigator and explorer rather than a zealous missionary or covetous settler, had no doubt that the line between France and Canada, between civilization and savagery, was sharply drawn and that civilization was on the march. 'From what we have been able to learn of these people,' Cartier concluded in his description of the society in which he and his men had lived during the winter of 1535–6, 'I am of opinion that they could easily be moulded in the way one would wish.' The sixteenth-century English translation is even more revealing: instead of 'moulded,' it said 'to bring them to some familiaritie and civilitie' (70).

Cartier's *Voyages* are rich in details about almost every aspect of the eastern North American environment and the people who inhabited it. But these details – these facts – are commented upon and organized into a story that was designed to make North America, and Cartier's actions there, understandable and even commendable to sixteenth-century French readers. That meant filtering the story through the cultural lenses that he and his countrymen wore. He provided an interpretation, a representation of what he saw and experienced on his travels. 'The innocent eye has never

13 J.R. Hale, *Renaissance Europe 1480–1520* (London: Fontana 1971), 19; Fernand Braudel, *The Structures of Everyday Life* (London: Fontana 1988), 133–43; Lucien Febvre, *Life in Renaissance France* (Cambridge, Mass.: Harvard University Press 1977), 27–32

14 Mandrou, *Introduction*, 237

existed,' the anthropologist Peter Mason writes, echoing Montaigne. 'Portrayal always involves at root a degree of betrayal.'[15]

III

Identifying, recognizing the familiar, naming the unfamiliar – places, birds, animals, people – is the challenge of a new land to a stranger. Naming makes the unfamiliar familiar, Europeanizing North American places.[16] Often, but not always, Cartier applied European place names: St John 'since we reached it on the anniversary of the beheading of that saint' (46–7), or 'la baye de Chaleur' because it was found to be 'more temperate than Spain' (22). Local names were adopted, too, when they were provided: Honguedo, Saguenay, even Canada (a region along the St Lawrence stretching from Grosse Ile west beyond Quebec City (43). Flora and fauna were almost always given their French names, and identification was made easier by the similarities of the two environments. On the Ile d'Orléans, where Cartier conducted a careful survey, he saw 'fine trees such as oaks, elms, pines, cedars and other varieties like our own' (51). The method was far from infallible. Looking for European birds sometimes meant finding them even when they were not there. At Hochelaga he listed 'cranes, swans, bustards, geese, ducks, larks, pheasants, partridges, blackbirds, thrushes, turtledoves, goldfinches, canaries, linnets, nightingales, sparrows and other birds, the same as in France.' Bustards were doubtless Canada Geese, while the nocturnal nightingale may have been the song sparrow or one of the varieties of thrush that sing so melodiously in the late evening in the St Lawrence region (57).[17]

Sometimes, as with the beluga whales performing at the mouth of the Saguenay River, no name could be imagined: 'This fish is as large as a porpoise but has no fin. It is very similar to a greyhound about the body and head and is as white as snow, without

15 Peter Mason, *Deconstructing America: Representations of the Other* (London and New York: Routledge 1990), 24. See also François-Marc Gagnon and Denise Petel, *Hommes effarables et bestes sauvaiges* (Montréal: Boréal 1986), 90. For the development of the French intellectual account of the 'sauvage,' mainly in the seventeenth and eighteenth centuries, see Cornelius Jaenen, 'France's America and Amerindians: Image and Reality,' *History of European Ideas* 6, 4 (1985): 405–20.

16 Paul Carter, *The Road to Botany Bay* (London and Boston: Faber and Faber 1987), 1–33

17 Eleanor Cook, a connoisseur of thrush song, suggested the thrush rather than the song sparrow.

a spot upon it' (48). His interpreters, who knew some French, could only supply the local name: *Adhothuys*. The astonishing 'sea horse' that appeared several times was never recognized as a walrus (73). Among the edible fruits and nuts Cartier recorded were figs and almonds – his interpreters even found a native word for fig! (25)

That Cartier attempted to understand the new world through similarities rather than differences is both understandable and, apparently, a characteristic sixteenth-century method.[18] But if, as some historians of the sixteenth century have argued, hearing, touching, and smelling took precedence over seeing, a sense associated with the science of classifying and ordering, then Cartier is an exception.[19] His observations were deliberate, not casual, and his descriptive abilities quite remarkable,[20] as illustrated by his memorable picture of the first step in the extinction of the Great Auk. On Funk Island he saw birds 'whose numbers are so great as to be incredible, unless one has seen them; for although the island is about a league in circumference, it is so exceedingly full of birds that one would think they had been stowed there ... Some of these birds are as large as geese, being black and white with a beak like a crow's. They are always in the water, not being able to fly in the air, inasmuch as they have only small wings about the size of half one's hand, with which however they move as quickly along the water as the other birds fly through the air. And these birds are so fat that it is marvellous. We call them apponats; and our two longboats were laden with them as with stones in less than half an hour. Of these, each of our ships salted four or five casks, not counting those we were able to eat fresh' (4–5). Cartier would return to this Island of Birds to replenish his larder on his second voyage, for he was convinced that nature's bounty was inexhaustible, there for exploitation.[21]

18 Michael T. Ryan, 'Assimilating New Worlds in the Sixteenth and Seventeenth Centuries,' *Comparative Studies in Society and History* 23 (1981): 525–6; Michel Foucault, *The Order of Things* (New York: Vintage Books 1973), 17–45

19 Febvre, *Problem*, 432; Mandrou, *Introduction*, 53–4

20 André Berthiume, *La découverte ambiquë* (Montréal: Pierre Tisseyre 1976), 93; Jean de Léry's *History of a Voyage to the Land of Brazil, Otherwise Called America* (Berkeley, Los Angeles, Oxford: University of California Press 1990), a classic of exploration literature, is also an exception to the Febvre-Mandrou thesis.

21 On his second trip to Funk Island, Cartier remarked: 'The island is so exceedingly full of birds that all the ships of France might load a cargo of them without perceiving that any of them had been removed' (40). The

The critical test of Cartier's representation of what he saw in eastern North America is not his natural history but rather his ethnology. For Cartier was, unwittingly, Canada's first ethnologist, an activity practised long before its invention as a science.[22] Cartier's *Voyages* can usefully be put to the test of a successful ethnographer set by Clifford Geertz: 'Ethnographers need to convince us ... not merely that they themselves have truly been there, but ... had we been there we should have seen what they saw, felt what they felt, concluded what they concluded.'[23] Historians, from Marc Lescarbot in the seventeenth century to Samuel Eliot Morison and Marcel Trudel in the twentieth, have given Cartier almost uniformly high marks by that standard.[24] Cartier's descriptions of the native people he met carry conviction. But the question may fairly be posed: is it necessary to *conclude* what Cartier concluded, even if his description bears the mark of authenticity? That question can best be approached by focusing on the well-known story of Cartier's troubled relationship with Donnacona, 'the lord of

---

last Great Auk was reported in 1844. On Cartier as a naturalist see W.F. Ganong, 'The Identity of Plants and Animals as Mentioned by the Early Voyages to Eastern Canada and Newfoundland,' *Transactions of the Royal Society of Canada*, 1909, section II, 197–221, and Jacques Rousseau, *La botanique canadienne à l'époque de Jacques Cartier* (Montréal: Institut Botanique, Université de Montréal 1937); Gagnon and Petel, *Hommes*, 15–88.

22 Numa Broc, *La géographie de la Renaissance 1420–1620* (Paris: Bibliothèque nationale 1980), where it is said of Renaissance explorers that 'par essence et par vocation, ils seront plus ethnologues que géographes' (80); Margaret Hogden, *Early Anthropology in the Sixteenth and Seventeenth Centuries* (Philadelphia: University of Pennsylvania Press 1964). Michèle Duchet in her *Anthropologie et histoire au siècle des lumières* (Paris: François Maspero 1971), argues that early travellers were not anthropologists in the modern sense because they failed to give up their civilized status 'to become participant-observers' (15). This is an elevated view of modern anthropologists, whose 'science' is effectively questioned in James Clifford, *The Predicament of Culture* (Cambridge, Mass.: Harvard University Press 1988), and by Clifford Geertz in *Work and Lives: The Anthropologist as Author* (Stanford: Stanford University Press 1988).

23 Geertz, *Work*, 16

24 Bruce Trigger's *The Children of Aataentsic: A History of the Huron People to 1660*, 2 vols. (Montreal and London: McGill-Queen's University Press 1976), I, 177–208, and Olive P. Dickason's *The Myth of the Savage* (Edmonton: University of Alberta Press 1984), 163–71, adopt a more sceptical approach to Cartier's evidence.

Canada,' and his two sons Dom Agaya and Taignoagny, always remembering that all the evidence about that relationship is provided by Cartier, a judge on his own case.[25]

Can that same evidence be used to discover the voices and motives of Cartier's protagonists, to tease out a dialogue where too often only a single voice has been heard in the past? It is worth attempting, even if the results must be tentative, even conjectural, since it must be constructed from limited, often obscure, clues.[26] Moreover, it is important to realize that, in attempting to reconstruct the Cartier-Donnacona dialogue, the problem of language and communication is enormous. Naturally, on Cartier's first trip, the language barrier was total and native speech was almost always described as a 'harangue' or a 'sermon.'[27] Yet in his account of his contacts with the local inhabitants he confidently describes actions, motives, and relationships as though communication had been fairly straightforward. But was it? For example, he describes the relationship among Donnacona, Dom Agaya, and Taignoagny as that of a 'father' and his 'sons.' How did Cartier know? The vocabulary compiled on the first voyage does not contain these words (32–4). On his second voyage he had, part of the time, the assistance of the two men he had carried off to France. How much French had they learned? How faithfully did they translate their own language that had developed in the North American context into an imperfectly understood European tongue? Many European concepts, as the missionaries would later discover, had no local

25 For a reconstruction of Amerindian views of European contact, based on sixteenth-century accounts and anthropological work, see Nathan Wachtel, *The Vision of the Vanquished: The Spanish Conquest of Peru through Indian Eyes 1530–1570* (New York: Barnes and Noble 1977). These rich sources are lacking for the sixteenth century in Canada. See Georges Sioui, *Pour une autohistoire amérindienne* (Québec: Les Presses de l'Université Laval 1989). For a brilliant discussion of the problems of documentation for nonliterate cultures see Inga Clendinnen, *Aztecs: An Interpretation* (Cambridge: Cambridge University Press 1991), 277–94. For an interpretation from an Amerindian perspective see Bernard Assiniw, *Histoire des Indiens du Haut et du Bas Canada* (Montréal: Leméac 1974).

26 On the 'conjectural model' and the use of clues see Carlo Ginzburg, 'Morelli, Freud and Sherlock Holmes: Clues and the Scientific Method,' *History Workshop* 9 (spring 1980): 5–36.

27 Cartier used several terms, including 'harangue' (26), 'sermon' (57), and 'prédictation et preschement' (54), all suggesting a hortatory tone, a characteristic of formal Amerindian speech.

equivalents.[28] The opposite was almost certainly true: the lack of European words for important Amerindian concepts. The more extensive vocabulary gathered during the second voyage still amounts to little more than a tourist's elementary phrase book: numbers, body parts, food, basic questions and commands (90–5). Writing of European accounts of contact with native people, Stephen Greenblatt remarks: 'The Europeans and the interpreters themselves translated such fragments as they understood or thought they understood into a coherent story, and they came to believe quite easily that the story was what they actually heard. There could be, and apparently were, murderous results.'[29] The *Voyages* certainly present a fairly coherent story of the Cartier-Donnacona relationship. The more that relationship is examined, however, the more obvious it becomes that it was based on a dialogue of incomprehension, a dialogue in which Donnacona's actions were

28 James Axtell, *The Invasion Within* (New York and Oxford: Oxford University Press 1985), 81–3

29 Stephen J. Greenblatt, *Learning to Curse: Essays in Early Modern Culture* (New York and London: Routledge 1990), 27; see also Stephen Greenblatt, *Marvellous Possessions: The Wonder of the New World* (Chicago: University of Chicago Press 1991), 86–118. For valuable insights into the problem of communications see Lois M. Feister, 'Linguistic Communication between the Dutch and the Indians in New Netherlands, 1609–94,' *Ethnohistory* 20, 1 (winter 1973): 25–38; David Murray, *Forked Tongues Speech: Writing and Representation in North American Indian Texts* (London: Pinter Publishers 1991), 1–48, and Robin Ridington, 'Cultures in Conflict: The Problem of Discourse,' in his *Little Bit Knowing Something* (Vancouver: Douglas and McIntyre 1990), 186–205. Charles Darwin's chapter on the Fuegians, in *The Voyages of the Beagle* (New York: Dutton 1977), is an interesting example of the way sixteenth-century attitudes to aboriginal peoples survived into the nineteenth century, though Darwin did recognize that 'wherever the European has trod, death seems to pursue the aboriginal' (418). Of particular interest is his comment on the problem of communication: 'Although all three could speak and understand, it was singularly difficult to obtain much information from them, concerning the habits of their countrymen: this was partly owing to their apparent difficulty in understanding the simplest alternative. Everyone accustomed to very young children knows how seldom one can get an answer even to so simple a question as whether a thing is black *or* white; the idea of black or white seems alternately to fill their minds. So it is with these Fuegians, and hence it was generally impossible to find out, by cross-questioning, whether one had rightly understood anything which they had asserted' (198). Inga Glendinnen, ' "Fierce and Unnatural Cruelty": Cortés and the Conquest of Mexico,' *Representations* 33 (winter 1991): 65–100

made to speak in European words. It ended, if not in murder, then certainly in tragedy.

IV

Cartier arrived in eastern North America already somewhat familiar with the character of its inhabitants.[30] That doubtless explains the matter-of-fact tone to his description of the scattered groups his expedition came across along the coast of Labrador. In 'the land God gave to Cain' he found a 'wild and savage folk' who painted themselves 'with certain tan colours' – Boethuk hunting seal (10). Before long he realized that these North American people were not all alike: they spoke different languages, practised contrasting lifestyles, and, he eventually realized, warred against one another. From first contact he feared them or at least doubted their trustworthiness, especially if he was outnumbered. He would retain that suspicion and fear even after numerous experiences of welcoming hospitality, though he would tell King Francis I of 'their kindness and peacefulness' (38). When forty or fifty canoe-loads of Micmac in the Bay de Chaleur signalled a desire to trade with a French party in one longboat, Cartier 'did not care to trust to their signs.' When they persisted, he drove them off with gunfire (20). French security and potential dominance was established.

This meeting also suggests that Cartier and his party may not have been the first Europeans whom the local native people had met. They wanted to trade and showed no fear. In fact, by 1534, trade between Europeans – Bretons, Basques, English, and other people who lived and fished on the Atlantic seaboard – had a history of several decades, possibly beginning before Columbus.[31] Cartier provides the first detailed description of the ceremonials surrounding trade when the people he had previously driven off returned on 7 July, 'making signs to us that they had come to barter.' Cartier had brought well-chosen trade goods: 'knives, and other iron goods, and a red cap to give their chief.' The first ex-

30 Michel Mollat, *Les explorateurs du XIIIe au XVIe siècles: Premiers regards sur des mondes nouveaux* (Paris: J.C. Lattès 1984), 184–5

31 David Beers Quinn, *England and the Discovery of America 1481–1620* (New York: Oxford University Press 1974), chap. 1, and James Axtell, 'At the Water's Edge: Trading in the Sixteenth Century,' in his *After Columbus* (New York: Oxford University Press 1988), 144–81; John Dickenson, 'Les précurseurs de Jacques Cartier,' in Braudel, *Le monde*, 127–48

change was brisk, the natives leaving stripped even of the furs that covered their bodies. Three days later, amid ceremonial gift exchanges, dancing and singing, business resumed. The young women hung back, suggesting earlier experiences with European sailors. Cartier watched these events with a careful eye, concluding that 'we perceived that they are a people who would be easy to convert' (22). This was not an immediate goal, but rather a thought for the future. It was an indication that from the outset the French were fishers of men as well as 'explorers,' and that Cartier saw no reason to accept these 'savages' on their own terms.

At Gaspé Harbour, later in July, Cartier made his first contact with members of the native community to which his future in Canada would be inextricably tied. These were people from Stadacona – Laurentian Iroquoians – making their annual fishing expedition to the east coast. Cartier's reports are the only record of these people who 'disappeared,' probably as a result of warfare and perhaps disease, by the end of the century.[32] His first impression of the Stadaconans is important because it illustrates Cartier's powers of observation again, and also provides a clear insight into his use of the term 'sauvaiges.' He wrote: 'This people may well be called savage; for they are the sorriest folk there can be in the world, and the whole lot of them had not anything above the value of five sous, their canoes and fishingnets excepted. They go quite naked, except for a small skin, with which they cover their privy parts, and for a few old skins which they throw over their shoulders. They are not at all of the same race or language as the first we met. They have their heads shaved all around in circles, except for a tuft on the top of the head, which they leave long like a horse's tail. This they do up upon their heads and tie in a knot with leather thongs. They have no other dwelling but their canoes, which they turn upside down and sleep on the ground underneath. They eat their meat almost raw, only warming it a little on the coals; and the same with their fish ... They never eat anything that has a taste of salt in it. They are wonderful thieves and steal everything they can carry off' (24–6).

For Cartier the word 'sauvaiges' was interchangeable with 'gens,' 'personnes,' 'peuple,' 'hommes du pays,' 'hommes,' 'femmes' – he never used 'Indiens.' This usage suggests that Cartier accepted the

32 Bruce G. Trigger, ed., *Handbook of North American Indians, vol. 15: Northeast* (Washington: Smithsonian Institution 1978), 357–61

Amerindians as human, like himself – a matter much disputed in the aftermath of Columbus's initial encounter with the people in America.[33] That impression is supported by Cartier's belief that the inhabitants of the St Lawrence region could be converted to Christianity; had they not been 'men,' that potential would have been denied. But still they were 'savages,' which apparently meant poverty stricken, lacking in worldly possessions and civic institutions, bereft of religion and culture. (They certainly fulfilled Montaigne's definition: 'we all call barbarous anything that is contrary to our own habits'!)[34] Because of their 'savage,' 'wild' state, their lack of culture, Cartier believed that native people could easily be 'dompter': subdued, subjugated, tamed,[35] or as Biggar says, 'moulded.' Consequently, while native people were accepted as 'human,' they were only potential, not actual, equals of the Europeans. Only if the 'savage' characteristics that made them different were 'tamed' or 'moulded' could they become actual equals. Different *and* equal was inconceivable.[36] Finally, since these Laurentian people were 'savages' without culture, religion, or government, Cartier, like those European explorers who had preceded him, saw no reason to ask permission to explore and eventually settle their lands.

Nothing better emphasizes Cartier's assumptions about his rights – and Donnacona's reaction – than the drama that was acted out on 24 July 1534 at the entrance to Gaspé Harbour. There Cartier presided over the raising of a thirty-foot wooden cross to which was fixed a coat-of-arms bearing the fleurs-de-lys and a board on which was emblazoned the words: 'VIVE LE ROI DE FRANCE.' In the presence of Donnacona's people, the French 'knelt down with our hands joined, worshipping it before them; and made signs to them, looking up and pointing towards heaven, that by means of this we had our redemption, at which they showed many marks of admiration, at the same time turning and looking at the cross' (26).

33 Anthony Pagden, *The Fall of Natural Man: The American Indian and the Origins of Comparative Anthropology* (Cambridge: Cambridge University Press 1986)

34 Gagnon and Petel, *Hommes*, 91–115; Kupperman, *Settling*, 197–40; Montaigne, *Essays*, 108

35 *Cassell's Concise French-English French Dictionary* (New York: Macmillan 1968), 121

36 Tzvetan Todorov, *The Conquest of America* (New York: Harper and Row 1984), 42

Any 'marks of admiration' Cartier thought he detected were soon erased by a vigorous act of protest by native leaders. Cartier's account of this reaction demonstrates that what was viewed as an arbitrary European intrusion into eastern North America was not passively accepted. The protest was led by the person Cartier identified as 'the leader' and 'three of his sons and his brother.' Even the language barrier did not prevent Cartier from understanding – or thinking he understood – the meaning of the demonstration: 'pointing to the cross he [the leader] made us a long harangue, making the sign of the cross with two of his fingers; and then he pointed to the land all around about, as if he wished to say that all this region belonged to him, and that we ought not to have set up this cross without his permission' (26).

Neither the action of the French, in raising the cross, nor the reaction of the native people is totally unambiguous. Cross-raising, beginning with Columbus, had already become something of a tradition in the Americas. It contained both religious and political symbolism. Cartier had previously raised at least one cross – an undecorated one at St Servan's Harbour in June – and he would raise others later. Some of these crosses were raised unceremoniously and doubtless were intended to function as 'a landmark and guidepost into the harbour' (27). Though Cartier explained the Gaspé cross that way, its bold symbols of church and state, and the accompanying ceremony, surely represented something more. If it was not an explicit legal claim, recognizable in international law, to French possession of this territory, it was surely at least what Trudel calls 'une affirmation solennelle des droits de la France sur cette terre.'[37] This was not an anonymous directional sign; it

37 Marcel Trudel, *Histoire de la Nouvelle-France: Les vaines tentatives* (Montréal: Fides 1963), 82; Brian Slattery, 'French Claims in North America, 1500–54,' *Canadian Historical Review* 59, 2 (June 1978): 139–69, argues convincingly that this act did not represent a legally recognizable claim, but in dismissing the symbolism he is, I think, too literal. Moreover, he underplays the importance of Cartier's remarks in the introduction to the Second *Voyage.* See also Olive P. Dickason, 'Concepts of Sovereignty at a Time of First Contacts,' in L.C. Green and Olive P. Dickason, *The Law of Nations and the New World* (Edmonton: University of Alberta Press 1989), 232. Cartier's action followed the precedent already set by Columbus on 12 October 1492, when he met his first group of 'naked people.' In his brilliant *Columbus* (Oxford and New York: Oxford University Press 1991), Felipe Fernandez-Armesto writes: 'This was not just a description, but a classification. A late fifteenth century reader

distinctly affirmed the French presence. It is also worth emphasizing that in introducing the account of his second voyage, Cartier related his exploration both to the protection and promotion of Catholicism against the threat of 'wicked Lutherans, apostates, and imitators of Mahomet' and to 'these lands of yours,' 'your possessions,' and 'those lands and territories of yours' (38). If, then, the crosses were merely traffic signals, they should at least be described as *French* traffic signals.

And what of the native people's protest? Cartier's interpretation of it as a rejection of the French right to act without permission can be seen, at the least, as a sign of a guilty conscience. Certainly he knew that no European sovereign would accept such an act on his or her territory. But did a North American 'leader,' especially one whose home territory was somewhere up the St Lawrence, have the same sense of sovereign or proprietary rights? Was the chief claiming the Gaspé harbour area as his people's fishing and hunting territory? It seems altogether likely. What is beyond doubt is that a protest did take place, a protest Cartier suspected was an expression of territorial jurisdiction. Moreover, Cartier acted quickly and deceptively to quell the protest.

When the chief – we later learn this was Donnacona[38] – completed his 'harangue,' a sailor offered him an axe in exchange for the black bear skin he was wearing. Responding to the offer of barter, Donnacona's party moved closer to the French ship only to have their canoe boarded and themselves taken prisoner, though Cartier did not use that term. On the second voyage he did, however, refer to them as 'captured' and 'seized' (43). Once on board they were cajoled – 'made to eat and drink and be of good cheer' (was the drink alcoholic?) – into accepting the sign-post explana-

---

would have understood that Columbus was confronting "natural men," not citizens of a civil society possessed of legitimate political institutions of their own. The registering of this perception thus prepared the way for the next step, the ritual appropriation of sovereignty to the Castilian monarchs, with a royal banner streaming and a scribe to record the act of possession' (82). For a fuller exposition of this argument see the same author's *Before Columbus: Exploration and Colonization from the Mediterranean to the Atlantic 1229–1492* (London: Macmillan 1987), 223–45.

38 Marcel Trudel, 'Donnacona,' DCB, I, 275–6. This biography, based on the only existing documentation, Cartier's *Voyages*, accepts unquestioningly Cartier's evaluation of Donnacona's actions.

tion. Cartier then announced that he intended to release only three of the prisoners – compensated with hatchets and knives. The other two, now decked out in shirts, ribbons, and red caps, would be taken 'away with us and afterwards would bring them back again to that harbour' (27). Since no destination was announced, it seems entirely unlikely that the two young men, or their father, understood this to mean an Atlantic crossing and a nine-month stay in France. Cartier made the final departure seem amicable, and perhaps it appeared that way to Donnacona's people who, if they understood what was taking place, probably recognized that resistance was hopeless. Cartier admitted that 'we did not understand the parting harangues,' and there is equally no reason to believe that Donnacona understood what Cartier had tried to tell him. At best the day ended in mutual misunderstanding – hardly the basis for an 'alliance.'[39]

In acting as he did – and the action seemed premeditated – Cartier followed an established European precedent. Europeans assumed a right to 'explore' new-found lands and to set up traffic crosses, indicating at least an intention to return and perhaps even staking a claim to possession. So, too, kidnapping native people began with Columbus, and Cartier may even have committed similar actions on earlier voyages to Brazil. Since at the time of the seizure of the natives Cartier had not determined whether to continue his explorations or to return to France before winter, his initial intention may have been simply to make use of the men as short-term guides (30). More plausible, however, is the view that Cartier planned to take the captives back to St Malo as concrete evidence of 'discovery' and to provide them with language training. With the aid of interpreters and go-betweens, the further penetration of North America, leading to the much sought after route to Asia – Cartier's primary goal – would be expedited. Or so Cartier doubtless hoped.

Exactly how Dom Agaya and Taignoagny, as the young men are identified in the account of the second voyage, spent their time between their arrival in St Malo on 5 September 1534 and their departure for home on 19 May 1535 is unrecorded. Nor is there

39 Trudel, 'Cartier,' 167. There is no documentation for the claim that an 'alliance' was made. Nor is there any evidence that 'Cartier also stated that he wished to take two of Donnacona's sons to France for the winter.' Trigger, *Children*, 182

any direct evidence revealing their reactions to their unexpected discovery of Europe. The harrowing experiences of an eighteenth-century Chinese visitor named John Hu, a man similarly untutored in French language and customs, offer some clues to the complexity of cultural contact: he was driven to such unpredictable behaviour that he was confined to the asylum at Charenton pondering the question, 'Why am I locked up?'[40] The two North Americans survived somewhat better, even though they must often have asked similar questions. They doubtless witnessed many strange and wonderful sights. Yet it seems unlikely that either the standard of living of ordinary Frenchmen – housing, food, or medical care – or the political and religious life of a country wracked with religious strife won their enthusiastic approval.[41] Perhaps they concluded, as Jean de Léry did after returning to France from Brazil, that 'one need not go beyond one's own country, nor as far as America, to see ... monstrous and prodigious things.'[42]

By the time of their return home, they spoke some French, though the level of fluency cannot have been very high. They had learned to dress in the French manner. They may have calculated, and filed for future use, the comparative values of French trade goods, a knowledge that would earn them the epithet of 'rogues' (70). They had not been baptized, though they had observed that ceremony and other Catholic rites (69). To Cartier they may have seemed at least partly 'moulded' or 'tamed,' though he would continue to call them 'sauvaiges.' He apparently believed they were ready and willing to work for him. It was not yet in their interest to disabuse him of that notion. That could wait until they were safely back in Stadacona. Then their actions and attitudes would reveal that they had no wish to go on their foreign travels again.

V

During the winter of 1534–5, Dom Agaya and Taignoagny provided Cartier with much useful information about eastern North America. The French navigator certainly wanted to know whether a route to Asia could be found by continuing westward from the

40 Jonathan Spence, *The Question of Hu* (New York: Knopf 1988), 126. Another suggestive source is Shusaku Endo's stories in *foreign studies* (Seven Oaks, England: Sceptre 1990).

41 Mandrou, *Introduction*, passim

42 De Léry, *History*, 133

mouth of the St Lawrence. Perhaps they encouraged his hopes that a route existed. What he obviously did learn from them was that their home was far inland, up an enormous river at Stadacona, beyond a rich region known as the Saguenay. It was there that they wished to be returned, not to the Gaspé as their father had been promised. Consequently it was from knowledge gained from the two native men, and as a result of their directions, that Cartier was able to attain his principal geographical achievement: 'he was,' Marcel Trudel noted, 'the first to make a survey of the coasts of the St Lawrence ... and, what is most to his credit, in 1535, he discovered the St Lawrence River.'[43] In fact, Cartier himself described what happened somewhat more accurately. On Friday, 13 August 1535, sailing from southwestern Anticosti, 'it was told us by the two savages whom we had captured on our first voyage, that this cape formed part of the land on the south which was an island; and that to the south of it lay the route from Honguendo where we had seized them ... and that two days journey from this cape and island began the kingdom of the Saguenay, on the north shore as one made one's way towards this Canada' (43). Four days later, when Cartier was in some doubt about the route, 'the two savages assured us that this was the way to the mouth of the great river of Hochelaga [St Lawrence] and the route towards Canada ... and that one could make one's way so far up the river that they had never heard of anyone reaching the head of it' (44). Cartier and his crew were the first known Europeans to be guided along the St Lawrence to Stadacona. They then insisted that the guide service be continued further up to Hochelaga. That demand resulted in a crisis in the hitherto satisfactory relationship with Dom Agaya, Taignoagny, and their father.

Not surprisingly, the return of the captives to their people in the Stadacona region was an occasion for great joy. At first the local inhabitants were cautious, even fearful, but once the returning men had identified themselves, the ceremonies and gift exchanges began. On 8 September, near the Ile d'Orléans, 'the lord of Canada' arrived alongside and began a 'harangue,' 'moving his body and his limbs in a marvellous manner as is their custom when showing joy and contentment.' Had Cartier interpreted the body

43 Trudel, 'Cartier,' 171, though earlier Trudel gives some credit to the guides. See also Samuel Eliot Morison, *The European Discovery of America: The Northern Voyages A.D. 500–1600* (New York: Oxford University Press 1971), 395–423.

language correctly? At this happy reunion, Cartier reported that the sons informed their father 'what they had seen in France, and the good treatment meted out to them there.' Donnacona expressed his gratitude with warm embraces for the French leader. Bread and wine were shared before the returning travellers departed with their father (50).

It was not until a week later, during which Dom Agaya and his brother had ample time to discuss their travels in more detail with their father, that Cartier met with them again. He was now impatient to move on, but he detected a marked, disturbing change in the mood of his former companions. Sailing towards Stadacona, Cartier met a large party of native people. 'All came over towards our ships,' he noted, 'except the two men we had brought with us ... who were altogether changed in their attitude and goodwill, and refused to come on board our ships, although many times begged to do so. At this we began somewhat to distrust them.' Cartier's attitude was obviously changing, too. Nevertheless he believed they were willing to guide him to Hochelaga, a place of whose existence they had apparently informed him (52).

During the next five days, until Cartier pushed on up-river without his guides, the issue of the continuing service of Dom Agaya and Taignoagny resulted in an almost total break in relations between the Stadaconans and the St Malouins. The issue in dispute was simple. Cartier believed that his interpreters had promised to continue on with him to Hochelaga. Donnacona and his sons (Taignoagny more consistently, it would seem, than his brother) either did not want the French to continue westward at all or at least not without first making some binding commitment or alliance with the Stadaconans. If it is true, as some have concluded, that Donnacona hoped to prevent Cartier from making contact with other native groups so that Stadacona could control trade between the French and the hinterland, or that Donnacona hoped to enlist French military aid against the Hochelagans, there is nothing in Cartier's account to support these speculations.[44] Nor is it fair to accept Cartier's claim that on their return to Stadacona, Dom Agaya and Taignoagny began to 'intrigue' against him.[45] They had, after all, painfully concrete reasons for distrusting Cartier, and legiti-

44 Trudel, 'Cartier,' 167; Trigger, *Children*, 187–8

45 Trudel, *Histoire*, 110; Cornelius Jaenen, *Friend and Foe: Aspects of French-Amerindian Cultural Contact in the Sixteenth and Seventeenth Centuries* (Toronto: McClelland and Stewart 1973), 13

mate grounds for looking to their own interests in the face of French incursions into their territory. To judge these confusing events – which make it plain that the language barrier had not been effectively breeched – solely from Cartier's perspective implicitly denies the legitimacy of Donnacona's stance. Yet what Cartier viewed as 'treachery,' from Donnacona's point of view was a perfectly reasonable insistence that foreign visitors conduct themselves with due respect for the wishes and customs of their hosts. This is not to argue that the actions of the Stadaconans were so straightforward that Cartier was simply obtuse in failing to understand them. It does have to be remembered that the account of these events is Cartier's and therefore reflects his confusion and suspicion; it does not necessarily represent faithfully the intentions of the other actors whose behaviour may have had a logic of its own. A tentative analysis of a series of events that left Cartier impatient, suspicious, and frightened helps to reveal this logic.

On 16 September Taignoagny informed Cartier that Donnacona was 'annoyed' (53) by the Frenchman's decision to visit Hochelaga and that he would not accompany him. Taignoagny then rejected Cartier's offer of a present – a bribe – in return for disobeying his father. The following day Donnacona appeared, and a ceremony – though Cartier may not have recognized it as such – took place in which the chief presented Cartier with a girl about twelve years old, said to be Donnacona's niece, and two younger boys, one of whom was said to be Taignoagny's brother, though these relationships seem confused. Cartier first understood these gifts as an attempt to convince him to forgo his Hochelaga trip – an apparent bribe. He refused that condition and was then told that the gifts were offered out of friendship and 'in sign of alliance' (54). Cartier attributed these conflicting stories to Taignoagny, 'as well by this as by other bad turns we had seen him do ... was a worthless fellow, who was intent upon nothing but treason and malice' (54). He ignored or disbelieved, or failed to understand, the meaning of a 'sign of alliance.'

It is possible that in order to cement an alliance with the French, Donnacona was proposing a reciprocal gift, an exchange of persons? Cartier was familiar with gift-giving, for he had engaged in it since his first arrival in North America. But he probably did not understand its ceremonial implications in North American native societies, especially that such ceremonies could include the exchange of people.[46] This interpretation is perhaps borne out by the fact that after the Stadaconans failed in what, from Cartier's account, seemed to be a clumsy attempt to invoke the aid of their divinity to frighten the French away from the western trip, a new proposal was advanced. 'Taignoagny and Dom Agaya told the Captain that Donnacona was unwilling that either of them should accompany him to Hochelaga unless he [Cartier] should leave a hostage behind on shore with Donnacona' (56). It is, of course, possible that Donnacona suspected another kidnapping and wanted a hostage. Alternatively, this proposal may have been a misunderstood attempt to explain the reciprocal nature of the gift-exchange treaty ceremony.

Cartier summarily rejected this new proposal, for he had now completely lost confidence in his former interpreters. He would go without them, sweeping Donnacona's objections aside. But the questions remain: Did Cartier misinterpret Donnacona's objections and the proposal he made? Had Donnacona merely been asking Cartier to complete the reciprocal action that had begun when Cartier accepted the children who had been offered as a 'sign of alliance'? If an alliance had been offered and rejected, was it not quite natural for Donnacona's people to suspect that the French expedition to Hochelaga might have results that would be detrimental to the interests of Stadacona? 'In these primitive and archaic societies' – one might prefer the term stateless societies – Marcel Mauss wrote in his *Essai sur le don*, 'there is no middle path. There is either complete trust or mistrust. One lays down one's arms, renounces magic and gives everything away, from casual hospitality to one's daughter or one's property. It was in such conditions that men, despite themselves, learnt to renounce what was theirs and made contracts to give and repay.'[47] Cartier had first refused to lay down arms ('to carry them ... was the custom in France' (53); had then insisted that their magic, not his, should be renounced ('their god Cudouagny was a mere fool ... Jesus would keep them safe' (56); and finally had refused the reciprocal gift

46 See Marshall Sahlins, 'The Spirit of the Gift,' in his *Stone Age Economics* (Chicago: Aldine 1972), 149–84, and also a brilliant application of this idea in Peter Hulme, 'John Smith and Pocahontas,' in his *Colonial Encounters: Europe and the Native Caribbean 1492–1797* (London and New York: Methuen 1986), 147–52.

47 Marcel Mauss, *The Gift: Forms and Functions of Exchange in Archaic Societies* (London: Cohen and West 1954), 80; Trigger, *Children*, 187–90

that would have sealed an alliance, even when the lord of Canada's own niece and son were offered to him (54). Where complete trust might have been established, mistrust, on both sides, resulted.

Unable to understand the framework in which the Stadaconans acted, Cartier was reduced to denunciation, charging his lost allies with ill-will and treason. But the problem was a much deeper one. Cartier had taken Dom Agaya and Taignoagny to France to train them as interpreters so they could act as go-betweens, easing him along his way. On their return to the St Lawrence region armed with their new language skills, they were to act in his interests and aid him in achieving his objectives. In a sense, he expected them to act as Frenchmen. What he failed to comprehend, or accept, was that after a brief nine months of total immersion, Dom Agaya and Taignoagny remained pretty much as they had always been: St Lawrence Iroquoians. Once reunited with their own people, they reverted completely to their own identities and refused to collaborate unconditionally with their former captors.[48] When Cartier learned that what had appeared to be friendship in France had disappeared – a friendship he thought had been affirmed by the welcome he received on his first arrival at Stadacona – he could only explain it by character defects in the native people. They were unreliable, untrustworthy, treacherous rogues – a typical European conclusion.[49] Yet the behaviour that Cartier condemned as 'treason' – a word implying that loyalty was owed to the French – was, by Donnacona's logic, a rejection of that very idea, a rejection of French mastery. The first act of resistance had taken place at Gaspé Harbour. The struggle over Cartier's trip to Hochelaga was but another action in the same drama. Everything was now in place for the dénouement.

VI

Cartier's Hochelaga trip, as he recorded it, stands in marked contrast to the gathering atmosphere of mistrust and confused signals

48 Marie-Christine Gomez-Géraud, 'Taignoagny et Dom Agaya: Portrait de deux truchements,' in Alain Parent, *La renaissance et le nouveau monde* (Québec: Musée de Québec 1984), 52–4. This is perhaps the only article on Cartier that attempts to understand the viewpoint of Donnacona's sons.

49 Hulme, *Colonial*, 163; Karen O. Kupperman, 'English Perceptions of Treachery, 1583–1640: The Case of the American Savages,' *Historical Journal* 20, 2 (1977): 263–87

between the French and the Stadaconans. That contrast is seen in the first contact he made with native people up the river: 'they come towards our boats in as friendly and familiar manner as if we had been natives of the country' (57). Further along Cartier felt the same easy relationship, and at one point allowed a powerful man to carry him ashore 'as if he had been a six-year-old child' (58). There were gift exchanges; one local leader presented Cartier with 'two of his children,' though only the girl, who was eight or nine, was accepted. The culmination of this almost royal progress came at Hochelaga. As the French approached the village on 2 October they were greeted by 'more than a thousand persons, men, women and children, who gave us as good a welcome as ever father gave to his son ... They brought us quantities of fish, and of their bread ... throwing so much of it into our longboats that it seemed to rain bread' (59).

Cartier accepted this treatment as perfectly natural, perhaps even to be expected from people whom he may have assumed were familiar with Europeans. But what he interpreted as signs of familiarity were quite likely just the opposite, as he may gradually have realized. In fact, the character of the reception the French received at Hochelaga bore the marks of a first contact, one in which the native people mistook the French, marshalled in their armour and speaking a strange language, for something other than ordinary men. Women repeatedly brought their children to be touched, and the women showed none of the shyness evident in those earlier trading sessions when their men kept them at a distance. The next day, within the pallisaded village, a remarkable ceremony took place, one in which Cartier found himself in the role of shaman or healer – and accepted his unexpected casting. Cartier and his men were ushered to the centre of the town square and seated on elaborately woven mats. Soon they were joined by the village's leader, carried in on the shoulders of nine or ten strong men. When he took his seat on a deerskin near Cartier, it became obvious that he was severely paralysed and that he expected to be 'cured and healed' by his visitor. Cartier, taking his cue, 'set about rubbing his arms and legs with his hands. Thereupon this *Agouhanna* took the band of cloth he was wearing as a crown and presented it to the Captain.' Then the sick, the lame, the blind, and the aged were brought forward for Cartier to 'lay his hands upon them, so that one would have thought Christ had come down to earth to heal them.' Cartier performed his appointed role in the only style he knew, 'making the sign of the cross over the poor sick people, praying God to give them knowledge of our holy faith' (63–4). So convincing was his interpretation that the local women tried to prevent the French from leaving by offering large quantities of food. Cartier rejected it for it was unsalted, though he was probably anxious to depart before being called for an encore.

Whether Cartier exaggerated these events of the early days of October 1535, and what exactly they meant to the St Lawrence Iroquoians, can only be guessed at. Certainly they were unlike any other ceremony recorded in the *Voyages*. It was obviously not an occasion for commerce, though some gifts were distributed by the French, for the Hochelagans showed none of the frenzied desire to exchange furs for European goods that was displayed at earlier meetings. Instead, the ritual performed in the village square bore the signs of some prophecy being fulfilled with the arrival of otherworldly healers.[50] Cartier's quick intelligence apparently allowed him to interpret the signals accurately. Perhaps it was the realization that his healing powers were at best untested that led to his hasty departure on the following day 'for fear of any misadventure' (66). Even the almost worshipful reception of the Hochelagans had not removed Cartier's distrust of the St Lawrence Iroquoians.

The French undoubtedly contrasted the respectful reception they had received at Hochelaga with what they interpreted as the cagey manoeuvring of Donnacona and his sons. Now they set out to return to Stadacona, convinced there was gold and silver to be found somewhere in the region and apparently under the impression that 'the Canadians and some eight or nine other peoples are subjects' of the Hochelagans. Perhaps this belief stiffened Cartier's determination to deal with Donnacona's people more firmly and, if necessary, harshly. The western trip had done nothing to dispel

50 George R. Hamell, 'Strawberries, Floating Islands, and Rabbit Captains: Mythical Realities and European Contact in the Northeast during the Sixteenth and Seventeenth Centuries,' *Journal of Canadian Studies* 21, 4 (winter 1986–7): 72–4; Christopher L. Miller and George R. Hamell, 'A New Perspective on Indian-White Contact: Cultural Symbols of Colonial Trade,' *Journal of American History* 73, 2 (Sept. 1986): 311–28. Bruce Trigger, in 'Early Native North American Responses to European Contact: Romantic versus Rationalistic Interpretations,' *Journal of American History* 77, 4 (March 1991): 1195–1215, criticizes the 'cultural' interpretation of early contact, though he admits that it may apply to first contacts. His position seems unnecessarily rigid.

his suspicion that even the friendliest of gesture on the part of the leaders at Stadacona only masked treacherous intentions.

VII

Cartier's peremptory departure for Hochelaga on 19 September doubtless left the Stadaconans displeased, suspicious, and perhaps even hostile. When the French party returned a week later they found that the men they had left behind had built themselves a fort 'with artillery pointing every way' (67). Obviously relations had deteriorated further. Still Donnacona issued an almost immediate invitation to visit Stadacona – something Cartier had not done before going to Hochelaga, which may have been another cause for Donnacona's earlier unease. On visiting Stadacona, Cartier received a warm and formal welcome. He attached no particular significance to a display of scalps that Donnacona explained had been harvested during a war with the 'Toudamans,' though this may have been a request for French assistance.

During this period Cartier began closer observation of local customs, and concluded that the St Lawrence Iroquoians had 'no belief in God that amounts to anything.' He attempted to inform them about Christianity, but when Donnacona and his sons rounded up the whole village for baptism 'an excuse was made to them': there were no priests to conduct the ceremony and there was no consecrated oil. Whether this was the whole truth is unclear. Cartier had told Donnacona earlier that he had consulted his 'priests' before going to Hochelaga, at the time when an attempt had been made to prevent Cartier's departure by an appeal to the local god (56). Moreover, a mass was 'said and sung' some months later (77). If the priests had not died in the interim – and that is possible – then Cartier prevaricated on one of these occasions. It is significant that Cartier refused baptism for two reasons: 'we did not know their real intention and state of mind and had no one to explain to them our faith' (68). Yet the incident further convinced him that conversion would be easy.

Still, Cartier continued to distrust the Stadaconans, especially his two former guides after they urged their fellows to bargain for better prices (70). Both on his trip to Hochelaga and after returning, the French had been encouraged by some native people to beware of Dom Agaya and his brother. After a number of small incidents had heightened Cartier's apprehensions, and 'fearing that they should attempt some treasonable design,' he reinforced the fort and ordered a round-the-clock watch, thus provoking annoyance and puzzlement among Donnacona's followers. Yet by the time winter had set in – and it was a terrible winter – relations had apparently been restored to 'as friendly a manner as before' (72).

December brought disaster in the shape of a scurvy epidemic, the best-known incident in Cartier's career. Disease was the scourge of sixteenth-century Europeans even more than for pre-contact North American people. In France disease was widespread, often epidemic, and cures were few. In March 1535, prior to Cartier's second trip, an 'epidemic and plague' broke out in St Malo and was perhaps carried up the St Lawrence. Europeans had, however, developed immunities, complete or partial, to a large number of communicable diseases, which meant they were no longer fatal. But European pathogens were largely unknown in America, making measles, small pox, tuberculosis, influenza, and other common diseases deadly. The cures – herbal and spiritual – that North Americans successfully applied to their own illnesses were impotent against the European biological invasion that silently accompanied Columbus.[51] Of course, Europeans could contact unexpected health problems in North America, too.

According to Cartier's account, the 'pestilence' that struck in December broke out first among the people of Stadacona and, despite efforts at quarantine, the French were soon infected. Since Cartier's graphic description of the disease makes it certain it was scurvy caused by a vitamin C deficiency, the suspicion of contagion was unfounded. Moreover, since the native people had an effective cure for scurvy, Cartier's assumption that both communities were suffering from the same illness may be questioned, especially when he reported 'more than fifty deaths' at Stadacona. Perhaps the native people had contracted a French imported virus. That the French brought diseases with them is documented by Cartier's observation that the scurvy remedy that was eventually used 'cured all of the diseases they had ever had. And some of the sailors who had been suffering for five or six years from the French pox [la grande vérole] were by the medicine cured completely' (80). What this

51 H.P. Biggar, ed., *A Collection of Documents relating to Jacques Cartier and the Sieur de Roberval* (Ottawa: Public Archives of Canada 1930), 51; see below, 119; Alfred W. Crosby, Jr, *The Columbian Exchange: Biological and Cultural Consequences of 1492* (Westport, Conn: Greenwood Press 1972).

disease really was – syphilis or small pox or something else – is impossible to say. But micro-organisms certainly entered the St Lawrence region with the French, likely began infecting the inhabitants by the early winter of 1535, and may even have played a part in the eventual disappearance of the St Lawrence Iroquoians.[52] Of course, native people suffered from vitamin C deficiencies, too; it is the reported fifty fatalities that suggests scepticism about Cartier's diagnosis.

What is incontestable is that while the scurvy raged through the French camp, afflicting all but three or four and killing twenty-five of the 110 members of the company, Cartier's fears and suspicions – his 'great dread' (78) of the Stadaconans – grew. Utterly convinced that the native people bore the French ill will, Cartier resorted to a series of ruses to disguise the weakness of his stricken contingent from them – instead of asking for assistance. When, for example, a party led by Donnacona set off for the annual winter hunt and did not return exactly when expected, Cartier concluded that 'a large force to attack us' was being assembled (81). Nor were those suspicions and fears erased by the most obvious sign of Iroquoian good will imaginable in the circumstances. Dom Agaya, who had apparently himself suffered severely from a scurvy-like disease, not only prescribed the cure he had used but even ordered two women to gather the 'Annedda' (white cedar) branches for him.[53] It was not Cartier 'skilfully questioning'[54] Dom Agaya that is noteworthy in this episode, but rather the young Iroquois' quick, willing response to the plight of his one-time kidnappers. That Cartier was blind to this generosity is perhaps seen in his enthusiastic thanks to God, rather than to Dom Agaya, for the miraculous cure.

What even more obviously reveals Cartier's almost paranoid suspicion of the Stadaconans is the evidence that Dom Agaya's gift of the cure did nothing to undermine the 'dread' that Donnacona was plotting an attack on the French. When the headman returned

52 Bruce G. Trigger and James F. Pendergast, 'The Saint Laurence Iroquoians,' in Bruce G. Trigger, ed., *Handbook of North American Indians*, vol. 15: *Northwest* (Washington, DC: Smithsonian Institute 1978), 36. On syphilis see Crosby, *Columbian*, 122–64, and Claude Quétel, *History of Syphilis* (Baltimore: Johns Hopkins University Press 1990), chap. 1.

53 Jacques Rousseau, 'L'Annedda et l'arbre de vie,' *Revue d'histoire de l'Amérique français* 7, 2 (Sept. 1954): 171–201

54 Trudel, 'Cartier,' 168

from his trip, accompanied by a large number of hunters, and showed some signs that Cartier interpreted as secretiveness and caution, those fears were heightened (81). When Cartier learned that 'a leader of that region named Agona' was somehow a problem for Donnacona, he made no offer of support to the old man and his sons or to draw any connection between this problem and Donnacona's mysterious movements. Instead Cartier, 'on being informed of the large number of people at Stadacona, though unaware of their purpose, yet determined to outwit them, and to seize their leader [Donnacona], Taignoagny, Dom Agaya, and the headmen. And moreover he had quite made up his mind to take Donnacona to France, that he might relate and tell to the king all he had seen in the west of the wonders of the world' (82). If Cartier believed that by removing Donnacona's party he could place Agona in power and thus establish French control of the St Lawrence region through a puppet, there is nothing in his account that even hints at such 'a plan for a revolution.'[55]

Every effort was now focused on drawing Donnacona and his supporters into a trap. When the Stadaconans, perhaps suspecting foul play, proved reluctant prey, Cartier took this as a further sign of 'knavishness' (83). That the Stadaconans had the uneasy feeling that the French were planning a trip for them was revealed by Taignoagny's expression of relief when Cartier assured him that the king had 'forbidden him to carry off to France any man or woman, but only two or three boys to learn the language' (83). Taignoagny, the supposed scheming roque, naïvely swallowed this blatant lie and promised to bring his father to the French fort the next day.

That day, 3 May, was Holy Cross Day, an appropriate occasion for a repetition of the events that had taken place at Gaspé Harbour two years earlier. First a cross raising, at a location where a traffic marker was hardly needed. Its Latin letters read: FRANCISCVS PRIMVS, DEI GRATIA, FRANCORVM REX, REGNAT.' Perhaps recalling the earlier ceremony, Donnacona was nervous and reluctant to enter the fort 'to eat and drink as usual' (84). Cartier became impatient with the cat-and-mouse game: he ordered his men to seize the chief, his two sons, and two others. A desperate attempt by Taignoagny to pull his father back came too late. Once the five 'had been captured and the rest had all disappeared, Donnacona and his companions were placed in safe custody' (84). They were prisoners.

55 Ibid.; Trudel, *Histoire*, 110–12

Donnacona's followers, fully aware of the deadly fire power of the French canon, probably concluded that any attempt to free their leader would result in disaster. One apparent threat was made, but Cartier ordered Donnacona brought on deck to calm his people with the promise that within 'ten or twelve moons' he would return to his homeland. Ceremonies followed on this and subsequent days when Cartier was presented with large quantities of *esnoquy* or wampum, 'the most valuable articles they possess in this world; for they attach more value to it than to gold or silver' (85). These gestures were surely not made in homage to the French explorer who had deceived them but rather as a pathetic attempt to purchase a guaranteed return passage for their chief and his companions. Cartier generously repeated his promise, for what it was worth, and on 6 May 1536 his ships and their human cargo sailed away.

Cartier probably intended to return to Stadacona the next year, but King Francis was preoccupied by a war with Spain. The return journey was delayed for more than three years. None of the ten native people – the five captives plus five others who were 'gifts' – ever returned to Canada. All but one woman died before Cartier set out again, and she remained in France. She might have brought some embarrassing news had she returned. Before he died, Donnacona had been to court, apparently performing as Cartier had hoped. According to Thevet, he died 'a good Christian, speaking French.'[56] The fate of his companions is unrecorded except that, in all, three were baptized, whether voluntarily, or *in articulo mortis*, is unknown.[57] Probably the diseases that Dom Agaya and Taignoagny had escaped on their first trip now took their toll. Four years was a long time to be away from home. The 'slips of trees and the seeds of the rarest [plants] of Canada' that Cartier presented to Francis I were planted in the garden at Fontainebleau.[58] The 'lord of Canada' and his companions were presumably interred in humbler ground.

When the navigator of St Malo finally reappeared before Stadacona on 23 August 1541, he offered a self-serving account of the fate of the men, girls, and boys he had so callously transported to France. When he met with Agona who, he noted, 'was appointed

56 Schlesinger and Stabler, eds., *Thevet*, 9; Ch.-A. Julien, *Les voyages de découvertes et les premiers établissements XVe–XVIe siècles* (Paris: PUF 1948), 138–9

57 Trudel, 'Donnacona,' 276

58 Schlesinger and Stabler, eds., *Thevet*, 83

king there by Donnacona,' Cartier told him that 'Donnacona was dead in France, and that his body rested in the earth, and that the rest stayed there as great Lords, and were married, and would not return back into their country.' The French leader was satisfied that the lie had been carried off convincingly, especially since Agona was now the unchallenged 'Lord and Governor of the Country' (97–8).

The third voyage, of which the record is so fragmentary, proved a complete fiasco. The settlement Cartier had been sent to help establish – leadership now rested with Sieur de Roberval – was short-lived. In the spring of 1542 the St Lawrence Iroquoians turned against him. Even Agona, whose loyalty the French so confidently believed had been bought by Donnacona's demise, apparently joined the opposition. Cartier, hoping a fistful of 'Canadian diamonds' would justify his desertion of Roberval, decided to flee.[59] Did he ever suspect that the St Lawrence Iroquoians had finally realized the true fate of Donnacona and the others?

Cartier's failure, for that is what it was, resulted from his ethnology, his attempt to understand the people who lived along the St Lawrence River. His description of them was careful and often perceptive. He leaves the impression of having truly 'been there.' But his judgment, and therefore his representation, of these people was mortally flawed. They existed only in European terms, never in their own, their *alterité* unrecognized because it was unaccepted. Though Cartier successfully mapped the St Lawrence, he misidentified the St Lawrence Iroquoians, who remained as mysterious as the *adhothuys* and 'seahorses' who played near the mouth of the Saguenay River. For Cartier, a flawed ethnology brought only failure; for Donnacona's people it proved fatal.

VIII

The Voyages of Jacques Cartier document the French discovery of the St Lawrence valley. They contain unique geographical, biological, and ethnological descriptions, but they also recount something else. Their pages record the St Lawrence Iroquoians' discovery of France, a country of overdressed and often underfed people, where men grew hair on their faces and did women's work in the fields. Women in France were said to be sexually voracious, babies

59 Trudel, *Histoire*, 142–68

consigned to wet nurses, and children subjected to harsh discipline. Most families lived huddled together while a few idle men enjoyed extensive estates, hunting and fishing for sport. Theirs was a religion of churches, priests, and preachers warring over dogma. From French ports sailed creaking ships filled with self-confident adventurers and sharp traders who carried arms, ignorant of local customs. These suspicious, scheming intruders brought unknown illnesses, frightened native women, told lies, and shamelessly kidnapped even those who helped them. The French, Donnacona's people might have concluded, 'are wonderful thieves and steal everything they can carry off.'

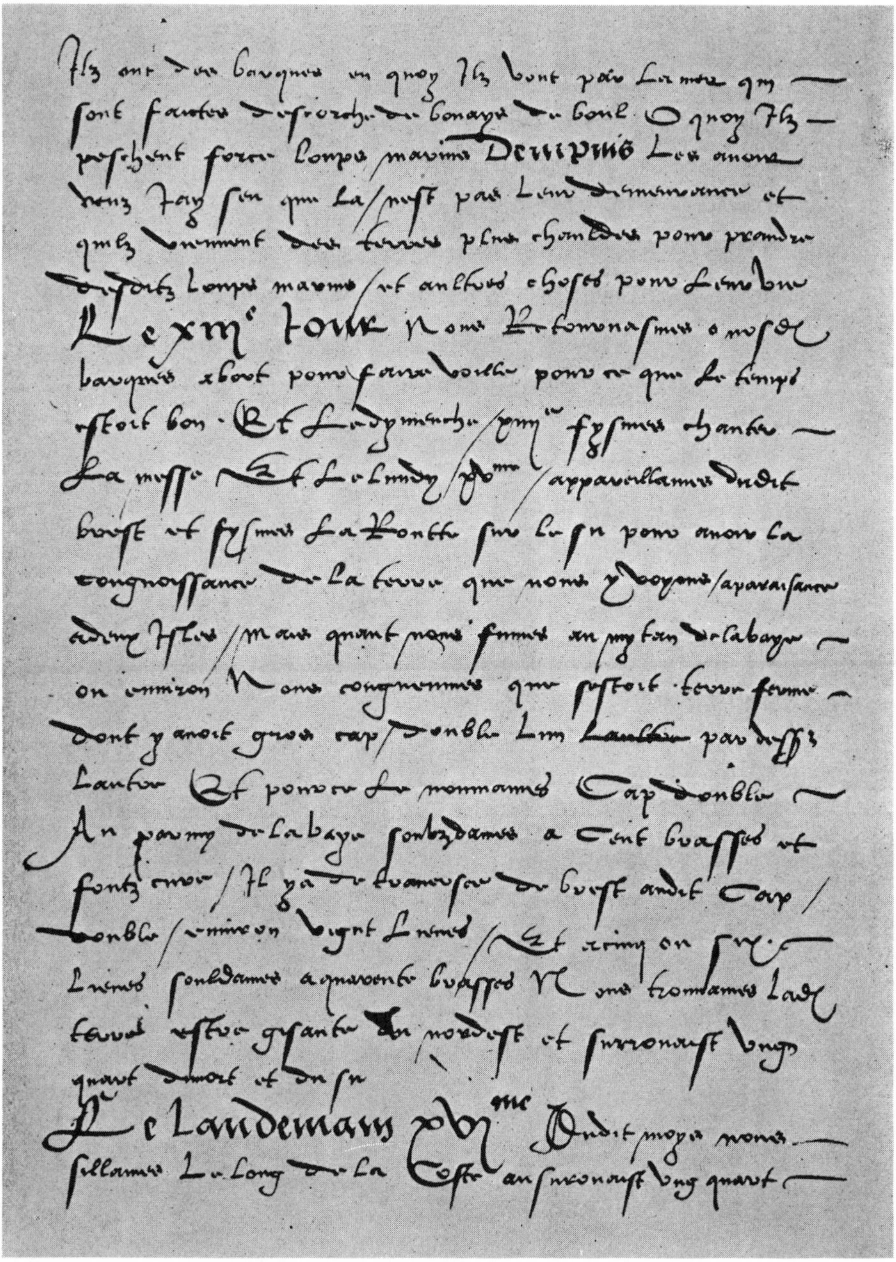

Ilz ont des barques en quoy ilz vont par la mer qui —
sont faictes descorche de bouays de boul o quoy ilz —
peschent force loups marins Depuis les avoir
veuz jay sceu que la nest pas leur demourance et
quilz viennent des terres plus chauldes pour prendre
desdits loups marins et aultres choses pour leur vie
Le xiii^{e} jour nous retournasmes o noz
barques a bort pour faire voille pour ce que le temps
estoit bon. Et le dymenche xiiii^{e} fysmes chanter —
la messe Et le lundy xvme appareillasmes dudit
hable et fysmes la routte sur le su pour avoir la
congnoissance de la terre que nous voyons apparaissant
a deux ysles mais quant nous fumes au my ban de la baye —
ou environ nous congneumes que cestoit terre ferme —
dont y avoit gros cap double lun lautre par dessus
lautre Et pour ce le nommames Cap double —
Au parmy de la baye sondames a cent brasses et
fonds cure Il y a de traverse de bout audit Cap
double environ vingt lieues Et a cinq ou six
lieues sondames a quarante brasses Nous trouvames la dite
terre estre gisante au nordest et surouaist ung
quart dnort et du su
Le lendemain xvime dudit moys nous —
sillames le long de la coste au surouaist ung quart —

Facsimile of a manuscript page of Cartier's first voyage. J.P. Baxter, *A Memoir of Jacques Cartier* (New York 1906)

MONTE REAL

Ramusio's plan of Hochelaga, 1556. Cartier is shown, bottom left centre, greeting a Hochelagan in European style.

MER OCCEANE:
MER DESPAIGNE:
MER DE FRANCE:
TERRE NEUFVE:
Grande baye
Terre du Laborador:

Pierre Descellier's 1550 planisphere depicting scenes of Cartier's second voyage

Though Cartier reported some unusual creatures, he did not mention either the pygmies or the ostrich-like birds depicted by Descellier.

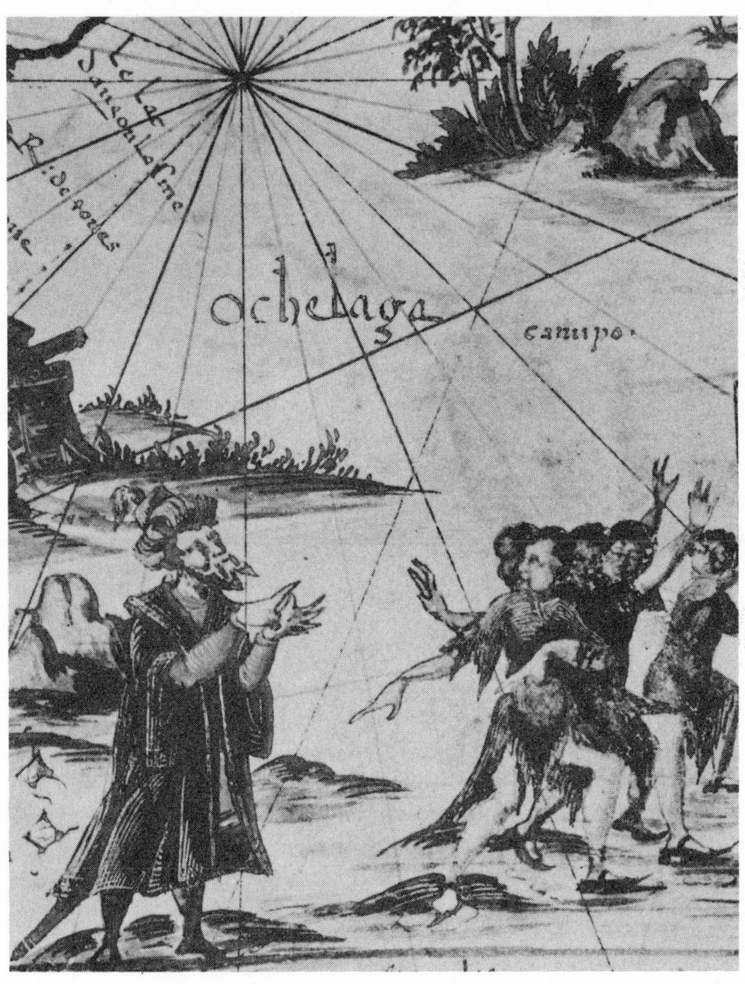

This detail from Descellier's map shows Cartier greeting a startled group of native people near Hochelaga.

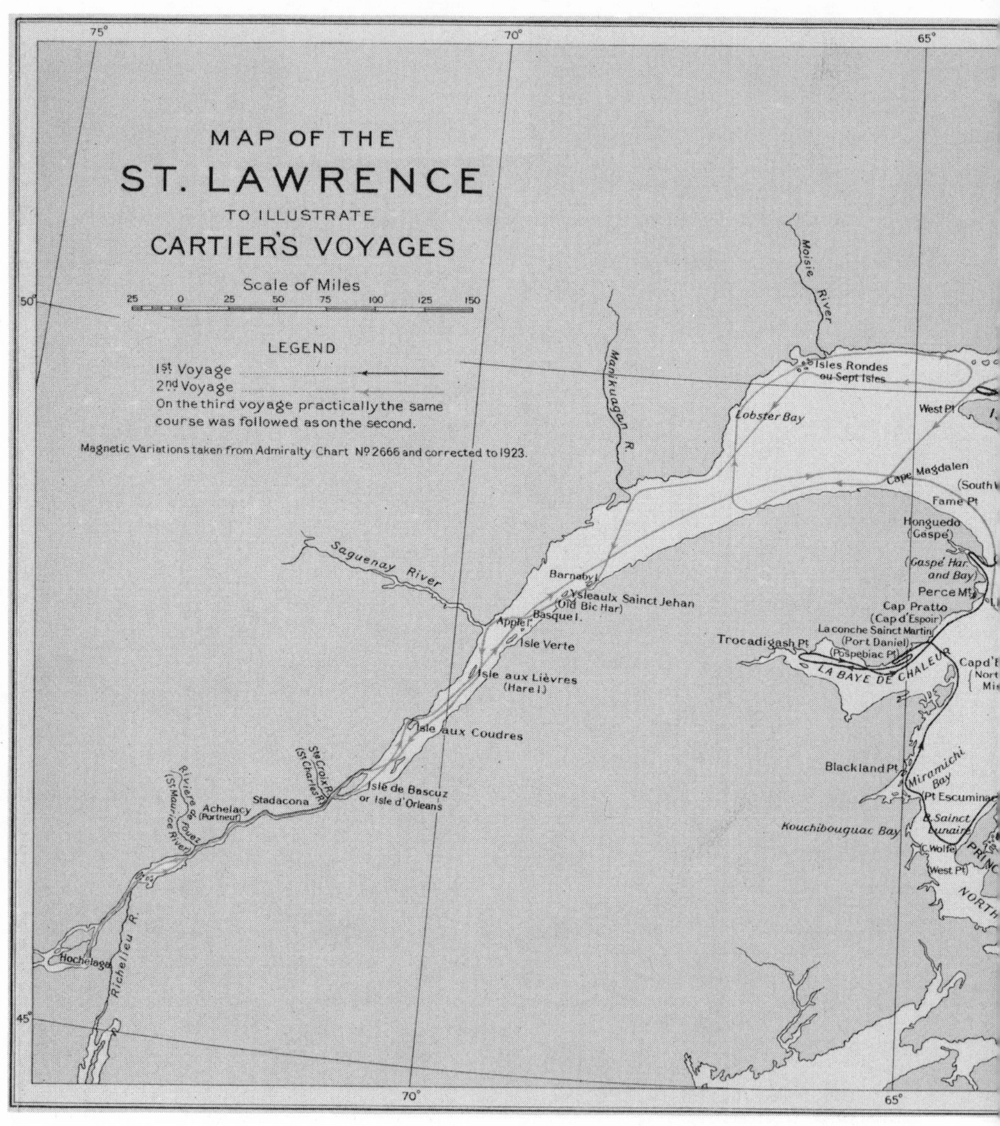

MAP OF THE
ST. LAWRENCE
TO ILLUSTRATE
CARTIER'S VOYAGES
Scale of Miles
25 0 25 50 75 100 125 150
LEGEND
1st Voyage
2nd Voyage
On the third voyage practically the same course was followed as on the second.
Magnetic Variations taken from Admiralty Chart No 2666 and corrected to 1923.
75°
70°
65°
50°
45°
Moisie River
Manikuagan R.
Isles Rondes ou Sept Isles
Lobster Bay
West Pt
Cape Magdalen
Fame Pt
Honguedo (Gaspé)
(Gaspé Har. and Bay)
Percé Mt
Cap Pratto (Cap d'Espoir)
La conche Sainct Martin (Port Daniel)
(Pospebiac Pt)
Trocadigash Pt
LA BAYE DE CHALEUR
Saguenay River
Barnaby I.
Ysleaulx Sainct Jehan (Old Bic Har)
Basque I.
Apple I.
Isle Verte
Isle aux Lièvres (Hare I.)
Isle aux Coudres
Blackland Pt
Miramichi Bay
Pt Escuminac
B. Sainct Lunaire
Kouchibouguac Bay
C. Wolfe
West Pt
Ste Croix R. (St Charles R)
Stadacona
Isle de Bascuz or Isle d'Orleans
Achelacy (Portneuf)
Riviere de Fouez (St Maurice River)
Hochelaga
Richelieu R.

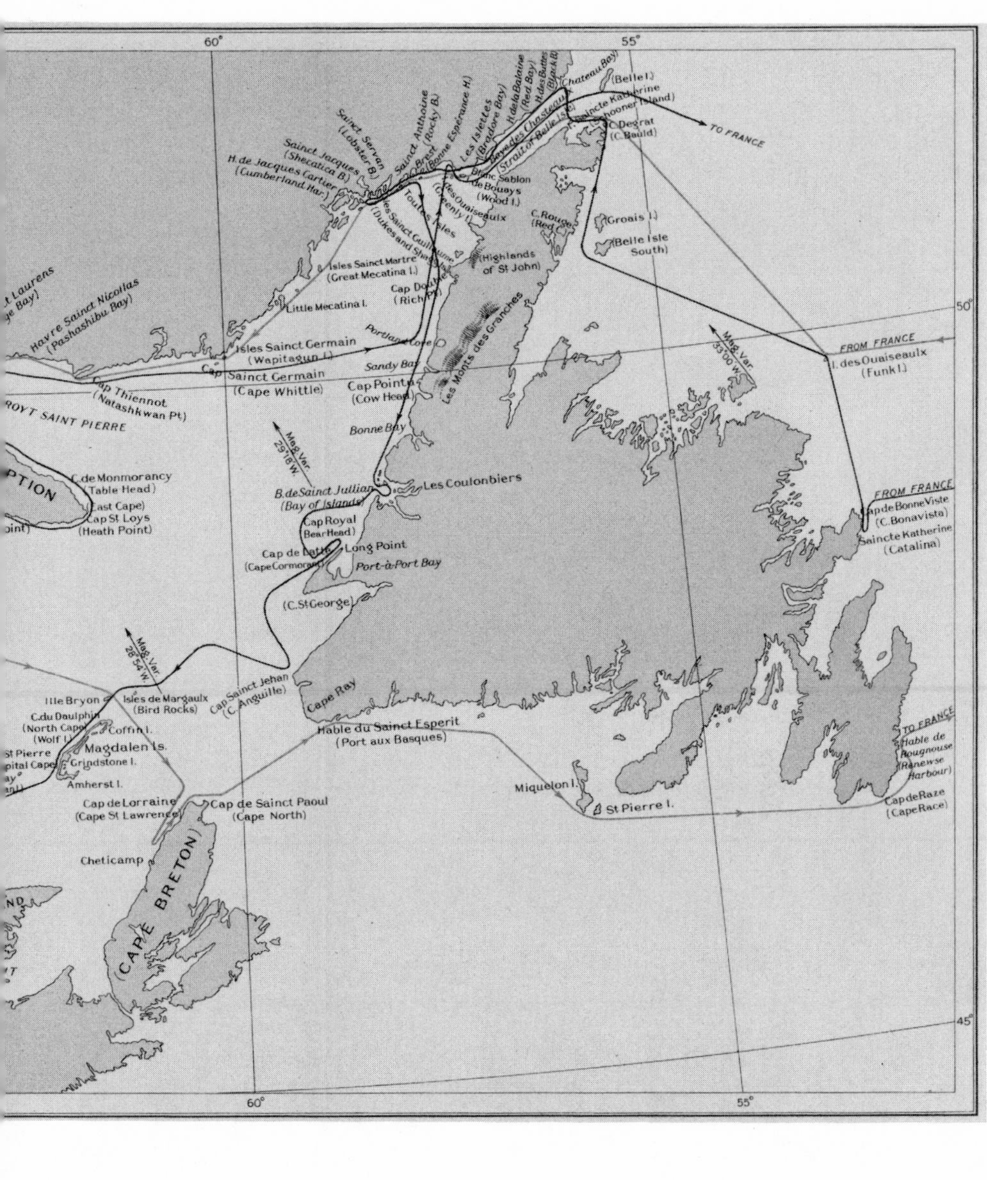

60°
55°
50°
45°
TO FRANCE
FROM FRANCE
FROM FRANCE
TO FRANCE
(Belle I.)
Chateau Bay
Saincte Katherine
(Schooner Island)
C. Degrat
(C. Bauld)
Strait of Belle Isle
Saint Servan
(Lobster B.)
Saint Anthoine
(Rocky B.)
Saincte Jacques
(Shecatica B.)
H. de Jacques Cartier
(Cumberland Har.)
Les Islettes
(Bradore Bay)
Blanc Sablon
de Bouays
(Wood I.)
Les Ouaiseaulx
Toutes Isles
C. Rouge
(Red C.)
(Groais I.)
(Belle Isle South)
(Highlands of St John)
Isles Saint Martre
(Great Mecatina I.)
Little Mecatina I.
Havre Saint Nicollas
(Pashashibu Bay)
Isles Saint Germain
(Wapitagun I.)
Cap Saint Germain
(Cape Whittle)
Cap Thiennot
(Natashkwan Pt)
DESTROYT SAINT PIERRE
Cap Double
(Rich Pt)
Portland Cove
Sandy Bay
Cap Pointu
(Cow Head)
Les Monts des Granches
Bonne Bay
Mag. Var. 33°00' W.
Mag. Var. 29°18' W.
Mag. Var. 28°54' W.
I. des Ouaiseaulx
(Funk I.)
C. de Monmorancy
(Table Head)
(East Cape)
Cap St Loys
(Heath Point)
B. de Saint Jullian
(Bay of Islands)
Les Coulonbiers
Cap Royal
(Bear Head)
Cap de Latte
(Cape Cormorant)
Long Point
Port-à-Port Bay
(C. St George)
Cap de Bonne Viste
(C. Bonavista)
Saincte Katherine
(Catalina)
Ile Bryon
Isles de Margaulx
(Bird Rocks)
Cap Saint Jehan
(C. Anguille)
Cape Ray
C. du Daulphin
(North Cape)
(Wolf I.)
Coffin I.
Magdalen Is.
Grindstone I.
Amherst I.
Hable du Sainct Esperit
(Port aux Basques)
Miquelon I.
St Pierre I.
Hable de Rougnouse
(Renewse Harbour)
Cap de Raze
(Cape Race)
Cap de Lorraine
(Cape St Lawrence)
Cap de Sainct Paoul
(Cape North)
Cheticamp
CAPE BRETON

The walled town of St Malo, as restored after its destruction during the Second World War. (July 1992)

Outside the walls of Limoëlou, Jacques Cartier's restored manor house (July 1992)

The Voyages

Cartier's First Voyage, 1534

JACQUES CARTIER'S FIRST ACCOUNT OF THE NEW LAND, CALLED NEW FRANCE, DISCOVERED IN THE YEAR 1534

How Captain Jacques Cartier, Having Set Forth from St Malo with Two Ships, Came to the New Land, Called Francis's Land, and Entered St Catherine's Harbour

When Sir Charles de Mouy, Knight, Lord of La Meilleraye and Vice-Admiral of France,[1] had received the oaths of the captains, masters, and sailors of the vessels, and had made them swear to conduct themselves well and loyally in the King's[2] service, under the command of the said Cartier, we set forth from the harbour and port of St Malo with two ships of about sixty tons' burden each, manned in all with sixty-one men, on [Monday] 20 April in the said year 1534; and sailing on with fair weather we reached Newfoundland on [Sunday] 10 May, sighting land at Cape Bonavista[3] in latitude 48° 30′ and in ...[4] degrees of longitude. And on account of the large number of blocks of ice along that coast,[5] we deemed it advisable to go into a harbour called St Catherine's

1 Charles de Mouy, Seigneur de La Meilleraye, was the fourth son of Jacques, Baron de Mouy, and Jacqueline d'Estouteville. He had been appointed vice-admiral on 26 February 1530, and died in 1562.

2 Francis I

3 It is still called Cape Bonavista and lies in latitude 48° 42′ 27″.

4 There is a blank here in the manuscript. In those days there were no accurate means of measuring the longitude.

5 *Cf.* Staff Commander W.F. Maxwell, RN, *The Newfoundland and Labrador Pilot*, 3rd edition (London 1897), 350: 'Field ice appears [in Bonavista Bay] about 15th February and disappears towards the end of May'; and also 377: 'Northern ice is irregular in its arrival seldom appearing before 15th January ... It generally leaves between 10th and 20th April but has known to remain as late as 10th June.'

Harbour,[6] lying about five leagues[7] south-southwest of this cape [Bonavista], where we remained the space of ten days, [11 to 21 May], biding favourable weather and rigging and fitting up our longboats.

How They Arrived at the Isle of Birds and of the Large Number of Birds Found There

And on [Thursday] the twenty-first of the said month of May we set forth from this [Catalina] harbour with a west wind, and sailed north, one quarter northeast of Cape Bonavista as far as the isle of Birds,[8] which island was completely surrounded and encompassed by a cordon of loose ice, split up into cakes. In spite of this belt [of ice], our two longboats were sent off to the island to procure some of the birds, whose numbers are so great as to be incredible, unless one has seen them;[9] for although the island is about a league in circumference, it is so exceeding full of birds that one would think they had been stowed there. In the air and round about are a hundred times as many more as on the island itself. Some of these birds are as large as geese, being black and white with a beak like a crow's. They are always in the water, not being able to fly in the air, inasmuch as they have only small wings about the size of half one's hand, with which however they move as quickly along the water as the other birds fly through the air. And these birds are so fat that it is marvellous. We call them apponats;[10]

6 Now called by the Spanish form Catalina Harbour. It lies about ten miles south of Cape Bonavista.

7 *Cf* S.E. Dawson, *The St. Lawrence Basin* (London 1905), 123: 'If then we would measure Cartier's courses on an Admiralty chart, we must allow only two and a half nautical miles for each league; for that is the equivalent value to a small fraction.'

8 Now Funk Island, in latitude 49° 45′ 29″

9 *Cf G. Cartwright, A Journal of Transactions and Events, etc.* (Newark 1792), III, 55: 'Innumerable flocks of sea-fowl breed upon it [Funk Island] every summer, which are of great service to the poor inhabitants of Fogo ... When the water is smooth, they make their shallop fast to the shore, lay their gang-boards from the gunwale of the boat to the rocks, and then drive as many penguins [great auks] on board, as she will hold; for, the wings of those birds being remarkably short, they cannot fly ... The birds which the people bring home thence, they salt and eat, in lieu of salted pork.'

10 The great auk (*Plautus impennis* (Linn.) Steenstr.), extinct since 1844. *Cf* F.A. Lucas, *The Expedition to Funk Island, with Observations upon the History and Anatomy of the Great Auk* in *Report of the U.S. National*

and our two longboats were laden with them as with stones in less than half an hour. Of these, each of our ships salted four or five casks, not counting those we were able to eat fresh.

Of Two Kinds of Birds, the One Called Tinkers and the Other Gannets; and How They [the Explorers] Arrived at Karpont

Furthermore, there is another smaller kind of bird that flies in the air and swims in the sea, which is called a tinker.[11] These stow and place themselves on this island underneath the larger ones. There were other white ones larger still that keep apart from the rest in a portion of the island and are very ugly to attack, for they bite like dogs. These are called gannets.[12] Notwithstanding that the island lies fourteen leagues from shore,[13] bears swim out to it from the mainland in order to feed on these birds; and our men found one as big as a calf and as white as a swan that sprang into the sea in front of them. And the next day, which was Whitsuntide,[14] on continuing our voyage in the direction of the mainland, we caught sight of this bear about half way, swimming towards land as fast as we were sailing; and on coming up with him we gave chase with our longboats and captured him by main force. His flesh was as good to eat as that of a two-year-old heifer.

On Wednesday, the twenty-seventh of the month [of May], we reached the mouth of the Bay of Castles,[15] but on account of the unfavourable weather and of the large number of icebergs we met with, we deemed it advisable to enter a harbour in the neighbourhood of that entrance called Karpont,[16] where we remained,

---

Museum under the direction of the Smithsonian Institution, for 1888 (Washington 1890), 493–530; Dawson, *The St Lawrence Basin*, 148–50.

11 The razor-bill auk, *alca torda* (Linn.). *Cf* C.E. Dionne, *Catalogue des oiseaux de la province de Québec* (Québec 1889), 9, no. 11; and P.A. Taverner, *Birds of Eastern Canada*, 2nd ed. (Ottawa 1922), 47.

12 *Sula bassana* (Linn.) Briss. *Cf* Dawson, *The St Lawrence Basin*; Dionne, *Catalogue*, 18, no. 34; and Taverner, *Birds*, 61–2.

13 Funk Island lies thirty-one miles north-northeast of Cape Freels on the main shore of Newfoundland, but only twenty-four miles east of Offer Wadham Island.

14 Sunday, 24 May, in 1534

15 The Strait of Belle Isle

16 Grand-Kirpon

without being able to leave, until [Tuesday] 9 June, when we set forth in order, with God's help, to proceed farther on. Karpont lies in latitude 51° 30′.[17]

Description of Newfoundland from Cape Rouge to Cape Dégrat

The coast from Cape Rouge to Cape Dégrat,[18] which is the point at the entrance to the bay,[19] runs from cape to cape north-northeast and south-southwest, and all this part of the coast has islands off it and near to one another, so that there are nothing but narrow channels where ships' boats may go and pass among them.[20] And on this account there are several good harbours of which the said Karpont Harbour[21] and the harbour of Dégrat[22] are in one of these islands, that which is the highest of all,[23] from the top of which one can see clearly the two Belle Isles that are near Cape Rouge,[24] whence to the harbour of Karpont the distance is twenty-five leagues. There are two entrances [to Grand-Kirpon], one to the east and the other to the south of the island. But one must beware of the eastern[25] [ie, western] shore and point; for there are bars and shallow water; and one must range the island[26] from the west at the distance of half a cable or closer if one wishes, and then head

17 Grand-Kirpon lies in lat. 51° 36′.

18 These capes still bear the same names: Cape Rouge is on the northeast coast of Newfoundland opposite Groais Island in latitude 50° 36′, while Cape Dégrat is on Kirpon Island, a few miles to the south of Cape Bauld, which forms the entrance to the Strait of Belle Isle. Cape Dégrat is much higher than Cape Bauld and, coming from the south, forms a much better landmark.

19 *Des Châteaux*, ie, the Strait of Belle Isle

20 This is by no means an accurate description of this coast.

21 Now Grand-Kirpon or Jacques-Cartier Harbour

22 It is still called *l'anse du Dégrat* and lies behind Cape Dégrat on the north side.

23 Kirpon Island

24 The Gray islands, ie, Groais (or Groix) Island and Belle Isle South (or *Belle Ile du Petit-Nord*), which lie just off Cape Rouge between 50° 45′ and 50° 56′ N. Cape Rouge lies in 50° 56′.

25 Pointe Duménil on the *west* side of Kirpon Island. The variation of the compass, which then attained some 14° W, may have led Cartier to think Kirpon Island ran northeast and southwest.

26 Jacques Cartier Island at the mouth of Grand-Kirpon or Jacques-Cartier Harbour

off to the south towards Karpont. And one must also beware of three shoals that lie under the water in the channel close to the island [of Jacques Cartier] on the east side. There is a depth of three or four fathoms[27] through the channel and good bottom [in Jacques-Cartier Harbour]. The other entrance [to Grand-Kirpon] lies east-northeast and south with a little westing and the passage is a narrow one.

Of the Island Now Called St Catherine's Island

Leaving Point Dégrat and entering the said bay,[28] heading west, one quarter northwest, one doubles two islands[29] which are left to port, one of which is three leagues from the said point [Dégrat] and the other[30] about seven leagues from the [two] first, which [Schooner] Island is flat and low, and looks as if it formed part of the main shore [of Newfoundland].[31] I named this island St Catherine's Island;[32] to the northeast of which are shoals and bad ground for about a quarter of a league,[33] for which reason one must give it a wide berth. The said [Schooner] island and Chateau Harbour[34] lie north-northeast and south-southwest, and are fifteen leagues apart. And from Chateau Harbour to the harbour of Hillocks, which is on the north shore of the said bay[35] running east-northeast and west-southwest, there are twelve and a half leagues. Two leagues from the said harbour of Hillocks is Whale Harbour,[36] abreast of which harbour, namely about three-quarters of the way through the said bay, there are thirty-eight fathoms and weedy bottom.

27 Although the French fathom is more than eight inches shorter than ours (1^{m} 62°), for the sake of convenience they are here treated as equivalent.

28 *Des Châteaux* or the Strait of Belle Isle

29 The *isles du Sacre* or Big and Little Sacred islands, which are five miles from Cape Bauld and lie one mile apart

30 A mistake of the redactor. It should be 'a third island,' *Ile à la Goélette* or Schooner Island, at the mouth of Pistolet Bay near Point Cook.

31 Newfoundland itself. Schooner Island is only separated from the main shore by Cook's harbour.

32 Now Schooner Island. The festival of St Catherine of Sienna had fallen on 30 April, when they were still at sea. The island was possibly so named in honour of Cartier's wife Catherine des Granches.

33 *Ile Verte* or Green Island and the shoals about it

34 Still called *baie des Châteaux* or Chateau Bay on the coast of Labrador in 51° 58′ opposite Belle Isle North

35 *Des Châteaux*, ie, the Strait of Belle Isle

36 *Baie Rouge* or Red Bay

From the said Whale Harbour to Blanc Sablon the distance is twenty-five leagues towards the west-southwest, and one must beware of a reef on the water like a ship's-boat to the southeast of Blanc Sablon, three leagues off.[37]

Of the Place Called Blanc Sablon, of Woody Island, of Bird Island, of the Kind and Numbers of Birds Found There; and of the Harbour Called the Islets

Blanc Sablon is a bight where there is no shelter from the south nor from the southeast. To the south-southwest of this bight there are two islands, one of which is called Woody Island[38] and the other, Bird Island,[39] where there are a great number of tinkers and puffins which have red beaks and feet and make their nests in holes under the earth like rabbits. On doubling a headland which is one league from Blanc Sablon, there is a harbour and passage called the Islets,[40] which is better than Blanc Sablon; and much fishing is carried on there. From the said Islets [Bradore Bay] to a harbour called Brest[41] in the same direction, there are ten leagues. This harbour lies in latitude 51° 55′, and in ... degrees of longitude. From the Islets to this place there are islands, and Brest lies among islands. And, furthermore, ranging the coast at a distance of three leagues out, there are islands all along for more than twelve leagues from Brest, which islands are low and one can see the high shore over the tops of them.

How They Entered Brest Harbour with the Ships and, Going on towards the West, Made Their Way among the Islands, Which They Found So Numerous That It Was Impossible to Count Them; and They Named Them 'All Isles'

On [Wednesday] 10 June we entered Brest Harbour with our ships to get wood and water[42] and to trim ship and proceed on beyond the said bay [of Castles, ie, the Strait of Belle Isle]. And on St

37 The modern charts give two fathoms on this patch, which lies four cables SSW3/4W from the western side of Pinware Bay east of Blanc Sablon.

38 It is still called *Ile au Bois* or Woody Island.

39 This second island is now called *Ile Verte* or Green Island.

40 Bradore Bay

41 Now Bonne Espérance Harbour in 51° 24′ 01″

42 Bonne Espérance Harbour

Barnabas's Day[43] after hearing mass, we went with our longboats beyond this harbour towards the west, to examine the coast and see what harbours there were. We made our way among the islands, which are so numerous that it is impossible to count them. They extend beyond the said harbour for some ten leagues. We slept on one of these islands overnight and found there ducks'[44] eggs in great quantity and those of other birds that nest on islands. We named these islands, 'All Isles.'[45]

Of the Harbour Called St Anthony's Harbour, of Port St Servan, Port Jacques Cartier, of the River Called St James's River; of the Costumes and Clothing of the Inhabitants on the Island of Blanc Sablon

The next day [Friday, June] the twelfth, we continued our way through these islands, and at the end of the thickest portion of them, we found a good harbour, which was named St Anthony's Harbour.[46] And further on, about a league or two, we came to a small, very deep passage with the land running southwest and with very high shores. It is a good harbour; and a cross was set up there, and it was named St Servan's Harbour.[47]About a league to the southwest of this harbour and passage there is an islet round like an oven, with several other small islets about it, which give indication of the said harbours. Ten leagues farther on there is another good opening somewhat larger and where there are many salmon. We named it St James's River.[48] While here we saw a large ship from La Rochelle that in the night had run past the harbour of Brest,[49] where she intended to go and fish; and they did not know where they were. We went on board with our longboats and brought her into another harbour, one league farther west than the said river St James. This harbour is in my opinion one of the best in the world. It was named port Jacques Cartier.[50] If the soil were as good as the harbours, it would be a blessing; but the land

43 Thursday, 11 June
44 The eider-duck, *Somateria dresseri*
45 Now called Eskimo, Old Fort, and Dog Islands
46 Rocky Bay
47 Lobster Bay. The festival of St Servan fell on 1 July. St Servan is practically a suburb of St Malo.
48 Shecatica Bay. The festival of St Jacques, Bishop of Toul, fell on 23 June.
49 Bonne Espérance Harbour
50 Cumberland Harbour

should not be called the New Land, being composed of stones and horrible rugged rocks; for along the whole of the north shore [of the gulf] I did not see one cart-load of earth and yet I landed in many places. Except at Blanc Sablon there is nothing but moss and short, stunted shrub. In fine, I am rather inclined to believe that this is the land God gave to Cain.[51] There are people on this coast whose bodies are fairly well formed, but they are wild and savage folk. They wear their hair tied up on the top of their heads like a handful of twisted hay, with a nail or something of the sort passed through the middle, and into it they weave a few bird's feathers. They clothe themselves with the skins of animals, both men as well as women; but the women are wrapped up more closely and snuggly in their skins; and have a belt at their waists. They [all] paint themselves with certain tan colours. They have canoes made of birch bark in which they go about, and from which they catch many seals. Since seeing them, I have been informed that their home is not at this place but that they come from warmer countries to catch these seals and to get other food for their sustenance.[52]

Of Some Capes, to Wit: Cape Double, Pointed Cape, Cape Royal, and Lath Cape; of the Barn Mountains, the Dovecot Islands, and of a Rich Cod-Fishing Ground

On [Saturday, June] the thirteenth we returned with our longboats on board [the ships] in order to make sail, as the weather was fine. On Sunday the fourteenth we had mass sung; and on Monday the fifteenth we set sail from Brest[53] and set our course towards the south in order to examine the land we saw there, in appearance like two islands. But when we were half-way across the bay[54] or thereabouts, we made out that it was mainland,[55] on which was a large cape doubled one part above the other, and on this account we named it Cape Double.[56] In the middle of the bay we sounded

51 Genesis 4, 12: 'When thou tillest the ground, it shall not henceforth yield unto thee her strength.'

52 According to J.P. Howley, *The Beothucks* (Cambridge 1915), 10, these were Beothuck.

53 Bonne Espérance Harbour

54 *Des Châteaux* ie, the Strait of Belle Isle

55 The northwest coast of Newfoundland

56 Now *pointe Riche* or Rich Point, which forms the northern end of Ingornachoix Bay in latitude 50° 42′. The double effect is increased by the highlands of Saint John in the rear.

in 100 fathoms and clean bottom.[57] The distance across from Brest to the said Cape Double is about twenty leagues; and at five or six leagues out we sounded in forty fathoms. We found the said coast [of Newfoundland] to run northeast and southwest, one quarter north and south.

The next day [Tuesday], the sixteenth of the month [of June], we ran along this coast to the southwest, one quarter south, for some thirty-five leagues from Cape Double, when we came to a region of very high and rugged mountains, among which was one in appearance like a barn and on this account we named this region the Barn Mountains.[58] These highlands and mountains are cut up and hewn out; and between them and the sea are low shores. On the day before this[59] we had had no further sight of the coast on account of the fog and thick weather we experienced. And in the evening[60] we caught sight of a break in the coast line, like the mouth of a river, between the said Barn Mountains and a cape[61] that lay to the south-southwest of us some three leagues off. This cape is all eaten away at the top, and at the bottom towards the sea is pointed, on which account we named it the Pointed Cape. To the north of it, one league off, lies a flat island.[62]

And as we wished to examine this opening, to see if there was any good anchorage and a harbour, we lowered the sails for the night.

The next day [Wednesday], the seventeenth of the said month [of June], we had a storm from the northeast, and we clewed up the mainsail to scud before it and housed the topmasts. We ran some thirty-seven leagues in a southwesterly direction until Thursday morning,[63] when we came abreast of a bay full of round islands like dovecots, and on this account we called them the Dove-cots and the bay St Julian's Bay.[64] From this bay to a cape that was named Cape Royal[65] lying to the south, one quarter southwest,

57 That is to say no sand, mud, shells, or coral came up in the lead. The modern charts give mud, and only a depth of sixty to seventy-five fathoms.
58 The highlands of Saint John
59 Monday, 15 June, the day they left Bonne Espérance Harbour
60 Tuesday, 16 June
61 Now *Tête-de-Vache* or Cow Head in latitude 49° 55′
62 Stearing Island
63 18 June
64 Now Bay of Islands
65 Now *pointe de l'Ours* or Bear Head in 49°

the distance is seven leagues. And to the west-southwest of this cape there is another cape,[66] which is much worn away at the bottom and round at the top, to the north of which about half a league there lies a low island.[67] This cape [Cormorant] was named Lath Cape.[68] Between these two capes [Bear Head and Cape Cormorant] are low shores, beyond which are very high lands with apparently rivers among them. Two leagues from cape Royal there is a depth of twenty fathoms and the best fishing possible for big cod. Of these cod we caught, while waiting for our consort, more than a hundred in less than an hour.

Of Some Islands between Cape Royal and Lath Cape

On the next day [Friday], the eighteenth[69] of the said month [of June], the wind came ahead and blew hard; and we put back towards Cape Royal [Bear Head] to try and find a harbour. We set out with our longboats to examine the coast between Cape Royal [Bear Head] and Lath Cape [Cape Cormorant], and found that on the other side of the low shores there is a large bay[70] running back a long way, with islands in it. It is land-locked to the south of the low shores, which form one side of the entrance, while Cape Royal [Bear Head] forms the other. These low shores stretch out into the sea for more than half a league, with shoal water and bad ground;[71] and in the middle of the entrance there is an island.[72] This [Port-à-Port] bay lies in latitude 48° 30′[73] and in ... degrees of longitude. That day[74] we found no harbour in which to anchor and headed out to sea for the night, the prow to the west.

66 Cape Cormorant
67 *Ile Rouge* or Red Island
68 Cape Cormorant lies five and a half miles north of Cape St George, which forms the northeast corner of St George's Bay. It was doubtless so named after *pointe de la Latte* on the French coast, a little to the west of St Malo. *Latte* means the batten or thin strip of wood or metal placed around the hatch to hold down the tarpaulin covering.
69 It should be nineteenth.
70 Now Port-à-Port Bay extending from latitude 48° 34′ to 48° 47′
71 Long Point
72 *Ile du Renard* or Fox Island
73 48° 35′
74 Friday, 19 June

Of an Island[75] Named St John's Island

From that day [Friday, 19 June] until [Wednesday] the twenty-fourth of the said month, which is St John's Day, we had stormy weather, head winds, and overcast sky to such an extent that we could not get sight of land until St John's Day, when we saw a headland to the southeast of us. By our reckoning it lay about thirty-five leagues to the southwest of Cape Royal [Bear Head]. That day we had mist and bad weather and could not draw near the said coast; and since it was St John's Day, we named the cape, Cape St John.[76]

Of Some Islands Named the Gannet Islands and of the Kinds of Birds and Beasts Found There; of Brion's Island and Cape Dauphin

The next day [Thursday], the twenty-fifth [of June], the weather was again bad, with overcast sky and much wind; and we headed west-northwest for part of the day, and in the evening hove to until the second watch,[77] when we once more made sail. By our reckoning we were then seventeen and a half leagues northwest, one-quarter west of Cape St John.[78] And when we hoisted sail, the wind was northwest, and we ran southwest about fifteen leagues, and [on Friday, 26 June] came to three islands,[79] two of which were small and as steep as a wall, so that it is impossible to climb to the top. Between these there is a narrow passage. These islands were as completely covered with birds, which nest there, as a field is covered with grass. The larger one was full of gannets, which are white and larger than geese. And on one part of the other was likewise a great number of them, and the other part was full of

75 Although it was a cape and not an island to which this name was given, one must remember that Newfoundland was then thought to form an extensive archipelago. It was indeed not represented as one island until 1599.

76 Probably Cape Anguille, the southwestern extremity of St George's Bay, although a cape still called *cap Saint-Jean* or Cape John lies four and a half miles up St George's Bay from Cape Anguille

77 This apparently began as now at midnight. *Cf* L. Estancelin, *Recherches sur les voyages et découveries des navigateurs normands* (Paris 1832), 242.

78 Cape Anguille

79 The Bird Rocks in 47° 50′

murres. And at the foot of the cliffs were likewise some of these murres and some large puffins, which are similar to those on the island mentioned above.[80] We landed on the lower part of the smaller island[81] and killed more than a thousand murres and great auks, of which we took away as many as we wished in our longboats. One might have loaded in an hour thirty such longboats. We named these islands, the Gannet Islands.[82] Five leagues to the west of these islands was the other island,[83] which is about two leagues long and as many in breadth. We sailed thither and anchored for the night [Friday–Saturday, 26–27 June] in order to get water and firewood. This island is fringed with sandbanks, and there is excellent bottom and anchorage all around it in six and seven fathoms. This island is the best land we have seen; for two acres[84] of it are worth more than the whole of Newfoundland. We found it to be covered with fine trees and meadows, fields of wild oats, and of pease in flower, as thick and as fine as ever I saw in Brittany, which might have been sown by husbandmen. There are numerous gooseberry bushes, strawberry vines, Provins[85] roses, as well as parsley and other useful, strong-smelling herbs. Round about this island are many great beasts, like large oxen,[86] which have two tusks in their jaw like elephant's tusks and swim about in the water. There was one asleep on shore near the water's edge, and we set out in our longboats to try and catch him; but as soon as we drew near he threw himself into the sea. We also saw there bears and foxes. This island was named Brion Island. In the neighbourhood of these islands the tides are strong and run to all appearance southeast and northwest. I am rather inclined to think from what I have seen that there is a passage between Newfoundland and the Breton's land. If this were so, it would prove a great saving both in time and distance, should any success be met with on this voyage.[87] Four leagues from the said [Brion] island to the

80 At Bird or Green Island

81 North Bird Rock

82 Now *Iles aux Oiseaux* or the Bird Rocks

83 Brion Island

84 The *arpent* fluctuated between three roods and two acres.

85 A small town in the department of Seine-et-Marne, fifty-nine miles southeast of Paris. The rose is a small red variety which, when brought into England by Edmund Crouchback, became the badge of the great House of Lancaster.

86 Walruses

87 That is to say, should they discover a new route to the east, the passage

west-southwest lies the mainland [the Magdalen Islands], which has the appearance of an island surrounded by islets of sand. On it stands a fine cape, which we named Cape Dauphin, as it is the beginning of the good land.[88]

On [Saturday] the twenty-seventh of the said month of June we ranged this coast, which runs east-northeast and west-southwest. From a distance it looks as if there were dunes, as the shores are low and sandy. We could not approach nor land there as the wind came off the shore.[89] We ranged it that day about fifteen leagues.

Of the Island Named Wedge Island[90] and of Cape St Peter

On the morrow[91] we followed that coast[92] about ten leagues, as far as a reddish headland,[93] that is eaten away and in behind which there is a shallow cove, running north.[94] A ridge of gravel stretches along between the sea and a lagoon.[95] From this [Hospital] cape and lagoon to another headland[96] the distance is four leagues. The shore runs in the form of a semicircle, and is skirted all along with sandhills and ditches, over the tops of and beyond which there appear to be lagoons and standing-pools, as far as the eye can reach. And before one reaches the first cape[97] there are two small islands, fairly close in shore.[98] Five leagues southwest from the second

---

to the south of Newfoundland would prove both shorter and quicker than the one through the Strait of Belle Isle by which they had come.

88 North Cape on Grosse Island of the Madgalen group, lying eight and three-quarter miles from the southwest corner of Brion Island

89 The wind was probably therefore south. The distance from Great Bird Rock to Deadman Islet is fifty-six miles.

90 The word *Allezay* seems to be derived from the verb *alaiser* or *élaiser* meaning 'to hammer out the edges on an anvil.' This represents exactly the appearance of Deadman Islet.

91 Sunday, 28 June

92 Wolf Island of the Magdalen group. The distance from North Cape to Hospital Cape is twenty miles.

93 Hospital Cape on Grindstone Island

94 *Etang du Nord* at Grindstone Island

95 This was probably House Harbour between Wolf, Grindstone, and Alright islands.

96 Southwest Cape on Amherst Island, which rises to a height of 300 feet. The distance to North Cape is thirty miles.

97 Hospital Cape

98 Hospital Rock and Gull Island or possibly Pierre de Gros Cap and White

cape[99] lies a very high pointed island, which was named by us Wedge Island. The first cape was named Cape St Peter, as we reached it on that saint's day.[100]

Of the Cape Called Cape Orleans, of Canoe River and Cape Savage; and of the Nature and Temperature of This Country

From Brion Island to this place there is fine sandy bottom and an even depth which gradually grows less as one approaches the shore. Five leagues from land there are twenty-five fathoms and one league out twelve fathoms; close in shore about six fathoms, rather more than less, and everywhere good bottom. And as we wished to make a fuller examination of this region, we lowered the sails and lay to.

And the next day, the last but one of the said month,[101] the wind came south, one quarter southwest, and we sailed west until sunrise on Tuesday, the last day of the said month, without seeing any land, except that in the evening at sunset, we caught sight of land in appearance like two islands, which lay some nine or ten leagues to the west-southwest of us.[102] And we made that day until sunrise the next morning[103] about forty leagues in a westerly direction. And pursuing our course we came in sight of what had looked to us like two islands, which was mainland,[104] that ran south-southeast and north-northwest as far as a very fine headland, named by us Cape Orleans.[105]

All this coast is low and flat but the finest land one can see, and full of beautiful trees and meadows. Yet we could find along it no

---

Horse shoals farther off shore, both near Grindstone Island and which then no doubt contained upland. These islands would identify this cape as being on Grindstone Island.

99 Southwest Cape on Amherst Island

100 Monday, 29 June

101 Monday, 29 June

102 This was probably the high land on Prince Edward Island near Grenville, between Charlottetown and Prince Town or possibly the capes Turner and Tryon, 120 and 110 feet high, respectively.

103 Tuesday, 30 June

104 Prince Edward Island. It was not known to be an island until after 1600.

105 Cape Kildare

harbour; for the shore is low and skirted all along with sandbanks, and the water is shallow. We went ashore in our longboats at several places, and among others at a fine river of little depth, where we caught sight of some savages in their canoes who were crossing the river. On that account we named this river Canoe River.[106] But we had no further acquaintance with the savages as the wind came up off the sea, and drove upon the shore, so that we deemed it advisable to go back with our longboats to the ships. We headed northeast until the next morning [Wednesday], the first day of July, at sunrise, at which hour came up fog with overcast sky, and we lowered the sails until about ten o'clock, when it brightened up and we had sight of Cape Orleans[107] and of another cape that lay about seven leagues north, one quarter northeast of it, which we named Savage Cape.[108] To the northeast of this cape, for about half a league, there is a very dangerous shoal and rocky bar. At this cape a man came in sight who ran after our longboats along the coast, making frequent signs to us to return towards the said point.[109] And seeing these signs we began to row towards him, but when he saw that we were returning, he started to run away and to flee before us. We landed opposite to him and placed a knife and a woollen girdle on a branch; and then returned to our ships. That day[110] we coasted this shore[111] some nine or ten leagues to try and find a harbour, but could not do so,[112] for, as I have already mentioned, the shore is low and the water shallow. We landed that day in four places to see the trees which are wonderfully beautiful and very fragrant. We discovered that there were cedars, yew-trees, pines, white elms, ash trees, willows, and others, many of them unknown to us and all trees without fruit. The soil where there are no trees is also very rich and is covered with pease, white and red gooseberry bushes, strawberries, raspberries, and

106 Cascumpeque Bay, a shallow opening five miles south of Cape Kildare. A number of small rivers flow into this bay.

107 Cape Kildare

108 North Point, the northwestern extremity of Prince Edward Island. It is eleven miles north of Cape Kildare.

109 North Point

110 Wednesday, 1 July

111 The west coast of Prince Edward Island down which they were evidently proceeding

112 There is no opening on the coast of Prince Edward Island from Tignish River, just north of Cape Kildare, all the way round to Egmont Bay in Northumberland Strait on the south coast.

wild oats like rye, which one would say had been sown there and tilled. It is the best-tempered region one can possibly see and the heat is considerable. There are many turtle-doves, wood-pigeons, and other birds. Nothing is wanting but harbours.

Of the Bay Called St Leonore's Bay and of Other Notable Bays and Capes; and of the Nature and Richness of These Lands

On the following day [Thursday], the second of July, we caught sight of the coast to the north of us[113] which joined that already explored, and we saw that this [mouth of the Northumberland Strait] was a bay about twenty leagues deep and as many in width. We named it St Leonore's Bay.[114] We went in our longboats to the cape on the north and found the water so shallow that at the distance of more than a league from shore there was a depth of only one fathom. Some seven or eight leagues to the northeast of this cape [Escuminac Point], lay another cape,[115] and between the two there is a bay,[116] in the form of a triangle, which ran back a long way; and so far as we could see the longest arm stretched northeast.[117] This [Miramichi] bay was everywhere skirted with sandbanks and the water was shallow. Ten leagues from shore the depth was twenty fathoms. From the last-mentioned cape to the said [?] point and headland the distance is fifteen leagues.[118] And when we were opposite to this cape we had sight of more land and a cape[119] which lay to the north of us, one quarter northeast

113 That is to say, on catching sight of Escuminac Point, the northern extremity of Kouchibouguac Bay on the New Brunswick coast, they thought this western mouth of Northumberland Strait must be a bay.

114 After a Breton bishop of the sixth century whose festival fell on 1 July

115 Escuminac Point at the northwest corner of the mouth of Northumberland Strait. It also forms the southeastern extremity of Miramichi Bay. Blackland point, the northeastern extremity of Miramichi Bay

116 Miramichi Bay

117 Looking into Miramichi River between Portage and Fox islands and allowing for the compass variation, this direction would be correct.

118 The redactor seems to have omitted several sentences here; for there is no previous mention of this *dit bout et cap de terre.* The distance given corresponds to that between Blackland Point and North Point on Miscou Island, at the mouth of Chaleur Bay, ie, forty-four and a half miles.

119 *Cap d'Espoir* on the north side of the mouth of Chaleur Bay, near Percé Mountain, which is 1,230 feet high

in full view. During the night [Thursday–Friday, 2–3 July] the weather turned bad with much wind; and we deemed it advisable to lie to until the morning of [Friday], the third day of July, when the wind came west; and we headed north in order to examine this coast, which was a high land lying to the north-northeast of us beyond the low shores. Between these low shores and the high lands was a large bay and opening, with a depth in some places of fifty-five fathoms and a width of about fifteen leagues.[120] On account of this depth and width of the alteration in the coastline, we had hopes of discovering here a strait like the one at the Strait of Castles.[121] This [Chaleur] bay runs east-northeast and west-southwest. The land along the south side of it is as fine and as good land, as arable and as full of beautiful fields and meadows, as any we have ever seen; and it is as level as the surface of a pond. And that on the north side is a high mountainous shore, completely covered with many kinds of lofty trees; and among others are many cedars and spruce trees, as excellent for making masts for ships of 300 tons and more, as it is possible to find. On this [north] shore we did not see a single spot clear of timber, except in two places near the water's edge, where there were meadows and very pretty ponds. The middle of this bay lies in latitude 47° 30′ and in longitude 73°.[122]

Of Hope Cape and St Martin's Cove; and How Seven Canoes of Savages Approached Our Longboat and Refusing to Withdraw Were Frightened Off by Two Small Cannon and Some Fire-Lances; and How They Fled in Great Haste

The cape on the south shore was named Hope Cape for the hope we had of finding here a strait.[123] And on [Saturday] the fourth of

120 *Baie de Chaleur* or Chaleur Bay, the mouth of which is twenty-five miles wide from North Point on Miscou Island to Cap d'Espoir

121 That is to say, they hoped to find here a passage similar to the Strait of Belle Isle. It should constantly be borne in mind that there then seemed no reason why they should not discover in the north a passage similar to the one discovered thirteen years previously by Magellan in the south.

122 The longitude extends from 67° to 68° 45′ west of Paris. It would be still less of course from St Malo and even less still from the island of Ferro in the Canaries, from which the longitude was generally reckoned.

123 North Point on Miscou Island

the said month [of July], being St Martin's Day, we coasted along the north shore [of Chaleur Bay] in order to find a harbour, and entered a small bay and cove[124] completely open to the south, with no shelter from that wind. We named it St Martin's Cove. We remained in this cove from [Saturday] the fourth until [Sunday] the twelfth of July. And while there, we set out on Monday the sixth [of July], after hearing mass, in one of our longboats to examine a cape and point of land that lay seven or eight leagues to the west of us,[125] and to see in which direction the coast ran. And when we were half a league from this point, we caught sight of two fleets of savage canoes that were crossing from one side [of Chaleur Bay] to the other, which numbered in all some forty or fifty canoes. Upon one of the fleets reaching this point, there sprang out and landed a large number of people, who set up a great clamour and made frequent signs to us to come on shore, holding up to us some skins on sticks. But as we were only one boat we did not care to go, so we rowed towards the other fleet which was on the water. And they [on shore], seeing we were rowing away, made ready two of their largest canoes in order to follow us. These were joined by five more of those that were coming in from the sea, and all came after our longboat, dancing and showing many signs of joy, and of their desire to be friends, saying to us in their language: *Napou tou daman asurtat,*[126] and other words we did not understand. But for the reason already stated, that we had only one of our longboats, we did not care to trust to their signs and waved to them to go back, which they would not do but paddled so hard that they soon surrounded our longboat with their seven canoes. And seeing that no matter how much we signed to them, they would not go back, we shot off over their heads two small cannon. On this they began to return towards the point, and set up a marvellously loud shout, after which they proceeded to come on again as before. And when they had come alongside our long-

124 Port Daniel, seven miles west of Maquereau Point on the north side of Chaleur Bay

125 Paspebiac Point, fourteen and a half miles west of Port Daniel

126 H.R. Schoolcraft, *American Indians, Their History, etc.* (Buffalo 1851), 335, note, concluded these Indians were Algonkin, but Father Pacifique, an excellent authority on the Micmac language, interprets these words as follows: N-apou tou dam-an as-ur-tat and Nit-ap gto- dem na gsa-lol-tôa, meaning in Micmac *Ami, ton semblable l'aimera.*

boat, we shot off two fire-lances which scattered among them and frightened them so much that they began to paddle off in very great haste, and did not follow us any more.

How these Savages Coming towards the Ships and Our People Going towards Them, Some from Each Party Went on Shore and How the Savages in Great Glee Began to Barter with Our Men

The next day [Tuesday, 7 July] some of these savages came in nine canoes to the point at the mouth of the cove, where we lay anchored with our ships.[127] And being informed of their arrival we went with our two longboats to the point where they were , at the mouth of the cove. As soon as they saw us they began to run away, making signs to us that they had come to barter with us; and held up some skins of small value, with which they clothe themselves. We likewise made signs to them that we wished them no harm, and sent two men on shore, to offer them some knives and other iron goods, and a red cap to give to their chief. Seeing this, they sent on shore part of their people with some of their skins; and the two parties traded together. They showed a marvellously great pleasure in possessing and obtaining these iron wares and other commodities, dancing and going through many ceremonies, and throwing salt water over their heads with their hands. They bartered all they had to such an extent that all went back naked without anything on them; and they made signs to us that they would return on the morrow with more skins.

How, When Our People Had Sent Two Men on Shore with Goods, about Three Hundred Savages Met Them in Great Glee; of the Nature of This Country and of Its Products; and of a Bay Named Chaleur Bay

On Thursday the eighth[128] of the said month [of July] as the wind was favourable for getting under way with our ships, we fitted up our longboats to go and explore this [Chaleur] bay; and we ran up it that day some twenty-five leagues. The next day [Friday, 10 July], at daybreak, we had fine weather and sailed on until about ten o'clock

127 West Point at the mouth of Port Daniel
128 Thursday was 9 July.

in the morning, at which hour we caught sight of the head of the bay, whereat we were grieved and displeased. At the head of this bay, beyond the low shore, were several very high mountains.[129] And seeing there was no passage, we proceeded to turn back. While making our way along the [north] shore, we caught sight of the savages on the side of a lagoon and low beach, who were making many fires that smoked. We rowed over to the spot,[130] and finding there was an entrance from the sea into the lagoon, we placed our longboats on one side of the entrance. The savages came over in one of their canoes and brought us some strips of cooked seal, which they placed on bits of wood and then withdrew, making signs to us that they were making us a present of them. We sent two men on shore with hatchets, knives, beads, and other wares, at which they showed great pleasure. And at once they came over in a crowd in their canoes to the side where we were, bringing skins and whatever else they possessed, in order to obtain some of our wares. They numbered, both men, women and children, more than 300 persons. Some of their women, who did not come over, danced and sang, standing in the water up to their knees. The other women, who had come over to the side where we were, advanced freely towards us and rubbed our arms with their hands. Then they joined their hands together and raised them to heaven, exhibiting many signs of joy. And so much at ease did they feel in our presence, that at length we bartered with them, hand to hand, for everything they possessed, so that nothing was left to them but their naked bodies; for they offered us everything they owned, which was, all told, of little value. We perceived that they are people who would be easy to convert, who go from place to place maintaining themselves and catching fish in the fishing-season for food. Their country is more temperate than Spain and the finest it is possible to see, and as level as the surface of a pond. There is not the smallest plot of ground bare of wood, and even on sandy soil, but is full of wild wheat, that has an ear like barley and the grain like oats, as well as of pease, as thick as if they had been sown and hoed; of white and red currant-bushes, of strawberries, of raspberries, of white and red roses and of other plants

129 These were Carleton, Scaumenac (1745 feet high), Dalhousie, and Sugar Loaf mountains with the other peaks near Dalhousie at the mouth of the Restigouche River.

130 Doubtless Tracadigash Point, where there is a lagoon

of a strong, pleasant odour. Likewise there are many fine meadows with useful herbs, and a pond where there are many salmon. I am more than ever of the opinion that these people would be easy to convert to our holy faith. They call a hatchet in their language, *cochy*, and a knife, *bacan*.[131] We named this bay, Chaleur Bay [ie, the Bay of Heat].

Of Another Nation of Savages and of Their Customs, Manner of Life, and Ways of Clothing Themselves

Being certain that there was no passage through this bay, we made sail and set forth from St Martin's Cove[132] on Sunday, 12 July, in order to explore and discover beyond this bay; and we sailed east some eighteen leagues along the coast, which runs in that direction, as far as Cape Pratto [or Meadow].[133] And there we found an extraordinary tide, shallow water,[134] and a very rough sea. And we deemed it advisable to hug the shore between that cape [d'Espoir] and an island,[135] which lies about one league east of it, where we dropped anchor for the night. And the next morning [Monday, 13 July], at daybreak, we set sail with the intention of following the coast, which ran north-northeast, but there arose such a headwind that we deemed it prudent to put back to the spot whence we had set out. We remained there that day [Monday, 13 July] and night until the following morning [Tuesday, 14 July], when we set sail and came abreast of a river[136] that lies five or six leagues to

131 *Cf* Father Pacifique, the Micmac missionary, in *Bulletin de la Société de Géographie de Québec* 16, 3 (août 1922): 143, notes 23 et 24: '*Cochy:* c'est ce qu'ils ont saisi de la fin du mot micmac, *Temigentijilj*, petite hache. *Bacan*: ici on a certainement mis un B à la place d'un O; le mot est encore *Oagan*, couteau.'

132 Port Daniel in Chaleur Bay.

133 *Cap d'Espoir*, thirty miles east of Port Daniel. The redactor has omitted to mention the naming of this cape, which doubtless took place on their arrival at the mouth of the bay.

134 Leander shoal, lying about a mile and a half S by E ½ E of cap d'Espoir

135 Bonaventure Island

136 Gaspé Bay into which empties Dartmouth River. *Cf* H.W. Bayfield, *The St. Lawrence Pilot*, vol. 1 (London 1894), 74: Gaspé bay possesses advantages which may hereafter render it one of the most important places, in a maritime point of view, in these seas. It contains an excellent outer roadstead off Douglastown; a harbour at its head [Gaspé Harbour], capable of holding a numerous fleet in perfect safety; and a basin [Gaspé Basin] where large ships might be hove down and refitted. The course up

the north of Cape Pratto. And when we were off this river the wind again came ahead, with much fog and mist, and we deemed it advisable to run into this river on Tuesday the fourteenth of the said month [of July]. We remained at anchor at the mouth of it until the sixteenth, hoping for fair weather and to set forth. But on the said sixteenth, which was a Thursday, the wind increased to such an extent that one of our ships lost an anchor, and we deemed it prudent to go farther up some seven or eight leagues, into a good and safe harbour,[137] which we had already explored with our longboats. On account of the continuous bad weather with overcast sky and mist, we remained in that harbour and river, without being able to leave, until [Saturday], the twenty-fifth of the said month [of July]. During that time there arrived a large number of savages, who had come to the river [Gaspé Basin] to fish for mackerel, of which there is great abundance. They numbered, as well men, women as children, more than 200 persons, with some forty canoes. When they had mixed with us a little on shore, they came freely in their canoes to the sides of our vessels. We gave them knives, glass beads, combs, and other trinkets of small value, at which they showed many signs of joy, lifting up their hands to heaven and singing and dancing in their canoes. This people may well be called savage; for they are the sorriest folk there can be in the world, and the whole lot of them had not anything above the value of five sous, their canoes and fishing-nets excepted. They go quite naked, except for a small skin, with which they cover their privy parts, and for a few old skins which they throw over their shoulders. They are not at all of the same race or language as the first we met. They have their heads shaved all around in circles, except for a tuft on the top of the head, which they leave long like a horse's tail. This they do up upon their heads

---

this bay ... is N. by W. and the distance 16 miles'; and J.A. Genand, *Notes de voyage – Le Golfe et les provinces maritimes* (Montréal 1872), 7: 'Quels sites enchanteurs de chaque côté du bassin! Quels superbes points de vue! Collines escarpées aux flancs desquelles de belles et gentilles résidences, vertes prairies couvertes de verdure et de moissons ondulantes, puis le long des côtes des cabanes de pêcheurs: le tableau est enchanteur.' The bay is seven miles and a quarter wide at its mouth.

137 Gaspé Harbour behind Sandy Beach point. F.J. Richmond,' The Landing Place of Jacques Cartier at Gaspé in 1534,' in *Annual Report of the Canadian Historical Association*, 1922 (Ottawa 1923), 38–46

and tie in a knot with leather thongs. They have no other dwelling but their canoes, which they turn upside down and sleep on the ground underneath. They eat their meat almost raw, only warming it a little on the coals; and the same with their fish. On St Magdalen's Day,[138] we rowed over in our longboats to the spot on shore where they were, and went on land freely among them. At this they showed great joy, and the men all began to sing and to dance in two or three groups, exhibiting signs of great pleasure at our coming. But they had made all the young women retire into the woods, except two or three who remained, to whom we gave each a comb and a little tin bell, at which they showed great pleasure, thanking the captain by rubbing his arms and his breast with their hands. And the men, seeing we had given something to the women that had remained, made those come back who had fled to the woods, in order to receive the same as the others. These, who numbered some twenty, crowded about the captain and rubbed him with their hands, which is their way of showing welcome. He gave them each a little tin ring of small value; and at once they assembled together in a group to dance; and sang several songs. We saw a large quantity of mackerel which they had caught near the shore with the nets they use for fishing, which are made of hemp thread, that grows in the country where they ordinarily reside; for they only come down to the sea in the fishing-season, as I have been given to understand. Here likewise grows corn like pease, the same as in Brazil, which they eat in place of bread, and of this they had a large quantity with them. They call it in their language, *Kagaige.* Furthermore they have plums which they dry for the winter as we do, and these they call, *honnesta*;[139] also figs, nuts, pears, apples, and other fruits; and beans which they call, *sahé*.[140] They call nuts, *caheya*,[141] figs, *honnesta*, apples ... If one shows them something they have not got and they know not what it is, they shake their heads and say, *nouda*, which means, they have none of it and know not what it is. Of the things they have, they showed us by signs the way they grow and how they prepare

138 Wednesday, 22 July

139 This word is given again in the vocabulary of Cartier's second voyage, which shows that this tribe was of the Huron-Iroquois family.

140 *Cf* Cartier's second voyage, and Sagard, *Dictionnaire*, 'Meures, *Sahiesse*.'

141 *Cf* Schoolcraft, *The American Indians*, 337: 'The language spoken by these Gaspé Indians is manifestly of the Iroquois type. "Cohehya" (sic) is, with a slight difference, the term for fruit in the Oneida.'

them. They never eat anything that has a taste of salt in it. They are wonderful thieves and steal everything they can carry off.

How Our People Set Up a Large Cross on the Point at the Mouth of This Harbour, and How the Captain of These Savages Came and after a Long Harangue was Quieted by Our Captain and Allowed Two of His Sons to Depart with the Latter

On [Friday] the twenty-fourth of the said month [July], we had a cross made thirty feet high, which was put together in the presence of a number of savages on the point at the entrance to this harbour,[142] under the crossbar of which we fixed a shield with three *fleurs-de-lys* in relief, and above it a wooden board, engraved in large Gothic characters, where was written, LONG LIVE THE KING OF FRANCE. We erected this cross on the point in their presence and they watched it being put together and set up. And when it had been raised in the air, we all knelt down with our hands joined, worshipping it before them; and made signs to them, looking up and pointing towards heaven, that by means of this we had our redemption, at which they showed many marks of admiration, at the same time turning and looking at the cross.

When we had returned to our ships, the captain, dressed in an old black bear-skin, arrived in a canoe with three of his sons and his brother; but they did not come so close to the ships as they had usually done. And pointing to the cross he made us a long harangue, making the sign of the cross with two of his fingers; and then he pointed to the land all around about, as if he wished to say that all this region belonged to him, and that we ought not to have set up this cross without his permission. And when he had finished his harangue, we held up an axe to him, pretending we would barter it for his skin. To this he nodded assent and little by little drew near the side of our vessel, thinking he would have the axe. But one of our men, who was in our dinghy, caught hold of his canoe, and at once two or three more stepped down into it and made them come on board our vessel, at which they were greatly astonished. When they had come on board, they were assured by the captain that no harm would befall them, while at the same time every sign of affection was shown to them; and they

142 Gaspé Harbour

were made to eat and to drink and to be of good cheer. And then we explained to them by signs that the cross had been set up to serve as a landmark and guidepost on coming into the harbour, and that we would soon come back and would bring them iron wares and other goods; and that we wished to take two of his sons away with us and afterwards would bring them back again to that harbour. And we dressed up his two sons in shirts and ribbons and in red caps, and put a little brass chain round the neck of each, at which they were greatly pleased; and they proceeded to hand over their old rags to those who were going back on shore. To each of these three, whom we sent back, we also gave a hatchet and two knives at which they showed great pleasure. When they had returned on shore, they told the others what had happened. About noon on that day;[143] six canoes came off to the ships, in each of which were five or six men who had come to say goodbye to the two we had detained, and to bring them some fish. These made signs to us that they would not pull down the cross, delivering at the same time several harangues which we did not understand.

How after Setting Forth from This Harbour and Making Their Way along that Coast, They Went in Quest of the Coast that Ran Southeast and Northwest

The next day [Saturday], the twenty-fifth of the said month [of July], the wind came fair and we set sail from that harbour,[144] and when we were outside the river we headed east-northeast, because, from the mouth of that river the coast ran back forming a bay,[145] in the shape of a semicircle, of which we could see the whole coastline from our ships.[146] And holding our course, we drew near that coast,[147] which ran southeast and northwest. This locality was distant from the last-mentioned river possibly some twenty leagues.[148]

143 Friday, 24 July
144 Gaspé Harbour
145 The passage between Gaspé and Anticosti Island
146 That is to say, after following the Gaspé shore for some distance, they thought, probably on account of a mirage, that this passage into the river St Lawrence was a bay, and they therefore stood over to the shore of Anticosti. These mirages are common in the gulf.
147 Anticosti Island near South-West Point
148 The distance from Cape Gaspé, at the mouth of Gaspé bay, to South-

Of Cape St Lewis, and Cape Montmorency, and of Some Other Coasts; and How One of Our Longboats Struck upon a Rock but Soon Passed On

We sailed along that [south] coast [of Anticosti], which as before mentioned ran southeast and northwest, from Monday afternoon, the twenty-seventh [of July] until Tuesday [28 July], when we had sight of another cape,[149] where the coast begins to run off to the east; and we ranged it fifteen leagues. Then the coast begins to fall away to the north.[150] Three leagues from this cape the depth is twenty-four fathoms, with muddy bottom. The whole of this coast is flat, and the most bare of timber that we have seen or found, with beautiful fields and marvellously green meadows. The above cape was named Cape St Lewis, on account of that day being the festival of this saint.[151] It lies in latitude 49° 15′ and in longitude 63° 30′.[152]

On Wednesday morning[153] we were to the east of that cape and headed northwest to examine that coast, until about sunset. The land here runs north and south. From Cape St Lewis[154] to another cape named Montmorency the distance is fifteen leagues. There the coast begins to run off towards the northwest. We thought we would take soundings three leagues or thereabouts from that cape but could not get bottom in 150 fathoms. We ranged that [north] coast [of Anticosti] about ten leagues, as far as fifty degrees latitude.[155]

At sunrise on Saturday the first of August, we descried and came in sight of another coast[156] that lay to the north and northeast of us. It was a marvellously high coast cut up into peaks; and between

---

West Point on Anticosti Island is about forty-four miles.

149 South Point on Anticosti Island

150 At Heath Point, the southeastern extremity of the island, twenty-two and a half miles from South Point

151 28 July, the festival of St Leobatius, abbot of Sennevières

152 Heath Point lies in lat. 49° 5′ and in long. 64° 2′ west of Paris.

153 29 July

154 Table Head, a densely wooded summit 260 feet high on the north coast of Anticosti Island and about twenty-three miles from Heath point

155 The parallel of fifty degrees runs up the middle of the passage between Anticosti Island and the Quebec coast opposite.

156 The Quebec coast opposite to Anticosti

them and us the shore was low with rivers and timber thereon. Heading northwest we ranged these coasts, first on one side and then on the other, to see if this[157] was a bay or a strait, until Wednesday of the fifth of the said month [of August] – the distance from shore to shore is about fifteen leagues and the centre is in latitude 50° 20′ – without ever being able to advance up it more than about twenty-five leagues, on account of the heavy headwinds and of the tides that set against us.[158] And we made our way as far as the narrowest part of it, where one can easily see the shore on both sides.[159] There it begins to broaden out again. And as we kept continually falling off before the wind, we set out for the shore in our longboats to try and make our way as far as a cape on the south shore, which stretched out the longest and the farthest of any we saw from the water, the distance to which was about five leagues.[160] On reaching the shore we found cliffs and a rocky bottom, which we had not met with in all the places visited towards the south since leaving Cape St John.[161] And at that hour the tide was running out, which caused a counter current to the west, to such an extent that in rowing along that coast one of our longboats struck upon a rock, but we immediately cleared it by all of us jumping out and pushing the boat into deep water.

How after Deliberating What was Best to Be Done, They Decided to Return Home; of the Strait Called St Peter's and of Cape Thiennot

When we had rowed along the said coast for some two hours, the tide began to turn and came against us from the west so violently that it was impossible to make a stone's throw of headway with thirteen oars. And we deemed it advisable to leave the longboats, with part of our men to stand guard over them, and for ten or twelve of us to go along the shore as far as that cape where we found that the coast began to turn off towards the southwest.[162]

157 The passage north of Anticosti

158 With southwest winds, a current of about a knot an hour sets eastward through the channel to the north of Anticosti.

159 The distance from North Point on Anticosti to Walrus Island, one of the Mingan Islands off the coast of Quebec, is only about fifteen miles.

160 North Point on Anticosti Island

161 Cape Anguille in St George's Bay

162 North Point, rechristened *Cap de Rabast.* See *17th Report of the Geo-*

When we had seen this, we made our way back to our longboats and returned on board the ships, which were still under sail, hoping always to make headway; but they had drifted more than four leagues to leeward from the spot where we had left them. And on arriving on board the said vessel,[163] we assembled all the captains, pilots, masters, and sailors to have their opinion and advice as to what was best to be done. When they had stated one after the other that, considering the heavy east winds that were setting in, and how the tides ran so strong that the vessels only lost way, it was not possible then to go farther; and also that as the storms usually began at that season in Newfoundland, and we were still a long way off, and did not know the dangers that lay between these two places, it was high time to return home or else to remain here for the winter; that nevertheless and moreover should a succession of east winds catch us, we should be obliged to remain. When these opinions had been heard, we decided by a large majority to return home. And as it was on St Peter's Day[164] that we had entered that strait, we named it St Peter's Strait.[165] We sounded it in many places and found in some 160 fathoms, in others 100, and closer in shore seventy-five fathoms, and everywhere clean bottom.

From that day [Saturday, 1 August] until Wednesday [5 August] we had a strong favourable wind and coasted this north shore east-southeast and west-northwest; for so it runs, except for a bight and a cape of low land[166] that takes more of a southeasterly direction. It lies about twenty-five leagues from the strait.[167] On this [Natashkwan] point we saw smoke rising from fires that the inhabitants of the coast were making at that spot. But because the wind blew towards the shore, we did not approach it; and seeing we kept away, some twelve men set off in two canoes and came as freely on board our vessels as if they had been Frenchmen. They

---

graphic Board of Canada (Ottawa 1922), 29.

163 No doubt Cartier's vessel

164 Saturday, 1 August

165 This is the passage to the north of Anticosti.

166 Natashkwan Harbour and point

167 *Saint-Pierre*, ie, the passage north of Anticosti. Natashkwan Point lies fifty-two miles from the Mingan Islands, opposite the west end of Anticosti.

gave us to understand that they had come from the Grand Bay,[168] and that they were captain Thiennot's people, who himself was on the cape [Natashkwan] making signs to us that they were returning to their own country in the direction whence we were coming; and that the ships had all set sail from the [Grand] bay laden with fish.[169] We named that cape, Cape Thiennot.[170]

From this cape onward the coast runs east-southeast and west-northwest, and is a very fine low shore but bordered with sand-banks. There are also a great number of shoals and reefs for the space of some twenty leagues, when[171] the coast begins to run east and east-northeast, and is all skirted with islands to a distance of two or three leagues off shore. In the neighbourhood of these are dangerous reefs to a distance of more than four or five leagues from shore.

How on 9 August They Entered Blanc Sablon and on 5 September Arrived at St Malo

From the said Wednesday [5 August] until Saturday [8 August] we had a heavy southwest wind and ran east-northeast, and that day we reached the west coast of Newfoundland between the Barn Mountains[172] and Cape Double.[173] And then the wind came out of the east-northeast with fury and violence, and we headed north-northwest and came to the north shore,[174] which is all bordered with islands like the part previously explored. And when we were off this coast and its islands, the wind calmed down and came out

168 The Strait of Belle Isle with that portion of the Gulf of St Lawrence lying just inside the strait. The name was a most natural one if it be borne in mind that those who first made their way from the Atlantic through this strait into the gulf were quite unaware both of the extension of that inland water as far as Cabot strait and of the existence of the river St Lawrence. This west end of the strait naturally appeared to them therefore to form a 'Big Bay.' It was this expedition of Cartier's which first made known the existence of open water over such a vast area and led to the supposition that this was a gulf with another entrance between Cape Breton Island and Newfoundland.

169 This shows that other vessels, besides the one met with from La Rochelle, came yearly from France to the Strait of Belle Isle for fish.

170 Natashkwan Point

171 At Cape Whittle, sixty-two miles from Natashkwan Point

172 The highlands of Saint John

173 Rich Point

174 The north shore of the gulf to the east of Cape Whittle

of the south; and we headed into the [Grand] bay.[175] And the next day [Sunday] 9 August, we arrived at Blanc Sablon, thanks be to God.

Conclusion of the Discovery

And afterwards, that is to say on [Saturday] 15 August, the day and feast of the Assumption of Our Lady, we set forth together from the harbour of Blanc Sablon, after hearing mass, and made our way in fine weather as far as mid-ocean between Newfoundland and Brittany, where we experienced a heavy storm of east winds for three consecutive days, but by God's help we bore up under it and rode it out. And afterwards we had such favourable weather that we reached the harbour of St Malo whence we had set forth, on [Saturday] 5 September in the said year [1534].

LANGUAGE OF THE LAND CALLED NEW FRANCE
RECENTLY DISCOVERED

Iddio	Dieu	...	God
Il Sole	Le Soleil	Isnez	The Sun
Idella ?(Stella)	Estoile	Suroé	Star
Cielo	Ciel	Camet	The Heavens
Giorno	Jour	...	Day
Notte	Nuyt	Aiagla	Night
Acqua	Eauë	Ame	Water
Sabbione	Sablon	Estogaz	Sand
Vela	Voile	Aganie	Sail
Testa	Teste	Agonazé	Head
Gola	Gorge	Conguedo	Throat
Naso	Nez	Hehonguesto	Nose
Denti	Dents	Hesangué	Teeth
Unghie	Ongles	Agetascu	Nails
Piedi	Piedz	Ochedasco	Feet
Gambe	Jambes	Anoudasco	Legs
Morto	Mort	Amocdaza	Dead
Pelle	Peau	Aionasca	Skin
Quello	Celuy	Yca	That one

175 *La Grande baie*, ie, the western end of the Strait of Belle Isle, or perhaps *la baie des Châteaux*

Un manaretto	Un hachot	Asogné	A hatchet
Molue pesce	Molue	Gadogourseré	Codfish
Buon da mangiar	Bon à mangier	Quesandé	Good to eat
Carne	Chair	...	Flesh
Amandole	Amandes	Anougaza	Almonds
Fighi	Figues	Asconda	Figs
Oro	Or	Henyosco	Gold
Il membro natural	Le vit	Assegnaga	Phallus
Un arco	Un arc	...	A bow
Latone	Laton	Aignetazé	Laton
La fronte	Le front	Anscé	The forehead
Una pluma	Une plume	Yco	A feather
Luna	La lune	Casmogan	Moon
Terra	Terre	Conda	Earth
Vento	Vent	Canut	Wind
Ploggia	Pluye	Onnoscon	Rain
Pane	Pain	Cacacomy	Bread
Mare	Mer	Amet	Sea
Nave	Navire	Casaomy	Ship
Huomo	Homme	Undo	Man
Capelli	Cheveux	Hochosco	Hair
Occhi	Yeux	Ygata	Eyes
Boca	Bouche	Heché	Mouth
Orecchie	Oreilles	Hontasco	Ears
Braccia	Bras	Agescu	Arm
Donna	Femme	Enrasesco	Woman
Mallato	Malade	Alouedeché	Ill
Scarpe	Souliers	Atta	Shoes
Una pelle da coprir le parti vergognose	Une peau pour couvrir les parties honteuses	Ouscozon uondico	A skin to cover the privy parts
Panno rosso	Drap rouge	Cahoneta	Red cloth
Coltello	Cousteau	Agoheda	Knife
Sgombro	Macquereau	Agedoneta	Mackerel
Noci	Noix	Caheya	Nuts
Pomi	Pommes	Honesta	Apples
Fave	Febves	Sahé	Beans
Spada	Espée	Achesco	Sword

Una frezza	Une fleche	Cacta	An arrow
Arbore verde	Arbre vert	Haueda	Green tree
Un pitaro di terre	Un pot de terre	Undaco	An earthen dish

Cartier's Second Voyage, 1535–1536

The second voyage undertaken by the command and wish of the Most Christian King of France, Francis the First of that name, for the completion of the discovery of the western lands, lying under the same climate[1] and parallels as the territories and kingdom of that prince, and by his orders already begun to be explored: this expedition carried out by Jacques Cartier, native of St Malo on the island[2], in Brittany, pilot of the aforesaid prince, in the year 1536.

To the Most Christian King[3]

Considering, O my most redoubted Prince, the great benefits and favours it has pleased God, the Creator, to grant to His creatures, and amongst others to place and fix the sun, upon which the lives and existence of all depend, and without which none can bring forth fruit nor generate, at that place where it is, where it moves and sets in a motion contrary and different from that of the other planets, by which rising and setting all the creatures on earth, no matter where they live, are able in the sun's year, which is 365 days and six hours, to have as much visual sight of it, the one as the other. Not that its beams and rays are as warm and hot in

1 The 'climate' was the zone of latitude of the ancient geographers within which the day was approximately of the same length.

2 At that time St Malo was only connected with the mainland by the *sillon* or ridge of sand.

3 Francis I. It is doubtful whether Cartier was the author of this dedication.

some places as in others, nor the division of days and nights of like equality everywhere, but it suffices that its heat is of such a nature and so temperate that the whole earth is or may be inhabited, in any zone, climate, or parallel whatsoever, and that these zones, with their waters, trees, plants, and all other creatures of whatever kind or sort they be, may through the sun's influence give forth fruit and offspring according to their natures for the life and sustenance of humanity. And should any persons wish to uphold the contrary of the above, by quoting the statements of the wise philosophers of ancient times, who have written that the earth was divided in five zones, three of which they affirmed to be uninhabitable, namely the torrid zone which lies between the two tropics or solstices, on account of the great heat and the reflection of the sun's rays, which passes over the heads of the inhabitants of that zone, and the arctic and antarctic zones, on account of the great cold which exists there, owing to their small elevation above the said sun's horizon, I confess that they have so written and firmly believe they were of that opinion, which they formed from some natural reasonings whence they drew the basis of their argument, and with these contented themselves without adventuring or risking their lives in the dangers they would have incurred had they tried to test their statements by actual experience. But I shall simply reply that the prince of those philosophers left among his writings a brief maxim of great import, to the effect that 'Experience is the master of all things,'[4] by which teaching I have dared to set before the eyes of Your Majesty this preface as an introduction to this little work; for the simple mariners of today, not being so afraid at your royal command to run the risk of those perils and dangers, as were the ancients; and being desirous of doing you some humble service to the increase of the most holy Christian faith, have convinced themselves by actual experience of the unsoundness of that opinion of the ancient philosophers.

I have set forth the above for the reasons that just as the sun which rises every day in the east and sets in the west, goes round and makes the circuit of the earth,[5] giving light and heat to everyone in twenty-four hours, which is a natural day, without any

4 The saying is Aristotle's. *Cf Metaphysics* I, 4.

5 Copernicus did not publish his *De revolutionibus orbium coelestium* until 1543.

interruption of its movement and natural course, so I, in my simple understanding, and without being able to give any other reason, am of opinion that it pleases God in His divine goodness that all human beings inhabiting the surface of the globe, just as they have sight and knowledge of the sun, have had and are to have in time to come knowledge of and belief in our holy faith. For first our most holy faith was sown and planted in the Holy Land, which is in Asia to the east of our Europe, and afterwards by succession of time it has been carried and proclaimed to us, and at length to the west of our Europe, just like the sun, carrying its light and its heat from east to west, as already set forth. And likewise also, we have seen this most holy faith of ours in the struggle against wicked heretics and false lawmakers here and there sometimes go out and then suddenly shine forth again and exhibit its brightness more clearly than before. And even now at present, we see how the wicked Lutherans, apostates, and imitators of Mahomet from day to day strive to cloud it over and finally to put it out altogether, if God and the true members of the same did not guard against this with capital punishment,[6] as one sees daily by the good regulations and orders you have instituted throughout your territories and kingdom. Likewise also one sees the princes of Christendom and the true pillars of the Catholic church, unlike the above infants of Satan, striving day by day to extend and enlarge the same, as the Catholic king of Spain[7] has done in the countries discovered to the west of his lands, and kingdoms, which before were unknown to us, unexplored and without the pale of our faith, as New Spain, Isabella, the Spanish Main[8] and other islands, where innumerable peoples have been found, who have been baptized and brought over to our most holy faith.

And now through the present expedition undertaken at your royal command for the discovery of the lands in the west formerly unknown to you and to us, lying in the same climates and parallels as your territories and kingdom, you will learn and hear of their fertility and richness, of the immense number of peoples living

6 The first Huguenot executed seems to have been Jacques Pauvan burnt at Paris in August 1528. During the winter of 1534–5, however, some twenty-four persons met a similar fate in the affair of the Posters.

7 Charles V

8 New Spain was Mexico: Isabella is the name given to Cuba on the Waldseemüller map, while the Spanish Main embraced the coast from the isthmus of Panama to the mouth of the Orinoco.

there, of their kindness and peacefulness, and likewise of the richness of the great river,[9] which flows through and waters the midst of these lands of yours, which is without comparison the largest river that is known to have ever been seen. These things fill those who have seen them with the sure hope of the future increase of our most holy faith and of your possessions and most Christian name, as you may be pleased to see in this present booklet wherein is fully set forth everything worthy of note that we saw or that happened to us both in the course of the above voyage and also during our stay in those lands and territories of yours, as well as the routes, dangers, and situation of those lands.

On Sunday, 16 May, the day and feast of Whitsuntide, in the year 1535, by command of the Captain[10] and the willing consent of all, each confessed himself and we all received our Creator together in the Cathedral of St Malo. After communion we went and kneeled in the choir of the church before the Reverend Father in God Monseigneur St Malo who, in his episcopal state, gave us his benediction.[11]

And on the Wednesday following, 19 May, the wind came fair and in our favour and we set sail with three vessels, namely, the *Great Ermine* of some 100 to 120 tons' burden, on board of which

9 The St Lawrence

10 Jacques Cartier

11 Denis Briçonnet, who had been made bishop of St Malo in 1513, suffered towards the close of his life so much in health that on 31 December 1534 Francis I gave permission for the former's nephew, 'François Bohier, abbé de l'abbaye de Nostre Dame de Bernay, de l'ordre sainct Benoist,' to take possession of the see. On 5 January 1535 this man took the oath of fidelity before the king at Paris. It was he who officiated on this occasion. Briçonnet died on 18 December 1535. See Archives de la Loire-Inférieure, série B 52, fols. 93v–94; P.P.B. Gams, *Series episcoporum ecclesiae catholicæ*, etc (Ratisbonae 1873), 618; and Guy Bretonneau, *Histoire généalogique de la maison des Briçonnets* (Paris 1620), 39, 225–78. In 1891 the following inscription was placed in the floor of the cathedral by Honoré Mercier:

Ici
s'est agenovillé
Jacques Cartier
Povr recevoir la bénédiction
de l'évêqve de Saint Malo
A son départ povr la découverte
dv Canada le 16 mai 1535

sailed the Commander, [Cartier] with Thomas Fromont[12] as mate, and Claud de Pontbriant,[13] son of the Lord of Montreal and cup-bearer to His Highness and Dauphin, Charles de La Pommeraye,[14] John Poulet,[15] and other gentlemen. In the second ship called the *Little Ermine* of about sixty tons' burden, went as captain under Cartier,[16] Macé Jalobert[17] and William Le Marié[18] as mate; and as captain of the third and smallest vessel named the *Merlin* of some forty tons' burden, went William Le Breton[19] with Jack Maingard as mate.[20] We sailed on in fine weather until [Wednesday] 26 May, when it turned bad and stormy and continued so for such a long time with incessant headwinds and overcast sky that no ships that have crossed the ocean ever had more of it; so much so that on [Friday] 25 June, on account of this bad weather and lowering sky, we all three became separated and had no news of one another until we reached Newfoundland, where we had agreed to meet.

And after separation, we in the commander's vessel had continual headwinds until [Wednesday] 7 July, when we sighted Newfoundland and made land at the isle of Birds,[21] which lies fourteen

12 He was from La Bouille near Rouen. See Joüon des Longrais, *Jacques Cartier* (Paris 1888), 128.

13 In all probability he was the son of Pierre de Pontbriant, seigneur de Montréal in the department of the Gers, who was captain of the famous castle of Bergerac under Francis I. François de Pontbriant, governor and seneschal of Limousin under Henri II, was doubtless his eldest brother. See M. Lainé, *Archives généalogiques et historiques de la noblesse de France*, tome 1er, art. Pontbriant (Paris 1828), 7ff; and Cabinet des titres, Pièces originales, vol. 2334, no. 52,557, no. 50, 57–63, 68–70, and 73–75.

14 According to Longrais, *Cartier*, 142 note 1, he was a nephew of Olivier de La Pommeraye, canon of St Malo and archdeacon of Dinan.

15 Though this man's name does not occur in any of the MSS, he was in all probability the redactor of this and of the former *Voyage*. He hailed from Dol near St Malo. See Biggar, *Early Trading Companies*, 215 note.

16 This is the only mention of Cartier by name in the whole *Voyage*. It is not surprising therefore that the edition of 1545 was not at first connected with him and his voyages.

17 He was married to Alison des Granches, the sister of Cartier's own wife. It is possible that Hermine Jalobert was his sister and that we have here the origin of the name of the two larger vessels. See Longrais, *Cartier*, 130.

18 The father of Jean Le Marié, a canon of St Malo

19 The son of Guillaume Le Breton, sieur de La Bastille near Limoilou at Paramé

20 The son of Allain Maingard and Collette des Granches

21 Funk Island, which Cartier had already visited on the first voyage

leagues from the main shore. This island is so exceeding full of birds that all the ships of France might load a cargo of them without one perceiving that any had been removed. We took away two boat-loads to add to our stores. This island lies in latitude 49° 40′ N. On [Thursday], 8 July, we set sail in fine weather from this island, and on [Thursday] the fifteenth of that month reached the harbour of Blanc Sablon, lying inside the Bay of Castles,[22] which was the point where we had agreed to meet. We stayed there awaiting our consorts until [Monday] the twenty-sixth of the month, on which day they both arrived together. Here we refitted and took on board wood, fresh water, and other necessaries. And at daybreak on [Thursday] the twenty-ninth of that month, we made sail and got under way to continue our voyage; and headed along the north shore [of the gulf], which ran east-northeast and west-southwest, until about eight o'clock in the evening, when we lowered sail opposite to two islands[23] which stretch farther out than the others. These we named 'St William's islands.'[24] They lie about twenty leagues beyond the harbour of Brest.[25] The whole coast from the Castles to this point runs east-northeast and west-southwest, and is bordered with numerous islands. The shore is broken and rocky having no soil nor timber except in some of the valleys.

On the following day, the last but one of the month,[26] we sailed westward to examine some other islands,[27] which lay some twelve leagues and a half from us. Between the two groups of islands, the coast forms a bight running north,[28] full of islands and large bays where to all appearance are some good harbours. We named these islands 'St Martha's islands.'[29] About a league and a half from them lies a very dangerous shoal,[30] and in the course east and west from St William's islands[31] are four or five patches lying off the above

22 The Strait of Belle Isle

23 Dukes and Shagg islands near Cumberland Harbour

24 The festival of St William, bishop of St Brieux near St Malo, fell on that day.

25 Bonne Espérance Harbour

26 Friday, 30 July

27 Great Mecatina and the islands about it, ie, Treble Hill, Flat, Dukes, and Murr islands that lie off Cape Mecatina. The last is fifty-five miles from Cape Whittle.

28 Ha-Ha Bay

29 *Marthe*, whose festival fell on Thursday, 29 July. The islands were Great Mecatina, Treble Hill, Flat, Dukes, etc.

30 Murr Rocks

31 Dukes and Shagg islands

bays. Some seven leagues to the west-southwest of St Martha's Islands lie more islands,[32] which we reached that day about one o'clock in the afternoon. And from that hour until the change of watch,[33] we made some fifteen leagues till we came opposite to a cape[34] on some low islands, which we named 'St German's Islands.'[35] Some three leagues to the southeast of this cape lies another very dangerous shoal,[36] and likewise between the said Cape St German[37] and St Martha's islands,[38] some two leagues from the latter, lies a shoal on which there is a depth of only four fathoms.[39] On account of the dangerous nature of this coast, we lowered the sails here and lay to for the night.

On the following day [Saturday], the last day of July, we continued our way along that coast, which runs east and west, one quarter southeast, and is skirted all along with islands and shoals and is very dangerous coast. The distance from the cape at St German's Islands[40] to the point where the islands end[41] is about seventeen and a half leagues. And at the point where the islands end, there is a fine headland, covered with large, high trees.[42] This coast is fringed all along with sandy beaches, and with no sign of a harbour, as far as Cape Thiennot,[43] where it turns northwest. This cape lies some seven leagues from the last of the islands,[44]

32 Little Mecatina and the Harrington islands

33 Probably eight o'clock in the evening; for though some of the sand glasses only took one hour to empty, others lasted three and four hours. *Cf* Père Georges Fournier, *Hydrographie* (Paris 1643), 30: 'Une horloge de trois ou quatre heures.'

34 Cape Whittle, 128 miles from Blanc Sablon

35 Wapitagun, Outer Wapitagun, and Lake islands. Cape Whittle forms the southwestern extremity of the latter. The festival of St German, bishop of Auxerre, fell on Saturday, 31 July.

36 South Makers ledge, six miles and a half southeast of Cape Whittle

37 Cape Whittle

38 Boat Islands are meant but as no name had been given to them, nor to Little Mecatina and the Harrington islands, the isles St Martha (ie, Great Mecatina, etc.) are mentioned, as they were the only ones to which a name had been given.

39 St Mary Reefs between Cape Whittle and Boat Islands and nine miles from South Makers ledge

40 Cape Whittle

41 The islands end at Kegashka Bay, about forty miles beyond Cape Whittle.

42 Kegashka Point

43 Natashkwan Point

44 The last islands along the coast lie off Curlew Point, the eastern extremity of Kegashka Bay, which is twenty-two miles to the east of Natashkwan

and we recognized it from our former voyage. On this account we sailed on all night [Saturday–Sunday, 31 July–1 August] to the west-northwest until daylight, when the wind came ahead, whereupon we looked out for a harbour in which to anchor. We found a nice little harbour[45] some seven and a half leagues beyond Cape Thiennot, lying among four islands which stretch out into the gulf. We named it 'St Nicholas's Harbour'; and on the nearest island we set up a large wooden cross for a landmark. One must keep this cross to the northeast, then head for it and leave it to starboard. You will find a depth of six fathoms and anchorage in the harbour in four fathoms. One must beware of two shoals, one on each side, half a league out. This whole coast is very dangerous and is full of reefs. Though one would think it contained many good harbours, there are shoals and reefs everywhere. We remained in that harbour from that day [Sunday, 1 August] until Sunday, 8 August, when we set forth and made our way towards Cape Rabast, on the coast towards the south.[46] This cape lies some twenty leagues southwest of the above [Pashashibu] harbour. On the following day[47] we had a headwind and since we found no harbours along this south coast, we sailed north to a point some ten leagues beyond the former [Pashashibu] harbour where we discovered a very fine large bay,[48] full of islands and with good entrances and anchorage for any weather that might prevail.[49] This bay may be known by a large island which stretches out beyond the others like a headland,[50] and on the mainland, some two leagues off, stands a mountain[51] having the form of a shock of wheat. We named this bay 'St Lawrence's Bay.'[52]

On [Friday] the thirteenth of that month we set out from St Lawrence's Bay and heading towards the west, made our way as

---

Point. Green Island and Black Islet, the very last islands, are in Kegashka Bay itself.

45 Pashashibu Bay, twenty miles west of Natashkwan Point

46 On Anticosti Island and still so called. It had been explored on the former voyage.

47 Monday, 9 August

48 Pillage Bay

49 The harbour is called Ste Geneviève Harbour and lies between Ste Geneviève Island and the mainland.

50 Ste Geneviève Island

51 Mount Ste Geneviève

52 Now Pillage Bay and Ste Geneviève Harbour. The festival of St Lawrence, archdeacon of Rome, fell on Tuesday, 10 August. It is an important festival in Brittany.

far as a cape on the south side,[53] which lies some twenty-five leagues west, one quarter southwest of St Lawrence's harbour. And it was told us by the two savages whom we had captured on our first voyage, that this cape formed part of the land on the south which was an island;[54] and that to the south of it lay the route from Honguedo,[55] where we had seized them when on our first voyage, to Canada;[56] and that two days' journey from this cape and island[57] began the kingdom of the Saguenay,[58] on the north

53 West Point on Anticosti Island. The depth of water, mentioned later, proves this.

54 Anticosti Island, which is 135 miles long and about thirty miles in width at the broadest part

55 Gaspé

56 As will be observed farther on, this word is always used to designate the region along the St Lawrence from Grosse Island on the east to a point between Quebec and Three Rivers on the west. It is so represented on the Vallard and Mercator maps and on Hakluyt's map of 1589. *Cf* also François de Belleforest, *La Cosmographie universelle de tout le monde*, 2 vols. (Paris 1575), II, 2190: 'Le pays de Canada est enuironné des hautes mõtaignes de Saguenai vers Septentrion, au Leuant luy gist le goulphe de saint Laurens, au Ponent le pays de Hochelaga, & au Midy la terre de Nurumbeg.' On the Harleian and Desceliers mappemondes and on the Desceliers planisphere, however, the name embraces the region on both sides of the St Lawrence down as far as Anticosti. It is also employed in this sense by André Thevet in *Les Singularitez de la France Antarctique* (Paris 1558, fols. 149 and 150v) as well as in his *Cosmographie de Levant* (Lyon 1554), II, 1010. The name 'river of Canada' by which the St Lawrence was frequently designated helped this extension, which seems to have been definitely ratified by Lescarbot. Although the real limits of Canada, he says (*History of New France* (1609), 250) were those given by Belleforest, 'Toutefois j'ay appris ... que les peuples de Gachepé, & de la baye de Chaleur ... se disent Canadoquoa c'est à dire Canadaquois ... Cette diversité a fait que les Geographes ont varié en l'assiette de la province de Canada, les uns l'ayant située par les cinquante, les autres par les soixante degrez. Cela presupposé, je dy que l'un & l'autre côté de ladite riviere [de Canada] est Canada'; and again, 'Voila comme de tout temps on a decrié le pais de Canada (souz lequel nom on comprend toute cette terre)' (843). Cartier gives the word in his Indian vocabulary as meaning 'town.' The old Mohawk word for castle given by Van Curler (*Report of the American Historical Association for 1895* [Washington 1896], 100) is *Canadaghi* and the old Huron form *Andata*. The modern Mohawk form is *Kanata*. See Schoolcraft, *The American Indians*, 256 no. 58; and compare Lescarbot, *History*, 250–1; J.B.A. Ferland, *Cours d'histoire du Canada* (Québec 1882), I, 25; and Rev. W.M. Beauchamp, *Indian Names in New York* (Fayetville 1893), 104.

57 West Point on Anticosti Island

58 The word Saguenay is perhaps derived from the Montagnais, *saki-nip*, 'water which issues forth.'

shore as one made one's way towards this Canada. Some three leagues from this cape, there is a depth of more than 100 fathoms; and none of us ever remembers having seen so many whales as we saw that day off this cape.

After passing through the strait [of St Peter] on the previous night,[59] the next day which was our Our Lady's day of August, [Sunday] the fifteenth of that month, we had sight of land towards the south, which turned out to be a coast with marvellously high mountains.[60] The above-mentioned [West] cape on the island [of Anticosti], which we named 'Assumption Island,'[61] and a cape on this high [Gaspé] shore, lie east-northeast and west-southwest; and the distance from one to the other is twenty-five leagues. The north shore, when one is some thirty leagues off, looks higher than the south shore. We coasted this south shore from that day, [Sunday],[62] until noon on Tuesday,[63] when the wind came out of the west. We then headed north in order to make our way towards the high coast we saw in that direction. And on reaching it, we found that the shore was low and flat at the water's edge, but that beyond this low shore there were mountains. This coast runs east and west, one quarter southwest.[64] Our savages told us that this was the beginning of the Saguenay and of the inhabited region; and that thence came the copper they call *caigneldaze*.[65] The distance from the south to the north shore is about thirty leagues; and there is a depth of more than 200 fathoms. The two savages assured us that this was the way to the mouth of the great river

59 Saturday–Sunday, 14–15 August. It is the passage to the north of Anticosti between it and the Quebec shore.

60 The south shore of the St Lawrence between Fame Point and Cape Magdalen. The mountains were Mont Louis and the Notre Dame chain.

61 The island of Anticosti

62 Sunday, 15 August

63 Tuesday, 17 August. They had in all probability made their way along the south shore to a point a little beyond cape Ste Anne.

64 The north shore near Lobster Bay, to judge from the distance run and the description of the coast

65 The old Mohawk form of this word was *Karistaji*, meaning 'iron, copper and lead.' *Cf* Gen. J.G. Wilson, *'Arent Van Curler and His Journal of 1634–1635,' Annual Report of the American Historical Association for the Year 1895* (Washington 1896), 99; Schoolcraft, *The American Indians*, 267, nos. 128 and 129.

of Hochelaga[66] and the route towards Canada, and that the river grew narrower as one approached Canada;[67] and also that farther up, the water became fresh, and that one could make one's way so far up the river that they had never heard of anyone reaching the head of it. Furthermore, that one could only proceed along it in small boats. In view of these statements and of their assertion that no other passage existed, the Captain [Cartier] was unwilling to proceed further until he had explored the remainder of the north shore to see if there was a strait there; for on account of our passing over to the south shore, the coast from St Lawrence's bay[68] onward had not been visited.

How the Captain Ordered the Ships to Head Back as Far as the Bay of St Lawrence, to Make Sure That No Strait Existed along the North Shore[69]

On Wednesday, 18 August, the Captain ordered the ships to head back and to steer in the opposite direction; and we coasted the north shore, which runs northeast and southwest in the form of a semicircle. It is a high shore though less so than the south shore. And on the following day, Thursday,[70] we came to seven very high islands, which we named the 'Round islands.'[71] They lie some forty leagues from the south shore, and stretch out into the gulf to a distance of three or four leagues. Opposite to them commences a low shore covered with trees, which we coasted with our longboats on the Friday [20 August]. Some two or more leagues from shore lie several very dangerous sandbars which become bare at low

66 This seems to have been the name given by Cartier to the St Lawrence.

67 At Quebec the St Lawrence is only 3,230 feet wide. Hence the name *kebec*, meaning 'where the stream is obstructed.'

68 Pillage Bay

69 It seems to be due to the misunderstanding of this heading by early writers that the river called by Cartier the 'river of Hochelaga' is called by us the St Lawrence. This name had been given by Cartier to Pillage Bay, where the festival of St Lawrence had been spent; but most readers, forgetting this, would understand the name to refer here to the expanse of water at the mouth of the river of which the Indian guides had just spoken.

70 The following day, Thursday, 19 August

71 Farther on he calls them the *Sept-Isles* and this is still their name, though in reality there are only six. The mistake was due to the peninsula of Seven Islands Bay, which from a distance looks like an island.

water.[72] At the end of this low shore, which continues for some ten leagues, is a fresh-water river [Moisie], which enters the gulf with such force that at a distance of more than a league from shore, the water is as fresh as spring water. We entered this river with our longboats and at the mouth of it found a depth of only a fathom and a half. Up this river were several fish in appearance like horses which go on land at night but in the daytime remain in the water, as our two savages informed us. We saw a great number of these fish up this river.[73]

At dawn on the following morning [Saturday], the twenty-first of the said month, we set sail and made our way along this shore until we had examined all the omitted portion, and had arrived at Assumption Island, which we had explored on leaving this coast.[74] And when we had made certain that we had examined the whole coast and that no strait existed, we returned to our ships, which were at the above-mentioned Seven Islands, where there are good harbours with eighteen and twenty fathoms and sandy bottom. We remained there, without being able to leave on account of fogs and headwinds, until [Tuesday] the twenty-fourth of that month, when we made sail and were under way, pursuing our course, until [Sunday] the twenty-ninth, when we came to a harbour on the south shore some eighty leagues from the said Seven Islands.[75] It lies opposite to three flat islands that stand in the middle of the stream.[76] About half-way between this harbour and the above-mentioned [Seven] islands, on the north shore, is a large river[77] with one bank high and the other low, which forms several shoals at a distance of more than three leagues from shore, which spot is very dangerous as there is only a depth of two fathoms and less. Off the edge of these shoals the depth is twenty-five and thirty fathoms steep-to. The whole of this north shore runs north-northeast and south-southwest.

The aforesaid [Old Bic] harbour, where we anchored, is on the south shore, and is a tidal harbour of little value. We named it the 'islets of St John,' since we reached it on the anniversary of the

72 Moisie Shoal and Rock and St Charles Reef

73 Walruses

74 Anticosti. They had now returned to the point at which they had left this north shore.

75 Old Bic Harbour

76 Bic and Bicquette islands and Northwest Reef

77 Manikuagan River

beheading of that saint.[78] And before coming to it, one passes an island[79] some five leagues to the east, with no passage between it and the mainland, except for small boats. The best spot in which to anchor vessels is to the south of a small islet in the middle of this [Old Bic] harbour and close to the islet.

On [Wednesday] September the first we set sail from this harbour to make our way towards Canada. Some fifteen leagues to the west-southwest of this harbour, in the middle of the stream, lie three islands,[80] and opposite to them there is a very deep and rapid river,[81] which is the river and route to the kingdom and country of the Saguenay, as we were informed by our two men from Canada.[82] This river issues from between lofty mountains of bare rock with but little soil upon them. Notwithstanding this, a large number of various kinds of trees grow upon this naked rock as in good soil, in such sort that we saw there a tree tall enough to make a mast for a ship of thirty tons, which was as green as possible, and grew out of the rock without any trace of earth about it. At the mouth of this river we found four canoes from Canada that had come there to fish for seals and other fish.[83] And when we had anchored in that river, two of the canoes came towards our ships but in such great fear and trembling that one of them finally went

78 Sunday, 29 August

79 Barnaby Island, seven and a half miles east of Old Bic Harbour

80 Basque, Apple, and Green islands. Basque Island lies twenty miles from Bicquette Island.

81 The Saguenay

82 Although Taignoagny and Dom Agaya had been seized in Gaspé Harbour, their home was in the region about Quebec.

83 *Cf*, however, Peter D. Clarke, *Origin and Traditional History of the Wyandotts* (Toronto 1870), 4: 'The ships of the first discoverer of Canada were first seen by the Delaware Indians, whom the Wyandotts had sent from about Quebec to the Gulf coast to look out for the strangers and guard the shores. One day the "coast guard" observed several objects appearing, one after another, like sea gulls, as they were scanning the gulf as far as the eye could reach, and which seemed, gradually, to increase in size, as the strange objects came on toward them, and after a while, the spread sails and dark hulls came in full view filling the Indians with wonder. The Delaware messengers sent to the first Wyandott village to inform them of this; represented the ships as some great dark animals, with broad white wings spitting out fire! and uttering the voice of thunder. The Indians on the St. Lawrence had heard, before this, of there being some "great, dark body and white winged animals," seen northeast and south of them, passing over the "big-waters." '

back but the other approached near enough to hear one of our savages who gave his name and told who he was and made them come alongside in all confidence.

On the morrow [Thursday], 2 September, we set forth again from this river[84] to make our way towards Canada, and found the tide extremely swift and dangerous on account of two islands[85] that lie to the south of this river [Saguenay]. At a distance of more than three leagues from these, there is a depth of only two and three fathoms, and the bottom is strewn with large boulders like casks and puncheons, so that with the tide running out between these islands, we thought we should lose our bark,[86] but saved her with the help of our longboats. On the edge of this shoal there is a depth of thirty fathoms and more. Some five leagues to the southwest, beyond the river of the Saguenay and these islands, lies another island.[87] Opposite to this island the north shore is extremely high, and when we tried to anchor there, to let the tide run out, we could not get bottom at a bowshot from shore in 120 fathoms. We were thereupon obliged to return to that [Hare] island, where we anchored in thirty-five fathoms with good bottom.

The next morning,[88] we made sail and got under way in order to push forward, and discovered a species of fish,[89] which none of us had ever seen or heard of. This fish is as large as a porpoise but has no fin. It is very similar to a greyhound about the body and head and is as white as snow, without a spot upon it. Of these there are a very large number in this river, living between the salt and the fresh water. The people of the country call them *Adhothuys* and told us they are very good to eat. They also informed us that these fish are found nowhere else in all this river and country except at this spot.

On [Monday] the sixth of that month, we ran with a favourable

84 The Saguenay

85 Red Islet and Green Island opposite the mouth of the Saguenay

86 The *Emérillon*

87 Cartier on his way home named this island *Ile aux Lièvres* or Hare Island, and this name has remained.

88 Friday, 3 September

89 *Encyclopaedia Britannica*, 9th ed. (Edinburgh 1888), vol. 24, 525: 'The beluga (*Delphinaplerus leucas*) is often called the "white whale," though scarcely exceeding the length of 12 feet. Its colour is almost pure white, and it has no dorsal fin, but a low ridge in its place.' A sketch of one 'from a specimen taken in the river St Lawrence, and exhibited in London in 1877,' will be found ibid., vol. 15, 339, fig. 50.

wind some fifteen leagues up this river, and came to anchor at an island near the north shore,[90] which here makes a small bay and inlet. In this bay and about this island are great numbers of large turtles. The people of the country also fish near this island for the above-mentioned *Adhothuys*. The current here is as strong as at Bordeaux on the ebbing and flowing of the tide. This [Coudres] island is some three leagues long by two in width.[91] The soil is rich and fertile, and the island is covered with several species of fine large trees. Amongst others we found many hazel-bushes, loaded with hazel-nuts as large as ours and better-tasting, though a little more bitter. On this account we named the island 'Hazel-bush Island.'

On [Tuesday], the seventh of the month, being our Lady's day,[92] after hearing mass, we set out from this [Coudres] island to proceed up stream, and came to fourteen islands[93] which lay some seven or eight leagues beyond Coudres Island. This is the point where the province and territory of Canada begins. One of these islands is large, being some ten leagues long and five leagues wide,[94] and is inhabited by people who are much employed in fishing for the many varieties of fish caught in this river, according to the season. Mention will be made of these fish farther on. After we had cast anchor between this large island and the north shore, we went on land and took with us the two men we had seized on our former voyage. We came upon several of the people of the country who began to run away and would not come near, until our two men had spoken to them and told them that they were Taignoagny and Dom Agaya. And when they knew who it was, they began to welcome them, dancing and going through many ceremonies. And some of the headmen came to our longboats, bringing us many eels and other fish, with two or three measures of corn, which is their bread in that country, and many large melons. And during

90 *Ile aux Coudres* or Coudres Island opposite baie St Paul, and so named by Cartier himself

91 Coudres Island is six miles long and two and a half in width.

92 The anniversary of the Virgin's birth really fell on Wednesday, 8 September.

93 There are in reality fifteen: Goose, Crane, Mill, Race, Middle, Canoe, Crowl, Margaret, Two Heads, Cliff, Grosse (the Quarantine station), Brothers, Patience, Reaux and Madame, without counting the island of Orleans.

94 The island of Orleans, so called by Cartier himself, though he also named it Isle of Bacchus

that day many canoes filled with the people of the country, both men as well as women, came to our ships to see and welcome our two men. The Captain received them all well and treated them to what he had to offer. And to ingratiate himself with them, he gave them some small presents of little value, at which they were much pleased.

On the morrow,[95] the lord of Canada, named Donnacona (but as leader they call him *Agouhanna*), came to our ships accompanied by many people in twelve canoes. He then sent back ten of these and came alongside our ships with only two canoes carrying sixteen men. And when he was opposite to the smallest of our three ships [*Emérillon*], this *Agouhanna* began to make a speech and to harangue us, moving his body and his limbs in a marvellous manner, as is their custom when showing joy and contentment. And when he came opposite to the Captain's vessel,[96] on board of which were Taignoagny and Dom Agaya, the leader spoke to them and they to him, telling him what they had seen in France, and the good treatment meted out to them there. At this the leader was much pleased and begged the Captain to stretch out his arms to him that he might hug and kiss them, which is the way they welcome one in that country. After this the Captain stepped down into this *Agouhanna's* canoe, and ordered bread and wine to be brought that the chief and his followers might partake thereof. When this had been done they were much pleased; but no other present was then made to the leader, pending a more suitable time and place. After these things had been thus carried out, they took leave of each other and separated, the said *Agouhanna* returning to his canoes to make his way home again. And the Captain likewise ordered out our longboats to make our way up the stream with the flood tide, to find a harbour and safe spot in which to lay up the ships. And we went some ten leagues up the river, coasting this island [of Orleans], at the end of which we came to a forking of the waters,[97] which is an exceedingly pleasant spot, where there is a small river and a harbour with a bar, on which at high tide, there is a depth of from two to three fathoms. We thought this river [St Charles] a suitable place in which to lay up our ships in safety. We named it 'Ste Croix,' as we arrived there that day.[98]

95 Wednesday, 8 September
96 *La Grande Hermine*
97 It is the fork formed by the St Charles and the St Lawrence.
98 The anniversary of the Elevation of the Cross fell on Tuesday, 14 September. This was still Wednesday, 8 September, but it was not until Tuesday

Near this spot lives a people of which this Donnacona is leader, and he himself resides there. The village is called Stadacona. This region is as fine land as it is possible to see, being very fertile and covered with magnificent trees of the same varieties as in France, such as oaks, elms, ash, walnut, plum-trees, yew-trees, cedars, vines, hawthorns, bearing a fruit as large as a damson, and other varieties of trees. Beneath these grows as good hemp as that of France, which comes up without sowing or tilling it. After visiting this river [St Charles] and finding it suitable, the Captain and the others returned to the longboats in order to go back to the ships.And as we came out of the river,[99] we saw one accompanied by several men, women, and children; and he began to make an harangue, expressing joy and contentment after the manner of the country, while the women danced and sang uninterruptedly, being in the water up to their knees. The Captain, seeing their great affection and good-will, ordered the longboat in which he was seated to go towards them, and gave them some knives and glass-beads, at which they showed wonderful pleasure. And when we were a league or so away, we still heard them singing, dancing, and rejoicing over our visit.

How the Captain Returned on Board the Ships, and Went to Visit the Island;[100] the Nature and Size of the Same; and How He Had the Ships Brought into the River Ste Croix[101]

When he had arrived with our longboats at the ships on our return from the river Ste Croix,[102] the Captain ordered the longboats to be manned again in order to go on shore at the island [of Orleans] to examine the trees, which appeared to be very fine, and also to see the nature of the soil of that island; which was done. And on reaching the island, we found it covered with very fine trees, such as oaks, elms, pines, cedars, and other varieties like our own; and

---

that the ships were brought to the mouth of the river St Charles or to 'Ste Croix harbour.' The two larger vessels were warped into the St Charles on Thursday, the sixteenth.

99 St Charles

100 The island of Orleans

101 The St Charles

102 Cartier farther on also called it *ile d'Orléans*, in all probability after Charles, Duke of Orleans, the third son of Francis I.

we likewise found there a great store of vines, which heretofore we had not seen in all this region. On that account we named the island 'Bacchus's Island.' This island is some twelve leagues in length, and in appearance is a fine flat land, covered with timber, without any of it being cultivated, except that there are a few small cabins which they use for fishing as has been mentioned above.

On the following day,[103] we set sail with our ships to bring them to the spot called Ste Croix, where we arrived the next day [Tuesday], the fourteenth of the month. And Donnacona, Taignoagny, and Dom Agaya came to meet us with twenty-five canoes filled with people who were coming from the direction whence we had set out and were making towards Stadacona, which is their home. And all came over towards our ships, showing many signs of joy, except the two men we had brought with us, to wit, Taignoagny and Dom Agaya, who were altogether changed in their attitude and goodwill, and refused to come on board our ships, although many times begged to do so. At this we began somewhat to distrust them. The Captain asked them if they were willing to go with him to Hochelaga,[104] as they had promised, and they replied that they were and that it was their intention to go there. Upon this each retired.

And on the following day [Wednesday], the fifteenth of the month, the Captain went ashore with a number of his men to set out buoys and landmarks that the ships might be laid up with more care. We found a large number of the people of the village coming to meet us, and among the rest, Donnacona, our two men, and their friends, who kept apart on a point of land on the bank of the river [St Lawrence], without one of them coming towards us, as did the others, who were not of their party. And the Captain, being informed of their presence, ordered some of his men to accompany him, and went towards the point of land where they were, and found Donnacona, Taignaogny, Dom Agaya, and several others of their party. After they had mutually saluted each other, Taignoagny began to make a speech and to say to the Captain, that Donnacona was vexed that the Captain and his people carried so many weapons when they on their side carried none. To this

103 According to the text this would be Thursday, 9 September, but several days are evidently omitted; for the day after the fourteenth is called Tuesday. It was therefore Monday, 13 September.

104 The region about the Lachine Rapids. The word in the Huron tongue means 'at the beaver-dam.'

the Captain replied that for all Donnacona's grief, he would not cease to carry them since such was the custom in France as Taignoagny well knew. But for all this the Captain and Donnacona were most friendly towards each other. Then we understood that what Taignoagny had been saying came solely from himself and his companion; for before we went away, the Captain and the leader made a compact together in the most strange manner; for the whole of Donnacona's people cried out all together, and gave three shouts in such a loud manner that it was awful to hear. After that they took leave of each other; and we returned on board our ships for that day.

On the morrow [Thursday], the sixteenth of that month, we placed our two largest vessels inside the harbour and river,[105] where at high water there is a depth of three fathoms, and at low tide, half a fathom. But the bark[106] was left in the roadstead to take us to Hochelaga. And as soon as the two vessels had been brought into the harbour and had grounded, Donnacona, Taignoagny, and Dom Agaya came about them with more than 500 people, both men, women, and children; and the leader came on board with ten or twelve of the headmen of the village, who were feasted and fêted by the Captain and others, according to their rank; and some small presents were given to them. And Taignoagny told the Captain that Donnacona was annoyed because he [Cartier] intended to go to Hochelaga, and was most unwilling that Taignoagny should accompany him, as he had promised to do; for the river was not worth exploring. To this the Captain made reply, that notwithstanding this he would use his efforts to reach there; for he had orders from the king his master to push on as far as possible; and that if Taignoagny were willing to come along, as he had promised, a present would be made to him which would please him, and he would be well entertained; and that they would merely go and see Hochelaga and return. Taignoagny answered that under no circumstances would he go. Upon this they retired to their houses.

And the next day [Friday], the seventeenth of the same month, Donnacona and the others came back and brought a quantity of eels and other fish, which are caught in great numbers in this river [St Lawrence], as shall be set forth farther on. And on arriving in front of our two ships, they began to dance and to sing as usual.

105 The St Charles. These were the *Grande Ermine* and the *Petite Ermine.*
106 The *Emérillon*

After this Donnacona had all his people place themselves on one side, and having made a ring in the sand, caused the Captain and his men to stand inside it. He then began a long harangue, holding by the hand a girl of about ten or twelve years of age, whom at length he presented to the Captain. Thereupon the whole of the leader's people raised three shouts and cries in sign of joy and alliance. He next made him a present of two small boys of tenderer age, one after the other, on which the people gave vent to the same shouts and cries as before. After the Captain had thanked the leader for the presents thus made to him, Taignoagny told the Captain that the girl was the daughter of Donnacona's own sister, and that one of the boys was his, the speaker's, brother; and that these children had been given to him to the intent he should not go to Hochelaga. To this our Captain replied that in case they had been given to him with that intent, they must be taken back; for that nothing would induce him to forgo the attempt to make his way to Hochelaga, since such were his orders. On hearing this Dom Agaya, Taignoagny's companion, told the Captain that Donnacona had given him these children out of pure affection and in sign of alliance; and that he [Dom Agaya] was willing to accompany the Captain to Hochelaga. At this Taignoagny and Dom Agaya had high words together, whereby we were convinced, as well from this as by other bad turns we had seen him do, that Taignoagny was a worthless fellow, who was intent on nothing but treason and malice. The Captain then ordered the children to be placed on board the ships, and had brought to him two swords, a large, plain, brass wash-basin and one that was worked, and of these he made a present to Donnacona, who was extremely pleased and thanked the Captain. And Donnacona called to his people to sing and to dance; and begged the Captain to have a piece of artillery discharged because Taignoagny and Dom Agaya had given him great accounts of it, and neither he nor his people had ever seen or heard of artillery. The Captain answered that he would do so, and ordered a dozen canon to be fired with their bullets into the wood that stood opposite to the ships and the people. These were all so much astonished as if the heavens had fallen upon them, and began to howl and to shriek in such a very loud manner that one would have thought hell had emptied itself there. And before they retired, Taignoagny sent word by others, that the sailors on board the bark [*Emérillon*], that lay out in the roadstead, had fired their cannon and had killed two of their people, whereupon all scurried off in such haste that one would have thought we had wished to destroy them. This report proved false; for no shot was fired that day from the bark.

How Donnacona, Taignoagny, and the Others Devised a Ruse, and Dressed Up Three Men as Devils, Who Pretended to Be Sent from Their God Cudouagny to Prevent Us from Going to Hochelaga

On the next day [Saturday], the eighteenth of the month, they devised a great ruse to prevent us still from going to Hochelaga. They dressed up three men as devils, arraying them in black and white dog-skins, with horns as long as one's arm and their faces coloured black as coal, and unknown to us put them into a canoe. They themselves then came towards our ships in a crowd as usual but remained some two hours in the wood without appearing, awaiting the moment when the tide would bring down the above-mentioned canoe. At that hour they all came out of the wood and showed themselves in front of our ships but without coming so near as they were in the habit of doing. And Taignoagny proceeded to greet the Captain, who asked him if he wished the ship's boat. Taignoagny answered that he did not wish it for the moment but that presently he would come on board the ships. Soon after arrived the canoe in which were the three men dressed as devils, with long horns on their heads. And as they drew near, the one in the middle made a wonderful harangue, but they passed by our ships without once turning their faces towards us, and proceeded to head for the shore and to run their canoe on land. Donnacona and his people at once seized the canoe and the three men, who had let themselves fall to the bottom of it like dead men, and carried them, canoe and men, into the wood which was distant a stone's throw from our ships; and not a soul remained in sight but all retired into the wood. And there in the wood they began a preaching and a speechifying that could be heard from our ships, which lasted about half an hour. After that, Taignoagny and Dom Agaya came out of the wood, walking in our direction, with their hands joined and their caps under their arms, pretending to be much astonished. And Taignoagny began to speak and repeated three times, '*Jesus*,' '*Jesus*,' '*Jesus*,' lifting his eyes towards heaven. Then Dom Agaya called out *'Jesus,' 'Maria,' 'Jacques Cartier,'* looking up to heaven as the other had done. The Captain, seeing their grimaces and gesticulations, began to ask them what was the matter, and what new event had happened? They replied that there was bad news, adding that indeed it was far from good. The Captain again asked them what was the trouble? They answered that their god, Cudouagny by name, had made an announcement at Hochelaga, and that the three above-mentioned men had come in his name to tell them the tidings, which were that there would be so much ice and snow that all would perish. At this we all began to laugh and to tell them that their god Cudouagny was a mere fool who did not know what he was saying; and that they should tell his messengers as much; and that Jesus would keep them safe from the cold if they would trust in him. Thereupon Taignoagny and his companion asked the Captain if he had spoken to Jesus; and he replied that his priests had done so and that there would be fine weather. On this they thanked the Captain extremely, and returned to the wood to tell the news to the others, who at once came forth pretending to be pleased at what the Captain had said. And to show their joy, as soon as they came opposite to the ships, they with one voice began to give three shouts and cries, which is their way of showing joy; and began to dance and to sing as usual. But by collusion Taignoagny and Dom Agaya told the Captain that Donnacona was unwilling that either of them should accompany him to Hochelaga unless he [Cartier] should leave a hostage behind on shore with Donnacona. To this the Captain replied that if they were not ready to go willingly, they could stay at home, and that on their account he would by no means give up his attempt to reach that place.

How the Captain and All the Gentlemen Set Forth from the Province of Canada with the Bark, the Two Longboats, and Fifty Sailors to Make Their Way to Hochelaga; and What They Saw along the River on the Way

The following day [Sunday], 19 September, we made sail and got under way with the bark [*Emérillon*] and the two longboats, as already stated, in order with the tide to push on up the river. Along both shores we had sight of the finest and most beautiful land it is possible to see, being as level as a pond and covered with the most magnificent trees in the world. And on the banks were so many vines loaded with grapes that it seemed they could only have been planted by husbandmen; but because they are never looked after nor pruned, the grapes are not so sweet nor so large as our own. We likewise noticed a large number of houses along the banks of the river, which are inhabited by people who catch great quantities of the numerous good fish in the river, according to the season. These people came towards our boats in as friendly and familiar a manner as if we had been natives of the country, bringing us great store of fish and of whatever else they possessed, in order to obtain our wares, stretching forth their hands towards heaven and making many gestures and signs of joy. And when we had come to anchor some twenty-five leagues from Canada, at a place called Achelacy, which is a narrow passage in the river where the current is swift and the navigation dangerous, both on account of the rocks as for other causes, there came several canoes to our ships; and among the rest came a great leader of this region, who made a long harangue as he came on board, pointing out to us clearly by signs and in other ways that the river was extremely dangerous a little higher up, and warning us to be on our guard. And this leader presented the Captain with two of his children; but the latter would only accept a girl of some eight or nine years of age and refused a little boy of two or three as being too young. The Captain fêted the leader and his party as well as he could and made him a small present, for which he thanked the Captain. Then the people went back on shore. And since then, this leader and his wife have come as far as Canada to see their daughter, and brought the Captain a small present.

From [Sunday] the nineteenth until [Tuesday] the twenty-eighth of the month,[107] we continued to make our way up the river without losing a day nor an hour. During this time we saw and discovered as fine a country and as level a region as one could wish, covered, as before mentioned, with the finest trees in the world, such as oaks, elms, walnuts, pines, cedars, spruce, ash, box-wood, willows, osiers, and, better than all, a great quantity of grape-vines, which were so loaded with grapes that the sailors came on board with their arms full of them. There are likewise many cranes,

107 Sunday, 19 September, to Tuesday, 28 September

swans, bustards, geese, ducks, larks, pheasants, partridges, blackbirds, thrushes, turtledoves, goldfinches, canaries, linnets, nightingales, sparrows and other birds, the same as in France, and in great numbers.

On [Tuesday] 28 September we reached a large lake[108] where for twelve leagues the river widens out to a distance of some five or six leagues. We made our way up this lake that day without finding anywhere a depth of more than two fathoms, neither more nor less. And on reaching the head of this lake we could see no passage nor outlet; but it seemed quite landlocked without any stream flowing into it; and at this end there was a depth of only a fathom and a half. On that account we had to heave to and drop the anchor, and to go and look for a way out with our longboats. And we discovered that there are four or five branches of the river entering the lake here from the direction of Hochelaga, but that they have bars and shoals in them formed by the current. At that time there was a depth here of only one fathom, but after passing these bars, there is a depth of four and five fathoms. This was the season of the year when the water was lowest, as we could see from the flood-mark of the river, which rises more than two fathoms higher.

These various branches encircle and enclose five or six fine islands[109] which form the terminus of the lake. Some fifteen leagues higher up, these branches all unite into one stream. The same day we visited one of these islands where we came across five men who were hunting for game. They came to meet our boats without fear or alarm, and in as familiar a manner as if they had seen us all their lives. And when our longboats grounded, one of those men took the Captain in his arms and carried him on shore as easily as if he had been a six-year-old child, so strong and big was that man. We discovered that they had a great heap of muskrats, which live in the water and are as large as rabbits and wonderfully good to eat. They made a present of these to the Captain, who in return gave them some knives and some beads. We asked them by signs if this was the way to Hochelaga? They made clear to us that it was, and that we had still a three days' journey thither.

108 Lake St Peter, which is twenty miles long and eight miles wide

109 Raisin, Monk, Boat, Stone, Grace, Bear, and Eagle islands at the head of Lake St Peter

How the Captain Gave Orders for the Longboats to Be Fitted Out for the Voyage to Hochelaga; and for the Bark to Be Left Behind, on Account of the Difficult Passage; and How We Reached Hochelaga; and of the Reception the People Gave Us on Our Arrival

On the morrow[110] our Captain, seeing it was impossible to get the bark past this spot at that season, ordered the longboats to be fitted out and provisioned, and stores to be put into them for as long a period as possible and as the longboats would hold. And he set out in them accompanied by a few of the gentlemen, to wit: Claude du Pontbriant, cup-bearer to His Royal Highness the Dauphin, Charles de La Pommeraye, John Guyon, John Poullet, with twenty-eight sailors including Macé Jalobert and William Le Breton, who had command, under Cartier, of the other two vessels, in order to make our way up the river as far as we possibly could. And we sailed on in as fine weather as one could wish until [Saturday] 2 October, when we arrived at Hochelaga,[111] which is about forty-five leagues from the spot where we had left our bark. During this interval we came across on the way many of the people of the country, who brought us fish and other provisions, at the same time dancing and showing great joy at our coming. And in order to win and keep their friendship, the Captain made them a present of some knives, beads, and other small trifles, whereat they were greatly pleased. And on reaching Hochelaga, there came to meet us more than a thousand persons, men, women, and children, who gave us as good a welcome as ever father gave to his son, making great signs of joy; for the men danced in one ring, the women in another, and the children also apart by themselves.[112] After this they brought us quantities of fish, and of their bread which is made of corn, throwing so much of it into our longboats that it seemed to rain bread. Seeing this the Captain, accompanied by several of his men, went on shore; and no sooner had he landed

110 Wednesday, 29 September

111 The Indian village on the island of Montreal

112 F.W. Hodge, *Handbook of American Indians*, I (Washington 1907), 382: 'These women ... form a circle round the song altar (the mat for the singer). Then outside of this circle the men form another circle at a suitable distance from that of the women,' etc. On the Iroquois dances, *cf* L.H. Morgan, *League of the Ho-dé-no-sau-nee or Iroquois* (New York 1904).

than they all crowded about him and about the others, giving them a wonderful reception. And the women brought their babies in their arms to have the Captain and his companions touch them, while all held a merry-making which lasted more than half an hour. Seeing their generosity and friendliness, the Captain had the women all sit down in a row and gave them some tin beads and other trifles; and to some of the men he gave knives. Then he returned on board the long-boats to sup and pass the night, throughout which the people remained on the bank of the river, as near the longboats as they could get, keeping many fires burning all night, and dancing and calling out every moment *aguyase*, which is their term of salutation and joy.[113]

How the Captain and the Gentlemen, Accompanied by Twenty-five Well-Armed and Marshalled Sailors, Went to Visit the Village of Hochelaga; and of the Situation of the Place

At daybreak the next day,[114] the Captain, having put on his armour, had his men marshalled for the purpose of paying a visit to the village and home of these people, and to a mountain which lies near the town. The Captain was accompanied by the gentlemen and by twenty sailors, the remainder having been left behind to guard the longboats. And he took three men of the village as guides to conduct them thither. When we had got under way, we discovered that the path was as well-trodden as it is possible to see, and that the country was the finest and most excellent one could find anywhere, being everywhere full of oaks, as beautiful as in any forest in France, underneath which the ground lay covered with acorns. And after marching about a league and a half, we met on the trail one of the headmen of the village of Hochelaga, accompanied by several persons, who made signs to us that we should rest at that spot near a fire they had lighted on the path; which we did. Thereupon this headman began to make a speech and to harangue us, which, as before mentioned, is their way of showing joy and friendliness, welcoming in this way the Captain and his

113 This word is given in the Indian vocabulary as meaning 'my friend,' but it seems more likely to be the same word as the *aquayesse* meaning 'to laugh.'

114 Sunday, 3 October

company. The Captain presented him with a couple of hatchets and a couple of knives, as well as with a cross and a crucifix, which he made him kiss and then hung it about his neck. For these the headman thanked the Captain. When this was done we marched on, and about half a league thence found that the land began to be cultivated. It was find land with large fields covered with the corn of the country, which resembles Brazil millet, and is about as large or larger than a pea. They live on this as we do on wheat. And in the middle of these fields is situated and stands the village of Hochelaga,[115] near and adjacent to a mountain, the slopes of which are fertile and are cultivated, and from the top of which one can see for a long distance. We named this mountain 'Mount Royal.' The village is circular and is completely enclosed by a wooden palisade in three tiers like a pyramid. The top one is built crosswise, the middle one perpendicular, and the lowest one of strips of wood placed lengthwise. The whole is well joined and lashed after their manner, and is some two lances in height. There is only one gate and entrance to this village, and that can be barred up. Over this gate and in many places about the enclosure are species of galleries with ladders for mounting to them, which galleries are provided with rocks and stones for the defence and protection of the place. There are some fifty houses in this village, each about fifty or more paces in length, and twelve or fifteen in width, built completely of wood and covered in and bordered up with large pieces of the bark and rind of trees, as broad as a table, which are well and cunningly lashed after their manner. And inside these houses are many rooms and chambers; and in the middle is a large space without a floor, where they light their fire and live together in common. Afterwards the men retire to the above-mentioned quarters with their wives and children.[116] And, furthermore, there are lofts in the upper part of their houses, where they store the corn of which they make their bread. This they call *carraconny*, and they make it in the following manner. They have wooden mortars, like those used [in France] for braying hemp, and in these with wooden pestles they pound the corn into flour. This they knead into dough, of which they make small loaves, which

115 James F. Pendergast and Bruce G. Trigger, *Cartier's Hochelaga and the Dawson Site* (Montreal and London 1972)

116 Peter Nabokov and Robert Easton, *Native American Architecture* (New York 1989), 76–92

they set on a broad hot stone and then cover them with hot pebbles. In this way they bake their bread for want of an oven. They make also many kinds of soup with this corn, as well as with beans and with pease, of which they have a considerable supply, and again with large cucumbers and other fruits. They have in their houses also large vessels like puncheons, in which they place their fish, such as eels and others, that are smoked during the summer, and on these they live during the winter. They make great store of these as we ourselves saw. All their food is eaten without salt. They sleep on the bark of trees, spread out upon the ground, with old skins of wild animals over them; and of these, to wit, otters, beavers, martens, foxes, wildcats, deer, stags, and others, they make their clothing and blankets, but the greater portion of them go almost stark naked. The most precious article they possess in this world is *esnoguy*, which is as white as snow. They produce it from shells[117] in the river in the following manner. When a man has incurred the death penalty or they have taken some prisoners in war, they kill one and make great incisions in his buttocks and thighs, and about his legs, arms, and shoulders. Then at the spot where this *esnoguy* is found, they sink the body to the bottom and leave it there for ten or twelve hours. It is then brought to the surface; and in the above-mentioned cuts and incisions they find these shells, of which they make a sort of bead, which has the same use among them as gold and silver with us; for they consider it the most valuable article in the world. It has the virtue of stopping nose-bleeding; for we tried it. This whole people gives itself to manual labour and to fishing merely to obtain the necessities of life; for they place no value upon the goods of this world, both because they are unacquainted with them and because they do not move from home and are not nomads like those of

117 *The Canadian Naturalist*, VI, 369: 'Only a single specimen of the shell wampum ... has been found. It is ... of small size, neatly formed, and the material is apparently the pearly shell of a Unio, probably *U. ventricosus* (or *U. Canadensis* of Lea) ... If this single specimen really represents the beads to which Cartier alludes, it accords with his statement that the material was obtained in the river.' See J.W. Dawson, *Fossil Men* (Montreal 1880), 141. Mr W.J. Wintemberg tells me that the shells usually found are *Pleurocera subulare* and *Goniobasis livascens.* See also his *Use of Shells by the Ontario Indians* in the *Annual Archeological Report*, 1906 (Toronto 1907), 62–4. See also Lynn Ceci, 'The Value of Wampum among the New York Iroquois: A Case Study in Artefact Analysis,' *Journal of Anthropological Research* 38 (spring 1982): 97–107.

Canada and of the Saguenay, notwithstanding that the Canadians and some eight or nine other peoples along this river are subjects of theirs.

How We Arrived at the Village and the Reception We Met With; and How the Captain Gave Them Presents and Other Things the Captain Did, as Will Be Seen in This Chapter

As we drew near to their village, great numbers of the inhabitants came out to meet us and gave us a hearty welcome, according to the custom of the country. And we were led by our guides and those who were conducting us into the middle of the village, where there was an open square between the houses, about a stone's throw or thereabouts in width each way. They signalled to us that we should come to a halt here, which we did. And at once all the girls and women of the village, some of whom had children in their arms, crowded about us, rubbing our faces, arms, and other parts of the upper portions of our bodies which they could touch, weeping for joy at the sight of us and giving us the best welcome they could. They made signs to us also to be good enough to put our hands upon their babies. After this the men made the women retire, and themselves sat down upon the ground round about us, as if we had been going to perform a miracle play. And at once several of the women came back, each with a four-cornered mat, woven like tapestry, and these they spread upon the ground in the middle of the square, and made us place ourselves upon them. When this had been done, the ruler and leader of this country, whom in their language they call *Agouhanna*, was carried in, seated on a large deer-skin, by nine or ten men, who came and set him down upon the mats near the Captain, making signs to us that this was their ruler and leader. This *Agouhanna*, who was some fifty years of age, was in no way better dressed than the others except that he wore about his head for a crown a sort of red band made of hedgehog's skin. This leader was completely paralyzed and deprived of the use of his limbs. When he had saluted the Captain and his men, by making signs which clearly meant that they were very welcome, he showed his arms and legs to the Captain motioning to him to be good enough to touch them, as if he thereby expected to be cured and healed. On this the Captain set about rubbing his arms and legs with his hands. Thereupon this

Agouhanna took the band of cloth he was wearing as a crown and presented it to the Captain. And at once many sick persons, some blind, others with but one eye, others lame or impotent and others again so extremely old that their eyelids hung down to their cheeks, were brought in and set down or laid out near the Captain, in order that he might lay his hands upon them, so that one would have thought Christ had come down to earth to heal them.

Seeing the suffering of these people and their faith, the Captain read aloud the Gospel of St John, namely, 'In the beginning,' etc., making the sign of the cross over the poor sick people, praying God to give them knowledge of our holy faith and of our Saviour's passion, and grace to obtain baptism and redemption. Then the Captain took a prayer-book and read out, word for word, the Passion of our Lord, that all who were present could hear it, during which all these poor people maintained great silence and were wonderfully attentive, looking up to heaven and going through the same ceremonies they saw us do. After this the Captain had all the men range themselves on one side, the women on another, and the children on another, and to the headmen he gave hatchets, to the others, knives, and to the women, beads and other small trinkets. He then made the children scramble for little rings and tin *agnus Dei*, which afforded them great amusement. The Captain next ordered the trumpets and other musical instruments to be sounded, whereat the people were much delighted. We then took leave of them and proceeded to set out upon our return. Seeing this the women placed themselves in our way to prevent us, and brought us some of their provisions, which they had made ready for us, to wit: fish, soups, beans, bread, and other dishes, in the hope of inducing us to partake of some refreshment and to eat with them. But as these provisions were not to our taste and had no savour of salt, we thanked them, making signs that we were in no need of refreshment.

On issuing forth from the village we were conducted by several of the men and women of the place up the above-mentioned mountain, lying a quarter of the league away, which was named by us 'Mount Royal.'[118] On reaching the summit we had a view of the land for more than thirty leagues round about. Towards the north there is a range of mountains, running east and west,[119] and an-

118 Hochelaga was thus about three-quarters of a mile from the mountain, Mount Royal.

119 The Laurentian hills

other range to the south.[120] Between these ranges lies the finest land it is possible to see, being arable, level, and flat. And in the midst of this flat region one saw the river [St Lawrence] extending beyond the spot where we had left our longboats.[121] At that point there is the most violent rapid it is possible to see, which we were unable to pass.[122] And as far as the eye can reach, one sees that river, large, wide, and broad, which came from the southwest and flowed near three fine conical mountains, which we estimated to be some fifteen leagues away.[123] And it was told us and made clear by signs by our three local guides that there were three more such rapids in that river,[124] like the one where lay our longboats; but through lack of an interpreter we could not make out what the distance was from one to the other. They then explained to us by signs that after passing these rapids, one could navigate along that river for more than three moons. And they showed us furthermore that along the mountains to the north[125] there is a large river,[126] which comes from the west like the said river [St Lawrence]. We thought this river [Ottawa] must be the one that flows past the kingdom and province of the Saguenay;[127] and without our asking any questions or making any sign, they seized the chain of the Captain's whistle, which was made of silver, and a dagger-handle of yellow copper-gilt like gold, that hung at the side of one of the sailors, and gave us to understand that these came from up that river [Ottawa], where lived *Agojuda*, which means bad people, who were armed to the teeth, showing us the style of their armour, which is made with cords and wood, laced and plaited together. They also seemed to say that these *Agojuda* waged war continually, one people against the other, but through not understanding their

120 The northern slopes of the Adirondacks and of the Green mountains of Vermont

121 This was possibly under the lee of a small island called Market Garden Island that then lay between the island of Montreal and St Helen's Island. It has since been incorporated with the docks.

122 The Lachine rapid. The descent is forty-two feet in two miles.

123 St Bruno, Beloeil, and Rougement. One can see Mt Johnson as well.

124 The Cascades (including Cedar and Coteau), Long Sault, and Galops rapids

125 The Laurentides

126 The Ottawa

127 What this mysterious 'kingdom of the Saguenay' was, with its 'infinite quantities of gold, rubies and other gems,' it is difficult to say, unless a confusion was made between copper and gold, and the region meant was the copper quarries of Lake Superior.

language we could not make out what the distance was to that country. The Captain showed them some copper, which they call *caigneldazé*, and, pointing towards the said region, asked by signs if it came thence? They shook their heads to say no, showing us that it came from the Saguenay, which lies in the opposite direction. Having seen and learned these things, we returned to our longboats, accompanied by a large number of these people, some of whom, when they saw that our people were tired, took them upon their shoulders, as on horseback, and carried them. And on our arrival at the longboats, we at once set sail to return to the bark,[128] for fear of any misadventure. Such a departure did not fail to cause the people great regret; for so long as they could follow us down the river, they did so. And we made such good headway that we reached our bark on Monday, 4 October.

On Tuesday, the fifth of that month, we hoisted sail and set forth with our bark and the longboats to return to the province of Canada and to Ste Croix Harbour,[129] where our ships had been left. And on [Thursday] the seventh we came to anchor opposite a stream[130] which enters the river [St Lawrence] from the north and at the mouth of which lie four small islands covered with trees.[131] We named this stream 'Lashing River.' And as one of these islands [St Quentin] stretches out into the river [St Lawrence], and can be seen from a distance, the Captain had a fine large cross erected upon the point of it.[132] He then commanded the longboats to be made ready to go up that river [St Maurice] at high tide to find out the depth and nature of the same. These orders were carried out; and they rowed up the river that day; but when it was discovered to be of no importance and shallow, they came back. We then made sail to continue our way down the river [St Lawrence].

128 The *Emérillon* in Lake St Peter

129 The river St Charles

130 The river St Maurice, which enters the St Lawrence at Three Rivers, twenty-five miles below the head of Lake St Peter, where the longboats had rejoined the *Emérillon*.

131 There are in fact six islands, although two of them, Iles Caron and Ogden, are quite small. The other four are now named St Quentin, La Potherie, St Christophe, and St Joseph, while their old names were Ile au Cochon, Bellerive, St Christophe, and La Croix. I am indebted to my friend Mr V.J. Hughes of Montreal for the modern names.

132 Ile St Quentin

How We Arrived at Ste Croix Harbour; and the State in Which We Found Our Ships; and How the Leader of That Region Came to See the Captain, and the Captain Went to See Him; and of Some of Their Customs in Detail

On Monday, 11 October, we arrived at the harbour of Ste Croix,[133] where our ships were lying, and found that the mates and sailors who had stayed behind had built a fort in front of the ships, enclosed on all sides with large wooden logs planted upright and joined one to the other, with artillery pointing every way, and in a good state to defend us against the whole countryside. As soon as the leader of that region [Donnacona] was informed of our arrival, he came on the following day, [Tuesday] the twelfth of the month, accompanied by Taignoagny, Dom Agaya, and several others, to see the Captain [Cartier], to whom they gave a hearty welcome, feigning to be much pleased at his return. The latter likewise received them fairly well, notwithstanding that they had not deserved it. Donnacona invited the Captain to visit him on the following day at Canada, and the Captain promised to do so. So on the morrow [Wednesday], the thirteenth of the month [October], the Captain, accompanied by the gentlemen and with fifty sailors drawn up, in order, went to visit Donnacona and his people at their home called Stadacona, which stood about half a league from the spot where lay our ships. And on drawing near the village, the inhabitants came out to meet us a stone's throw or more from their houses, where they ranged and seated themselves after their manner and custom, the men on one side and the women and girls on the other, standing up and singing and dancing unceasingly. And when all had mutually saluted and welcomed each other, the Captain presented the men with knives and other wares of small value, and had all the women and girls pass before him, to whom he gave each a tin ring, for which they thanked him. He was then conducted by Donnacona and Taignoagny to see their houses which were well stored with the provisions they use in winter. Donnacona showed the Captain the scalps of five men, stretched on hoops like parchment, and told us they were Toudamans from the south, who waged war continually against his people. He informed us also that two years previously these Toudamans had come and attacked them in that very river, on an island which lies opposite

133 The river St Charles

to the Saguenay, where they were spending the night on their way to Honguedo,[134] being on the war-path against the Toudamans with some two hundred men, women, and children, who were surprised when asleep in a fort they had thrown up, to which the Toudamans set fire round about and slew them all as they rushed out, except five who made their escape. Of this defeat they still continued to complain bitterly, making clear to us that they would have vengeance for the same. After seeing these things, we returned to our ships.

Of the Manner of Life of the People of This Region; and of Some of Their Customs, Beliefs, and Habits

This people has no belief in God that amounts to anything; for they believe in a god they call *Cudouagny*, and maintain that he often holds intercourse with them and tells them what the weather will be like. They also say that when he gets angry with them, he throws dust in their eyes. They believe furthermore that when they die they go to the stars and descend on the horizon like the stars. Next, that they go off to beautiful green fields covered with fine trees, flowers, and luscious fruits. After they had explained these things to us, we showed them their error and informed them that their *Cudouagny* was a wicked spirit who deceived them, and that there is but one God, Who is in Heaven, Who gives us everything we need and is the Creator of all things and that in Him alone we should believe. Also that one must receive baptism or perish in hell. Several other points concerning our faith were explained to them which they believed without trouble, and proceeded to call their *Cudouagny, Agojuda*, to such an extent that several times they begged the Captain to cause them to be baptized. And one day the leader [Donnacona], Taignoagny, and Dom Agaya came with all the people of their village to receive baptism; but since we did not know their real intention and state of mind, and had no one to explain to them our faith, an excuse was made to them; and Taignoagny and Dom Agaya were requested to tell them that we should return another voyage and would bring priests and

134 Gaspé. We thus see that expeditions from Quebec to Gaspé were frequent and that there was nothing unusual in the expedition of the previous summer in the course of which Taignoagny and Dom Agaya had been carried off from Gaspé Bay by Cartier.

some chrism, giving them to understand, as an excuse, that no one could be baptized without his chrism. This they believed; for they [Taignoagny and Dom Agaya] had seen several children baptized in Brittany. And at the Captain's promise to return, they were much pleased and thanked him.

These people live with almost everything in common, much like the Brazilians. They go clothed in beasts' skins, and rather miserably. In winter they wear leggings and moccasins made of skins, and in summer they go barefoot. They maintain the order of marriage, except that the men take two or three wives. On the death of their husband the wives never marry again, but wear mourning all their lives by dyeing their faces black with brayed charcoal and grease as thick as the back of a knife-blade; and by this one knows they are widows. They have another very bad custom connected with their daughters, who as soon as they reach the age of puberty are all placed in a brothel open to every one, until the girls have made a match. We saw this with our own eyes; for we discovered houses as full of these girls as is a boys' school with boys in France. And furthermore betting, after their fashion, takes place in these houses in which they stake all they own, even to the covering of their privy parts. They are by no means a laborious people and work the soil with short bits of wood about half a sword in length. With these they hoe their corn which they call *ozisy*, in size as large as a pea. Corn of a similar kind grows in considerable quantities in Brazil. They have also a considerable quantity of melons, cucumbers, pumpkins, pease, and beans of various colours and unlike our own. Furthermore, they have a plant, of which a large supply is collected in summer for the winter's consumption.[135] They hold it in high esteem, though the men alone make use of it in the following manner. After drying it in the sun, they carry it about their necks in a small skin pouch in lieu of a bag, together with a hollow bit of stone or wood. Then at frequent intervals they crumble this plant into powder, which they place in one of the openings of the hollow instrument, and, laying a live coal on top, suck at the other end to such an extent that they fill their bodies so full of smoke that it streams out of their mouths and nostrils as from a chimney. They say it keeps them warm and in good health, and never go about without these things. We made a trial of this smoke. When it is in one's mouth, one would think

135 Tobacco

one had taken powdered pepper, it is so hot. The women of this country work beyond comparison more than the men, both at fishing, which is much followed, as well as at tilling the ground and other tasks. Both the men, women, and children are more indifferent to the cold than beasts; for in the coldest weather we experienced, and it was extraordinary severe, they would come to our ships every day across the ice and snow, the majority of them almost stark naked, which seems incredible unless one has seen them. While the ice and snow last, they catch a great number of wild animals such as fawns, stags, and bears, hares, martens, foxes, otters, and others. Of these they brought us very few; for they are heavy eaters and are niggardly with their provisions. They eat their meat quite raw, merely smoking it, and the same with their fish. From what we have seen and been able to learn of these people, I am of opinion that they could easily be moulded in the way one would wish. May God in His holy mercy turn His countenance towards them. Amen.

How Day by Day These People Brought Fish and Whatever Else They Had to Our Ships; and How on the Advice of Taignoagny and Dom Agaya They Ceased Coming; and How There Was a Certain Coldness between Us

After this, these people used to come day by day to our ships bringing us plenty of eels and other fish to get our wares. We gave them in exchange knives, awls, beads, and other trinkets, which pleased them much. But we perceived that the two rogues whom we had brought with us[136] were telling them and giving them to understand that what we bartered to them was of no value, and that for what they brought us, they could as easily get hatchets as knives, although the Captain had made them many presents, which indeed they never for a moment ceased begging from him. The latter was warned by the leader of the village of Hagouchonda, who had presented him with a little girl when he was on his way to Hochelaga, to be on his guard against Donnacona and these two rogues, Taignoagny and Dom Agaya, who were *Agojuda*, that is to say traitors and rogues, and he [Cartier] was also warned against them by some of the people of Canada. Besides this we ourselves

136 Taignoagny and Dom Agaya

perceived their malice, when they wished to take away the three children whom Donnacona had given to the Captain; and the older girl in truth was induced by them to run away from the ship. After her escape, the Captain had a watch kept over the others. And on Taignoagny's and Dom Agaya's advice, the Canadians ceased coming to see us for four or five days, except a few who used to come in great fear and trembling.

How the Captain, Fearing Lest Some Treachery Should Be Attempted, Had the Fort Strengthened, and How They Came to Parley with Him; and of the Restoration of the Girl Who Had Run Away

Seeing their malice, and fearing lest they should attempt some treasonable design and come against us with a host of people, the Captain gave orders for the fort to be strengthened on every side with large, wide, deep ditches, and with a gate and drawbridge, and with extra logs of wood set crosswise to the former. And fifty men were told off for the night-guard in future, in four watches, and at each change of watch the trumpets were to be sounded. These things were done according to the above orders. And when Donnacona, Taignoagny, and Dom Agaya were informed of this, and of the good watch and ward that was being kept, they were annoyed to be in the Captain's bad graces, and several times sent some of their people to see if any harm would befall them. No attention was paid to the latter, and no sign shown or exhibited of anything unusual. And several times Donnacona, Taignoagny, Dom Agaya, and others came to speak to the Captain from the other side of the river, asking him if he were angry and why he did not go and visit them at Canada. The Captain answered that they were nothing but traitors and rogues, as had been reported to him, and as he himself had seen on several occasions, as for example in not keeping their promise to go to Hochelaga, and in taking away the girl that had been offered to him, and in other bad turns which he mentioned; but for all that, if they were willing to behave properly and to lay aside their evil thoughts, he would forgive them, and they might come on board in all security and have some good cheer as formerly. For these words they thanked the Captain and promised that, within three days, the girl who had run away would be given back. And on [Thursday] 4 November, Dom Agaya, accompanied by six other men, came to our ships to tell the Captain that Donnacona had gone up country to look for the girl who had run away, and that she would be brought to him on the morrow. He also stated that Taignoagny was very ill and begged the Captain to send him a little bread and salt. The Captain did so and told them to tell him that it was Jesus who was angry with him for the bad turns he had tried to play.

And on the following day,[137] Donnacona, Taignoagny, Dom Agaya, and several others came and brought the girl and offered her anew to the Captain, but the latter paid no attention and said he would have nothing to do with her, and that they might take her away again. Thereupon they excused themselves, saying they had not counselled her to run away and that she had done so because the cabin-boys had beaten her, and she had informed them; and again they begged the Captain to take her back and themselves brought her as far as the ship. After this the Captain ordered bread and wine to be brought and entertained them. Then they took leave of one another, and thenceforward both they and we came and went between our ships and their village in as friendly a manner as before.

Of the Size and Depth of This River in General; and of the Beasts, Birds, Fishes, Trees, and Other Things We Saw along It; and of the Situation of the Villages

This river[138] begins just beyond the island of Assumption[139] opposite to the high mountains of Honguedo[140] and the Seven islands,[141] and the width across is some thirty-five or forty leagues, with a depth in the middle of 200 fathoms. The deeper side and the safer to navigate is along the south shore. And on the north shore, namely about seven leagues on each side of the Seven Islands, are two large rivers[142] which flow down from the mountains of the Saguenay[143] and form several very dangerous shoals in the

137 Friday, 5 November
138 The St Lawrence
139 Anticosti Island
140 Notre-Dame Mountains in Gaspé
141 Seven Islands. The distance across to Cape Ste Anne on the Gaspé shore is about fifty-six miles.
142 Pentecost River on the west and Moisie River to the east of the Seven Islands
143 The Laurentides

gulf.[144] At the mouths of these rivers we saw a large number of whales and sea horses.[145]

Opposite to the Seven Islands is a small river,[146] which passes through swamps for some three or four leagues from the coast and up which are a marvellous number of all kinds of water fowl. The distance from the mouth of this river [St Lawrence] to Hochelaga is 300 leagues and more.[147] It begins at the tributary which comes from the Saguenay, which issues from between lofty mountains and flows into this river on the north side before one arrives at the province of Canada. This [Saguenay] tributary is extremely deep and narrow and is very difficult to navigate.

Above this tributary lies the province of Canada where live several peoples in open villages. Several large and small islands lie in the river within the limits of Canada, and among the rest is one[148] more than ten leagues in length which is covered with fine high trees and with many vines upon it. There is a passage on both sides of this island, but the better and safer one is on the south side. And at the western extremity of this island [of Orleans] there is a forking of the waters which is a fine pleasant spot for laying up vessels. Here the river [St Lawrence] becomes narrow, swift and deep, and but a quarter of a league in width.[149] Opposite to this spot the shore rises to a good height in two ridges of cultivated land,[150] and is as good soil as it is possible to find. There[151] stands the village and abode of Donnacona and of our two men. [Taignoagny and Dom Agaya] whom we had seized on our first voyage. This village is called Stadacona. And before reaching this point there are four peoples and villages, namely: Ajoaste, Starnatam, Tailla, which is on a mountain, and Sitadin. Then the village of Stadacona. Beneath this high land on the north lies the river and harbour of Ste Croix [St Charles], where we remained with our

144 Moisie shoal and rock

145 Walruses

146 St Margaret River a few miles to the west

147 The distance from Montreal to the Atlantic is 873 miles. The distance from Cape Chatte opposite pointe des Monts to Montreal is 373 miles, and from the Saguenay to Montreal, 243 miles.

148 The island of Orleans, which is twenty-one miles long

149 The St Lawrence is only some 3230 feet wide at Quebec.

150 Quebec rises in two ridges, the first ending at Dufferin terrace, while on top of the second stands the Citadel. Cape Diamond is 350 feet in height.

151 Evidently on Cape Diamond itself, though the exact site is not stated

ships hauled out, as before mentioned, from 15 September [1535] until 6 May 1536. Beyond this point lies the abode of the people of Tequenonday and of Hochelay, the former on a mountain and the latter in a flat region.

The whole country on both sides of the river [St Lawrence] up as far as Hochelaga and beyond is as fine a land and as level as ever one beheld. There are some mountains visible at a considerable distance from the river, and into it several tributaries flow down from these. This land is everywhere covered and overrun with timber of several sorts and also with quantities of vines, except in the neighbourhood of the tribes, who have cleared the land for their village and crops. There are a large number of big stags, does, bears, and other animals. We beheld the footprints of a beast with but two legs, and followed his tracks over the sand and mud for a long distance. Its paws were more than a palm in size. Furthermore, there are many otters, beavers, martens, foxes, wild-cats, hares, rabbits, squirrels, wonderfully large [musk-] rats, and other wild beasts. The people wear the skins of these animals for want of other apparel. There are also great numbers of birds, to wit: cranes, bustards, swans, white and gray wild geese, ducks, drakes, blackbirds, thrushes, turtle-doves, wood-pigeons, goldfinches, tarins, canaries, linnets, nightingales, sparrows, and other birds the same as in France. Again this river, [St Lawrence] as has been already stated in the preceding chapters, is the richest in every kind of fish that any one remembers having ever seen or heard of; for from its mouth to the head of it, you will find in their season the majority of the [known] varieties and species of salt and fresh-water fish. Up as far as Canada, you will meet with many whales, porpoises, sea-horses, walruses, and *Adhothuys*,[152] which is a species of fish that we had never seen or heard of before. They are as white as snow and have a head like a greyhound's. Their habitat is between the ocean and the fresh-water that begins between the river Saguenay and Canada.[153]

Moreover, you will find in this river [St Lawrence] in June, July, and August great numbers of mackerel, mullets, maigres, tunnies, large-sized eels, and other fish. When their [spawning] season is over you will find as good smelts as in the river Seine. In spring again there are quantities of lampreys and salmon. Up above Can-

152 The beluga or white whale

153 The fresh water begins at Grosse Ile.

ada are many pike, trout, carp, breams, and other fresh-water fish. All these varieties are caught, each in its season, in considerable quantities by these people for their food and sustenance.

A Chapter of Some Information Which the Native People Gave Us after Our Return from Hochelaga

On our return from Hochelaga with the bark and the longboats, we held intercourse and came and went among the peoples nearest to our ships in peace and friendship, except for a few quarrels now and then with some bad boys, at which the others were very angry and much annoyed. And we learned from Donnacona, from Taignoagny, Dom Agaya, and the others that the above-mentioned river, named the 'river of the Saguenay,' reaches to the [kingdom of the] Saguenay, which lies more than a moon's journey from its mouth, towards the west-northwest; but that after eight or nine days' journey this river is only navigable for small boats; that the regular and direct route to the [kingdom of the] Saguenay, and the safer one, is by the river [St Lawrence] to a point above Hochelaga, where there is a tributary[154] which flows down from the [kingdom of the] Saguenay and enters this river [St Lawrence], as we ourselves saw, from which point the journey takes one moon. And they gave us to understand that in that country the people go clothed and dressed in woollens like ourselves; that there are many towns and peoples composed of honest folk who possess great store of gold and copper. Furthermore, they told us that the whole region from the first-mentioned river[155] up as far as Hochelaga and the [the kingdom of the] Saguenay is an island, which is encircled and surrounded by rivers and by the said river [St Lawrence];[156] and that beyond the [kingdom of the] Saguenay, this tributary[157] flows through two or three large, very broad lakes,[158] until one reaches

154 The Ottawa

155 The river Saguenay

156 The head waters of the Gatineau, a tributary of the Ottawa, lie in fact within a very short distance of the head waters of the Chamouchouan, which flows into lake St John, whence the Saguenay takes its rise. The region between the Ottawa and the Saguenay rivers is therefore virtually encircled by the Gatineau, the Ottawa, the St Lawrence, the Saguenay, and the Chamouchouan.

157 The Ottawa

158 These lakes were Nipissing, Des Allumettes, and the others of the chain leading from the Ottawa to Georgian Bay via the Mattawan. This route

a fresh-water sea,[159] of which there is no mention of anyone having seen the bounds, as the people of the [kingdom of the] Saguenay had informed them; for they themselves, they told us, had never been there. They also informed us that at the place where we had left our bark when on our way to Hochelaga[160] there is a river [Richelieu] flowing from the southwest, and that along it they likewise journey in their canoes from Ste Croix [the St Charles] for one month to a land where ice and snow never come; but in which there are continual wars of one people against the other. In that country grow in great abundance oranges, almonds, walnuts, plums, and other varieties of fruit. They also told us that the inhabitants of that land were dressed and clothed in skins, like themselves. On inquiring if gold and copper were to be found there, they said no. From these statements, and judging from their signs and the indications they gave us, I am of opinion that this land lies towards Florida.

Of a Great Sickness and Pestilence Which Visited the People of Stadacona, by Which, for Having Frequented Them, We Were Attacked to Such an Extent that There Died as Many as Twenty-five of Our Men

In the month of December we received warning that the pestilence had broken out among the people of Stadacona to such an extent that already, by their own confession, more than fifty persons were dead. Upon this we forbade them to come either to the fort or about us. But notwithstanding we had driven them away, the sickness broke out among us accompanied by most marvellous and extraordinary symptoms; for some lost all their strength, their legs became swollen and inflamed, while the sinews contracted and turned as black as coal. In other cases the legs were found blotched with purple-coloured blood. Then the disease would mount to the hips, thighs, shoulders, arms, and neck. And all had their mouths so tainted that the gums rotted away down to the roots of the

---

to Lake Huron via the Ottawa, Mattawan, and the above lakes continued to be the only one used througout the whole of the sixteenth and the first half of the seventeenth centuries.

159 Lake Huron

160 At the head of Lake St Peter

teeth, which nearly all fell out. The disease spread among the three ships[161] to such an extent that, in the middle of February [1536], of the 110 men forming our company, there were not ten in good health so that no one could aid the other, which was a grievous sight considering the place where we were. For the people of the country who used to come daily to the fort saw few of us about. And not only were eight men dead already but there were more than fifty whose case seemed hopeless.

Our Captain, seeing the plight we were in and how general the disease had become, gave orders for all to pray and to make orisons, and had an image and figure of the Virgin Mary carried across the ice and snow and placed against a tree about a bowshot from the fort, and issued an order that on the following Sunday, mass should be said at that spot, to which all who could walk, both sick and well, should make their way in a procession, singing the seven psalms of David[162] with the Litany,[163]praying the Virgin to be good enough to ask her dear Son to have pity upon us. And when the mass had been said and sung before the image, the Captain made a vow to go on a pilgrimage to Our Lady of Racamadour,[164] if God would allow him to return to France in safety. On that day there died Phillip Rougemont, aged some twenty-two years, a native of Amboise.

And because the disease was a strange one, the Captain had the body opened to see if anything could be found out about it, and the rest, if possible, cured. And it was discovered that his heart

161 This would seem to indicate that the *Emérillon* had also been brought into the St Charles after their return from Hochelaga.

162 The seven Psalms were numbers 6, 31, 37, 50, 101, 129, 142 in the Vulgate, but 6, 32, 38, 51, 102, 130, and 143 in the Protestant versions.

163 The Litany of all the Saints comes immediately after these psalms in the *Livre d'heures d'Anne de Bretagne*, 203–21.

164 Rocamadour near Gamat is the department of the Lot. It was one of the most famous sanctuaries of the later Middle Ages, from 1166 onwards. It was even the theme of the *jongleurs*:

La douce mère au Creatour
As église Rochemadour
Fait tant miracles, tant biaus fais
C'uns moult biax livres en est fais.

It was sacked by the Huguenots in 1572 when over 1,500 quintals of gold and silver were taken away. See G. Servois, *Notice et estraits du recueil des miracles de Nostre-Dame de Roc-Amadour*, in the *Bibliothèque de l'Ecole des Charles*, 4me série, III (Paris 1857), 21–44 and 228–45.

was completely white and shrivelled up, with more than a jug full of red date-coloured water about it. His liver was in good condition but his lungs were very black and gangrened; and all his blood had collected over his heart; for when the body was opened, a large quantity of dark, tainted blood issued from above the heart. His spleen for some two finger breadths near the backbone was also slightly affected, as if it had been rubbed on a rough stone. After seeing this much, we made an incision and cut open one of his thighs, which on the outside was very black, but within the flesh was found fairly healthy. Thereupon we buried him as well as we could. May God in His holy grace grant forgiveness to his soul and to those of all the dead. Amen.

After this the disease increased daily to such an extent that at one time, out of the three vessels, there were not three men in good health, so that on board one of the ships there was no one to go down under the quarter-deck to draw water for himself and the rest. And already several had died, whom from sheer weakness we had to bury beneath the snow; for at that season the ground was frozen and we could not dig into it, so feeble and helpless were we. We were also in great dread of the people of the country, lest they should become aware of our plight and helplessness. And to hide the sickness, our Captain, whom God kept continually in good health, whenever they came near the fort, would go out and meet them with two or three men, either sick or well, whom he ordered to follow him outside. When these were beyond the enclosure, he would pretend to try to beat them, and vociferating and throwing sticks at them, would drive them back on board the ships, indicating to the savages by signs that he was making all his men work below the decks, some at calking, others at baking bread and at other tasks; and that it would not do to have them come and loaf outside. This they believed. And the Captain had the sick men hammer and make a noise inside the ships with sticks and stones, pretending that they were calking. At that time so many were down with the disease that we had almost lost hope of ever returning to France, when God in His infinite goodness and mercy had pity upon us and made known to us the most excellent remedy against all diseases that ever has been seen or heard of in the whole world, as will be set forth in this [second] chapter [following].

The Length of Time We Remained in Ste Croix Harbour Frozen Up in the Ice and Snow; and the Number of Men who Died of the Pestilence from the Time It Began until the Middle of March[165]

From the middle of November [1535] until [Saturday] the fifteenth of April [1536], we lay frozen up in the ice, which was more than two fathoms in thickness, while on shore there were more than four feet of snow, so that it was higher than the bulwarks of our ships. This lasted until the date mentioned above, with the result that all our beverages froze in their casks. And all about the decks of the ships, below hatches and above, there was ice to the depth of four finger breadths. And the whole river [St Lawrence] was frozen where the water was fresh up to beyond Hochelaga. During this period there died to the number of twenty-five of the best and most able seamen we had, who all succumbed to the aforesaid malady. And at that time there was little hope of saving more than forty others, while the whole of the rest were ill, except three or four. But God in His divine grace had pity upon us and sent us knowledge of a remedy which cured and healed all in the manner that will be told in this next chapter.

How by God's Grace We Received Knowledge of a Tree Which Cured Us and Gave Back Health to All the Sick; and the Manner of Using It

One day our Captain, seeing the disease so general and his men so stricken down by it, on going outside the fort to walk up and down on the ice, caught sight of a band of people approaching from Stadacona, and among them was Dom Agaya whom he had seen ten or twelve days previous to this, extremely ill with the very disease his own men were suffering from; for one of his legs about the knee had swollen to the size of a two-year-old baby, and the sinews had become contracted. His teeth had gone bad and decayed, and the gums had rotted and become tainted. The Captain, seeing Dom Agaya well and in good health, was delighted, hoping to learn what had healed him in order to cure his own men. And when they had come near the fort, the Captain inquired of him [Dom Agaya] what had cured him of his sickness. Dom Agaya

165 From the context it should evidently be April.

replied that he had been healed by the juice of the leaves of a tree and the dregs of these, and that this was the only way to cure sickness. Upon this the Captain asked him if there was not some of it thereabouts, and to show it to him that he might heal his servant who had caught the disease when staying in Donnacona's house at Canada, being unwilling that he should know how many sailors were ill. Thereupon Dom Agaya sent two women with our Captain to gather some of it; and they brought back nine or ten branches. They showed us how to grind the bark and the leaves and to boil the whole in water. Of this one should drink every two days, and place the dregs on the legs where they were swollen and affected. According to them this tree cured every kind of disease. They call it in their language *Annedda*.[166]

The Captain at once ordered a drink to be prepared for the sick men but none of them would taste it. At length one or two thought they would risk a trial. As soon as they had drunk it they felt better, which must clearly be ascribed to miraculous causes; for after drinking it two or three times they recovered health and strength and were cured of all the diseases they had ever had. And some of the sailors who had been suffering for five or six years from the French pox were by this medicine cured completely. When this became known, there was such a press for the medicine that they almost killed each other to have it first; so that in less than eight days a whole tree as large and as tall as any I ever saw was used up, and produced such a result that had all the doctors of Louvain and Montpellier been there, with all the drugs of Alexandria, they could not have done so much in a year as did this tree in eight days; for it benefited us so much that all who were willing to use it recovered health and strength, thanks be to God.

How Donnacona, Accompanied by Taignoagny and Several Others, Set Off from Stadacona on a Deer Hunt and Remained Away Two Months; and How on Their Return They Brought with Them a Number of People Whom We Had Not Hitherto Seen

During the time that sickness and death were holding sway on board our ships, Donnacona, Taignoagny, and several others set

166 Jacques Rousseau, 'L'Annedda et l'Arbre de Vie,' *Revue d'histoire de l'Amérique française* 7, 2 (Sept. 1954): 171–201

off, pretending to be going to hunt stags and other animals, which in their language they call *Ajounesla* and *Asquenondo*, as the snow was deep and yet they could paddle along the river [St Lawrence] where the ice had broken up. Dom Agaya and the others told us that they [Donnacona, etc.] would be gone about a fortnight, which we believed, but they did not return for two months. At this we became suspicious lest they should be gone to collect a large force to attack us, when they saw we were so weak; although we had put everything in such good order that had the whole of the armed forces of their country come against us, they would have been able to do nothing but gaze at us. Meanwhile every day there came to our ships as usual a considerable number of people with fresh meat, venison, and all varieties of fresh fish, which they bartered for a good price or otherwise preferred to carry them away again; for they were themselves in need of provisions on account of the winter having been a long one, during which they had consumed their provisions and supplies.

How Donnacona Came Back to Stadacona with a Large Number of People, and Feigned to Be Ill, because He Was Afraid to Come and See the Captain, Thinking the Latter Would Go and Visit Him

On [Friday] 21 April, Dom Agaya came on board our vessels with several fine-looking, powerful men whom we had not been in the habit of seeing, and told us that Donnacona would be back on the following day and would bring with him a quantity of deer's meat and other venison. And the next day, the twenty-second of the month, Donnacona did arrive at Stadacona accompanied – why or for what purpose we did not know – by a great number of men. But as the proverb says, 'He who is on guard against everything escapes something,' which with us was a case of necessity, so weakened were we by the disease and by the men we had lost that we were obliged to leave one of our ships at Ste Croix. The Captain, being informed how on their return they had brought back so many people, and how Dom Agaya, on coming to tell us of this, had been unwilling to cross the river lying between us and Stadacona,[167] and had refused to come over, a thing he was not in the habit of doing, became suspicious of treason, as did the rest of us.

167 The St Charles

And in view of this the Captain sent his servant, named Charles Guyot, accompanied by John Poullet, who were greater favourites with the people of that region than any of the others, to find out who was in the village and what they were doing, pretending they had come to see Donnacona; for they had passed a long time in the village with him; and they brought him a small present.[168] And on being informed of their arrival, Donnacona played the sick man and went to bed, telling the servant [Guyot] that he was very ill. After this the servant went to Taignoagny's house to pay him a call, and everywhere found the houses so full of people whom he had not been in the habit of seeing that one could not turn around inside them. Taignoagny would not allow the servant to visit the other houses, but accompanied them almost half-way to the ships. And he informed them that if the Captain would do him a good turn and would seize a leader of that region named Agona, who had slighted him [Taignoagny] and would carry him [Agona] off to France, that he [Taignoagny] would be in the Captain's debt and would do anything he asked; and that on the morrow the servant should return with the captain's answer.

The Captain, on being informed of the large number of people at Stadacona, though unaware of their purpose, yet determined to outwit them and to seize their leader [Donnacona], Taignoagny, Dom Agaya, and the headmen. And moreover he had quite made up his mind to take Donnacona to France, that he might relate and tell to the king all he had seen in the west of the wonders of the world; for he assured us that he had been to the land of the Saguenay where there are immense quantities of gold, rubies, and other rich things, and that the men there are white as in France and go clothed in woollens. He told us also that he had visited another region where the people, possessing no anus, never eat nor digest, but simply make water through the penis. He told us furthermore that he had been in the land of the Picquenyans, and to another country whose inhabitants have only one leg and other marvels too long to relate. This leader is an old man who has never ceased travelling about the country by river, stream, and trail since his earliest recollection.

When Poullet and the servant had delivered their message and told the Captain what Taignoagny had asked them to say, the Captain on the morrow[169] sent back his servant to tell Taignoagny

168 Probably on Friday, 28 April

169 Saturday, 29 April

to come and see him and let him know what he wished; and that he [Cartier] would treat him well and would perform part of what he asked. Taignoagny sent back word that he would come on the following day, and would bring with him Donnacona and the man who had done him the bad turn.[170] But he did not do so and for two days no one from Stadacona came near the ships, as they had been in the habit of doing, but used to flee as if we were trying to kill them. Upon this we became convinced of their knavishness. But on learning that the people of Sitadin[171] came and went among us, and that we had let them have the hull of the vessel we were abandoning, that they might secure the old nails, the people of Stadacona all came on the third day[172] to the riverbank, and most of them crossed in their canoes without hesitation. But Donnacona would not come over; and Taignoagny and Dom Agaya debated together for more than an hour before they would cross, but in the end they did so and came and spoke to the Captain. And Taignoagny begged the Captain to consent to seize that man and carry him off to France. This the Captain refused, saying that the king [Francis I], his master, had forbidden him to carry off to France any man or woman but only two or three boys to learn the language; but that he would willingly take him to Newfoundland and set him upon an island.[173] The Captain spoke thus in order to calm their fears and to induce Donnacona, who still kept on the other side of the river, to cross over. Taignoagny was much pleased at these words, which made him hope he should never go back to France, and he promised the Captain to return on the following day, which was Holy Cross Day[174] and to bring with him Donnacona and all the people of Stadacona.

How on Holy Cross Day the Captain Had a Cross Set Up Inside Our Fort; and How Donnacona, Taignoagny, Dom Agaya, and Their Party Came, and of the Capture of This Leader

On [Wednesday] 3 May, which was the festival of the Holy Cross, the Captain in celebration of this solemn feast had a beautiful cross

170 Agona

171 It doubtless lay on the Beauport shore.

172 Tuesday, 2 May

173 It should be borne in mind that at that time Newfoundland was supposed to form an archipelago.

174 Wednesday, 3 May 1536

erected some thirty-five feet high, under the cross-bar of which was attached an escutcheon, embossed with the arms of France, whereupon was printed in Roman characters: LONG LIVE FRANCIS I. BY GOD'S GRACE KING OF FRANCE. And that day about noon several persons arrived from Stadacona, both men, women, and children, who told us that Donnacona with Taignoagny, Dom Agaya, and the rest of their party were on their way, which pleased us, as we were in hopes of being able to capture them. They arrived about two o'clock in the afternoon; and as soon as they came opposite to our ships the Captain went and greeted Donnacona, who likewise was friendly enough but kept his eye constantly fixed on the wood and was wonderfully uneasy. Soon after Taignoagny came up and told Donnacona that on no account should he go inside the fort. Thereupon one of their men brought out some embers and lit a fire for their leader outside the fort. Our Captain begged him to come on board the ships to eat and to drink as usual, and also invited Taignoagny, who replied that they would go presently. This they did and came inside the fort. Before this, however, our Captain had been warned by Dom Agaya that Taignoagny had spoken adversely and had told Donnacona by no means to go on board the ships. And our Captain, knowing this, went outside the fort where he had been keeping and saw that at Taignoagny's warning the women were hurrying away and that none but men were left, who were present in considerable numbers. At this the Captain issued his orders for the seizure of Donnacona, Taignoagny, Dom Agaya, and two other headmen, whom he pointed out, and he commanded that the others should be driven away. Soon after the leader [Donnacona] entered the fort in company with the Captain, whereupon Taignoagny immediately rushed in to make him go out again. Seeing there was no other chance, our Captain proceeded to call to his men to seize them. At this they rushed forth and laid hands upon the leader and the others whose capture had been decided upon. The Canadians, beholding this, began to flee and to scamper off like sheep before wolves, some across the river,[175] others into the wood, each seeking his own safety. When the above-mentioned had been captured and the rest had all disappeared, Donnacona and his companions were placed in safe custody.

175 St Charles

How at Nightfall the Canadians Came Opposite to Our Ships to Look for Their Men, and Howled and Cried All Night like Wolves; and of the Parley and Agreement Made Next Day and the Presents They Offered to Our Captain

At nightfall a large number of Donnacona's people came opposite to our ships, the river [St Charles] between us, howling and crying like wolves all night long, calling out incessantly, *Agouhanna, Agouhanna*, in the hope of being able to speak to him [Donnacona]. This the Captain would not then allow, nor during the whole of the following morning[176] until about noon, on which account they made signs to us that we had killed or hanged them. And about noon they returned in as great numbers as we had seen during the voyage, prepared for a move of some sort, and remained hidden in the wood, except a few who called out and shouted aloud to Donnacona. At this the Captain gave orders for Donnacona to be brought on deck to address them. And the Captain told him [Donnacona] to be of good cheer, for that after he had had an interview with the king of France, his master, and had related what he had seen at the Saguenay, he would be able, within ten or twelve moons, to come back, and that the king would make him a fine present. At this Donnacona was much pleased and in his speech mentioned it to the others, who gave three great shouts in sign of joy. Then these people and Donnacona made several harangues and went through various ceremonies which, as we did not understand them, it is impossible to describe. Our Captain told Donnacona that his people might cross the river [St Charles] in all security in order to converse with greater comfort, and that he might reassure them. On learning this from Donnacona, several of the headmen came alongside our vessels in a canoe and began once more their harangues, praising our Captain and making him a present of twenty-four strings of wampum, which is the most valuable article they possess in this world; for they attach more value to it than to gold or silver. When they had chatted and discussed matters together to their heart's content, and had seen that there was no chance for their chief to escape and that he would be obliged to go to France, the latter commanded them to fetch provisions to eat at sea and to bring them to him on the following day. Our Captain presented

176 Thursday, 4 May

Donnacona with two brass kettles, eight hatchets, and some smaller objects such as knives and beads, at which to all appearance he was much pleased, and sent them to his wives and children. The Captain likewise gave some small presents to the people who had come to speak with Donnacona, who thanked him extremely for the same. After that they left and went back to their houses.

How on the Morrow, 5 May, These People Came Back to Speak with Their Leader, and How Four Women Brought Provisions on Board to Him

On the following day, [Friday] 5 May, at daybreak, the people returned in considerable numbers in order to speak with their leader, and sent over a canoe, which in their language is called *casnouy*, with four women but no men for fear lest we should detain them. These women brought a large quantity of food, to wit: corn (which is their wheat), fresh meat, fish, and the other provisions they use. The Captain received these women well on board the ships. And Donnacona begged the Captain to say to them that he would return within twelve moons, and would bring Donnacona to Canada. He spoke thus to set their minds at rest. The Captain did as requested, whereupon the women pretended to be much pleased, and have him to understand by signs and words that should he ever return and bring back Donnacona and the rest, the whole people would give him many presents. After this each of them offered the Captain a string of wampum. Then they retired to the opposite bank of the river [St Charles], where the whole population of Stadacona was collected; and all withdrew waving farewell to their leader Donnacona.

On Saturday, 6 May, we set sail from Ste Croix Harbour[177] and came to anchor at the foot of the island of Orleans, some twelve leagues from Ste Croix. And on Sunday[178] we reached Coudres Island, where we remained until Monday, the fifteenth of the month, to allow the spring-flood to moderate, for it was too swift and dangerous to sail down the river; and we were also waiting for fine weather. During this interval arrived several canoes with people who were Donnacona's subjects, who came from the river Saguenay. And on being informed by Dom Agaya of their capture

177 St Charles
178 Thursday, 4 May

and how and in what manner Donnacona was being taken to France, they were extremely astonished; but nevertheless came alongside to speak to Donnacona, who told them that within twelve months he would come back and that he was well treated by the Captain and the sailors. At this all with one voice thanked the Captain. And to Donnacona they gave three bundles of beaver and seal-skins, with a large copper knife from the Saguenay and other gifts, and presented the Captain with a string of wampum. In return for these things the Captain had ten or twelve hatchets given to them, which made them very happy and contented; and they thanked the Captain and then left.

The channel is safer and better to the north of this island[179] than to the south of it, where there are a large number of shoals, bars, and boulders, and where the water is shallow.

On the following day [Tuesday], 16 May, we set sail from Coudres Island and came to anchor at an island[180] lying some fifteen leagues below Coudres Island. This island is about five leagues in length. Here we anchored for the night, hoping on the morrow to make our way through the dangers of the Saguenay [river], which are great. In the evening we rowed over to this [Hare] island where we found a great number of hares, and captured a quantity of them. On this account we named the island 'Hare Island.' In the night the wind veered around into a head wind and blew with such violence that [on Wednesday, 17 May] we had to run back under the lee of Coudres Island, whence we had set out, as there is no other passage among these islands. And there we remained until [Sunday] the twenty-first of the month, when the wind came fair; and we made such good headway each day that we passed down as far as Honguedo,[181] between the island of Assumption[182] and this Honguedo, which passage had never before been discovered. And we ran on until we came opposite cape Pratto [or Meadow],[183] which is the entrance to Chaleur Bay. And as the wind was fair and entirely in our favour, we carried sail both night and day. And

179 *Ile aux Coudres*

180 Hare Island, forty-one miles below Coudres Island. It is eight miles long and half a mile wide.

181 Gaspé

182 Anticosti Island. On their way up they had gone north of the island, so this was the first time they had been through the passage to the south of it between Anticosti and Gaspé.

183 Cap d'Espoir at the mouth of Chaleur Bay

on the morrow[184] we found we were heading straight for the middle of Brion Island, which was what we wished in order to shorten our route.[185] These coasts [Gaspé and Brion Island] lie southeast and northwest, one quarter east and west, while the distance between them is fifty leagues. This [Brion] island lies in latitude 47° 30′.[186]

On Thursday the twenty-fifth of the month [of May], the anniversary of the festival of our Lord's Ascension, we crossed to a coast and narrow strip of low sandy shore lying some eight leagues to the southwest of Brion Island. Beyond this low coast are high lands covered with trees. And there is also a lagoon[187] into which we saw no entrance or opening, by which to enter the same. And on Friday the twenty-sixth, as the wind began to blow off the sea, we went back to Brion Island, where we remained until [Thursday] 1 June. And [setting sail that day] we came to a high shore [Cape Breton Island], lying southeast of this [Brion] island, which appeared to us to be an island, which we coasted for some twenty-two leagues. While holding this course we described three other islands[188] lying near the sandbars,[189] and likewise perceived that these sandbars formed an island.[190] This coast [of Cape Breton Island], which is high and flat, we saw to be mainland, which ran northwest. After discovering this we made our way back to the point of this coast where there are two or three very very high capes[191] with great depth of water, and the tide as strong as it is possible to meet. We named this cape, which lies in 46° 30′, 'Cape Lorraine.'[192] To the south of it the shore in one place is low as if a river entered the sea there; but there is no harbour of any value.

184 In all probability Wednesday, 24 May. It would take them quite three days to sail from Coudres Island the Chaleur Bay.

185 They wished to see if there was really a passage into the Atlantic between Newfoundland and Cape Breton, as they had supposed on their first voyage.

186 47° 48′

187 The Great Lagoon or Grand Entry Harbour inside Grosse, East, and Coffin islands

188 Alright, Entry, and Amherst islands of the Magdalen group

189 The Magdalens

190 That is to say, the Magdalens were not mainland as they had supposed on their first voyage but were really a group of islands.

191 Cape St Lawrence, Black Point, Cape North, Money Point

192 Probably Cape St Lawrence, the northwestern extremity of Cape Breton Island

Beyond these headlands towards the south stands another cape named by us.' Cape St Paul,' which lies in 47° 15'.

On Sunday, the fourth of that month [of June], which was the feast of Whitsuntide, we came in sight of the coast of Newfoundland, which runs east-southeast and is distant some twenty-two leagues from the above cape [North]. And as the wind was against us, we went into a harbour, which we named the 'harbour of the Holy Ghost.'[193] Here we remained until Tuesday [6 June], when we set sail and coasted along that [south] shore [of Newfoundland] as far as the islands of St Pierre.[194] On our way along that coast, which runs east-southeast and west-southwest, we saw several islands[195] and some dangerous shoals, lying at a distance of two, three, and four leagues out to sea. We remained at these islands of St Pierre, where we met several ships both from France and from Brittany, from [Sunday] 11 June, St Barnabas's Day, until [Friday] the sixteenth of that month, when we set sail from these islands of St Pierre. And we came to Cape Race and entered a harbour called Rougnouse, where we took on board wood and fresh water for consumption at sea. Here we left one of our longboats. And on Monday, the nineteenth of that month [of June], we set forth from this [Renewse] harbour and were favoured at sea with such good weather that we reached St Malo on [Sunday] 16 July 1536, thanks be to God, whom we implore on bringing our voyage to an end, to give us His grace and His paradise hereafter. Amen.

193 Probably *port aux Basques* or Port Basque, seven miles and a half southeast of Cape Ray

194 Still called St Pierre and Miquelon islands, which belong to France to this day. Formerly with Langlade they formed three islands.

195 Dead, Burnt, Wreck, Great Bruit, Burger, Ramea, Penguin, etc. islands

HERE FOLLOWS THE LANGUAGE OF THE COUNTRIES AND KINGDOMS OF HOCHELAGA AND CANADA, OTHERWISE CALLED NEW FRANCE

First Their Numerals

Un	One	Segada
Deux	Two	Tigneny
Trois	Three	Asche
Quatre	Four	Honnacon
Cinq	Five	Ouyscon
Six	Six	Judaié
Sept.	Seven	Aiaga
Huit	Eight	Addegué
Neuf	Nine	Wadellon
Dix	Ten	Assem

Next the Names of the Different Parts of the Body

Le teste	The head	Aggonosy
Le frons	The forehead	Hetguenyascon
Les yeulx	The eyes	Hegata
Les oreilles	The ears	Ahontascon
La bouche	The mouth	Escahé
Les dentz	The teeth	Esgongay
La langue	The tongue	Esnache
La gorge	The throat	Agonhon
Le menton	The chin	Hebbehin
Le visaige	The face	Hegouascon
Les cheveulx	The hair	Aganyscon
Les bras	The arms	Ayaiascon
Les esselles	The armpits	Hetnenda
Les coustez	The sides	Aissonné
L'esthomach	The stomach	Aggoascon
Le ventre	The belly	Eschehenda
Les cuysses	The thighs	Hetnegoadascon
Les genoilz	The knees	Agochinegodascon
Les jambes	The legs	Agouguenehondé
Les piedz	The feet	Ouchidascon
Les mains	The hands	Aignoascon
Les doidz	The fingers	Agenoga

Les ongles	The nails	Agedascon
Le vyt	Phallus	Agnascon
Le con	The womb	Chastaigné
La barbe du menton	The beard	Ostoné
La barbe du vyt	Hair of Phallus	Aggonsson
Les coillons	The testicles	Xista
Vng homme	A man	Aguehan
Vne femme	A woman	Aggouetté
Vng garçon	A boy	Addegesta
Vne fille	A girl	Agnyaquesta
Vng petit enfant	A small child	Exiasta
Vne robbe	A dress	Cabata
Vn prepoinct	A doublet	Coza
Des chausses	Stockings	Henondoua
Des soulliers	Shoes	Atha
Des [chemises]	Shirts	Anigoua [or Anigona]
Vng bonnet	A cap	Castrua [or Castona]
Ilz appellent leur bled	They call their corn	Ozisy
Pain	Bread	Carraconny
Eaue	Water	Ame
Chair	Flesh	Quahouachon
Poisson	Fish	Quejon
Prunes	Plums	Honnesta
Figues	Figs	Absconda
Raisins	Grapes	Ozaha
Noix	Nuts	Quaheya
Senelles de buisson	Bush fruits	Aesquesgoua
Petites noix	Small nuts	Undegonaha [or Undegocaha]
Vne poulle	A hen	Sahonigagoa
Vne lamproye	A lamprey	Zisto
Vng saulmon	A salmon	Ondaccon
Vne ballaine	A whale	Ajunehonné
Vne anguille	An eel	Esgneny [or Esgue ny]
Vng escureul	A squirrel	Caiognen
Vne couleuvre	A snake	Undegnesy
Des tortues	Turtles	Heuleuzonné [or Heulenzonné]
Des ollyves	Olives	Honocohonda
Ils appellent le boys	They call wood	Conda
Feulhes de boys	Leaves	Honga [or Houga]

Ilz appellent leur dieu	They call their god	Cudonaguy
Donnez moy à boire	Give me a drink	Quazohoa quea
Donnez moy à desiune[r]	Give me breakfast	Quazahoa quascahoa
Donnez moy à soupper	Give me supper	Quazahoa quatirean
Allons nous coucher	Let us go to bed	Quasigno, agnydahoa
Bon jour	Good day	Aigay
Allons jouer	Let us go and bet	Quasigno caudy
Venez parler à moy	Come and speak to me	Asigny quadadya
Regardez moy	Look at me	Quatgathoma
Taisez vous	Silence	Aista
Allons au bateau	Let us go to the canoe	Quasigno quasnouy
Cela ne vault rien	That's no good	Sahauty quahonquey [or quahouquey]
Donnez moy vng cousteau	Give me a knife	Quazahoa aggoheda
Vng achot	A hatchet	Addogué
Vng arc	A bow	Ahena
Vne flesche	An arrow	Quahetan
Des plumes	Feathers	Heccon
Allons à la chasse	Let us go a hunting	Quasigno donassené
Vng serf	A stag	Ajonuesta [or Ajonnesta]
[De dains ilz dient que se sont moutons, & les appellent]	They speak of does as sheep and call them	Asquenondo
Vng liepvre	A hare	Sonohamda
Vng chian	A dog	Aggayo
Des oayes	Geese	Sadeguenda
[ilz appellent] le chemin	They call a trail	Addé
Ilz appellent la graine de coucombres et mellons	They call the seed of cucumbers and mellons	Cascouda [or Casconda]
Quant ilz veullent dire demain, Ilz dient	When they wish to say tomorrow they say	Achidé

Quant ilz veulent dire à Dieu à quelcun ilz dient	When they wish to say good-bye to any one they say	Hedgagnehanyga
Chanter	To sing	Thegnehoaca
Rire	To laugh	Cahezem
Pleurel[r]	To cry	Agguenda
Danscer	To dance	Thegoaca
Le ciel	The heavens	Quemhya
La terre	The earth	Damga
Le soleil	The sun	Ysnay
La lune	The moon	Assomaha
Les estoilles	The stars	Signehoan
Le vent	The wind	Cahona
La mer	The sea	Agougasy
Eaue doulce	Fresh water	Amé
Les vagues de la mer	Sea waves	Coda
Vne ille	An island	Cohena
Vne montaigne	A mountain	Ogacha
La glace	The ice	Honnesca
La neige	The snow	Canysa
Froyt	Cold	Athau
Chault	Hot	Odayan
Grand merciz	Many thanks	Adgnyeusce
Mon amy	My friend	Aguiase
Courez	Run	Thodoathady
Venez nagez	Come for a paddle	Cazigahoatte
Feu	Fire	Asista
Fumée	Smoke	Quea
La fumée me faict mal ès yeulx	The smoke hurts my eyes	Quea quanoagné egata
Vng tel est mort	So and so is dead	Camedané
Vne malson	A house	Quanocha
Ilz appellent leurs febvres	They call their beans	Sahé
Vng pot de terre	The earthen pot	Undaccon
Ilz appellent une ville	They call a town	Canada
Nota que leur seigneur a nom Donnacona et quant ilz le veullent appeller seigneur ilz l'appellent	Note that their chief is named Donnacona and when they wish to call him chief they say	Agouhanna

Quant ilz veullent dire injure à quelcun ilz l'appellent *Agojuda*, qui est à dire merschant et traystre	When they wish to insult anyone they call him *agojuda* which means bad and treacherous	Agojuda
Villain	Ugly	Aggousay
Cheminez	Walk along	Quedaqué
D'où venez vous?	Whence come you?	Canada undagneny [or undagneuy]
Donnez cela à quelcun	Give that to someone	Taquenonde
Gardez moy cecy	Keep that for me	Sodanadegamesgamy
Oû est allé cestuy?	Where had he gone?	Quanehoesnon
Fermez la porte	Shut the door	Asnodyan
Va quérir de l'eaue	Go and fetch some water	Sagithemmé
Va quérir quelcun	Go and fetch someone	Achidascoué
Ilz appellent l'erbe de quoy ilz usent en leurs cornetz durant l'yver	They call the plant which they use in their pipes during the winter	Quyecta
Il y a de groz ratz en leur pays, qui sont gros comme connyns, lesquelz sentent le musq et les appellent	There are large rats in their country the size of rabbits, which smell of musk and are called	Hoatthe
Herbe commune	Common plant	Hanneda
Quant une personne est si viel qu'il ne peult plus chemyner, ilz l'appellent	When a person is so old that he can no longer walk they call him	Agondesta
Mon père	My father	Addhaty
Ma mère	My mother	Adhanahoé
Mon frère	My brother	Adhadguyn
Ma seur	My sister	Adassene
Mon cousin	My cousin	Hegay
Mon nepveu	My nephew	Yuadin

Ma femme	My wife	Ysaa
Mon enffent	My child	Aguo or Agno
Grand	Big	Estahezy
Petit	Small	Estahagao
Gros	Large	Hougauda
Gresle	Thin	Houcquehin
Quant ilz veullent faire quelque exclamation ilz dient	When they wish to make an exclamation they say	Aggondée
Le soir	The evening	Angau
La nuyt	The night	Anhena
Le jour	The day	Adegahon

Here Follow the Names of the Towns Subject to Donnacona

Ajoasté	Thegadechoallé
Thoagahen	Tella
Sitadin	Thequenondahy [or Thequenoudahy]
Stadaconé	Stagoattem
Deganonda	Agouchonda
Thegnignoudé [or Theguignondé]	Ochela

Note that their chief named Donnacona has been to a country distant from Canada by canoe one moon, in which land grow much cinnamon and clover.

Ilz appellent ladicte canelle	They call this cinnamon	Adotathny
Le giroffle	Clover	Canonotha

Cartier's Third Voyage, 1541

The Third Voyage of Discovery Made by Captaine Jacques Cartier, 1540[1] *– unto the Countreys of Canada, Hochelaga, and Saguenay*

King Francis the first having heard the report of Captaine Cartier his Pilot generall in his two former Voyages of discovery, as well by writing as by word of mouth, touching that which hee had found and seene in the Westerne partes discovered by him in the parts of Canada and Hochelaga, and having also seene and talked with the people, which the sayd Cartier had brought out of those Countreys, whereof one was king of Canada, whose name was Donnacona and others: which after that they had bene a long time in France and Britaine[2] were baptized at their owne desire and request, and died in the sayd countrey of Britaine. And albeit his Maiestie was advertized by the sayd Cartier of the death and decease of all the people which were brought over by him (which were tenne in number) saving one little girle about tenne yeeres old, yet he resolved to send the sayd Cartier his Pilot thither againe, with John Francis de la Roche,[3] Knight, Lord of Roberval,[4] whome hee appointed his Lieutenant and Governour in the Countreys of

The text here given is that first published in *The Third and Last Volume of the Voyages, Navigations, Traffiques and Discoveries of the English Nation*, etc., collected by Richard Hakluyt (London 1600), 232–7.

1 The true date is 1541. Easter fell that year on 17 April.
2 Brittany
3 His name was Jean François de La Roque, seigneur de Roberval.
4 A small village near the forest of Compiègne in the department of the Oise

Canada and Hochelaga, and the sayd Cartier Captaine generall and leader of the shippes, that they might discover more then was done before in the former voyages, and attaine (if it were possible) unto the knowledge of the Countrey of Saguenay, whereof the people brought by Cartier, as is declared, made mention unto the King, that there were great riches, and very good countreys. And the King caused a certaine summe of money to be delivered to furnish out the sayd voyage with five shippes: which thing was performed by the sayd Monsieur Roberval and Cartier. After that they had agreed together to rigge the sayd five ships at Saint Malo in Britaine, where the two former voyages had beene prepared and set forth. And the said Monsieur Roberval sent Cartier thither for the same purpose. And after that Cartier had caused the said five ships to bee built and furnished and set in good order, Monsieur Roberval came downe to S. Malo and found the ships fallen downe to the roade, with their yards acrosse full ready to depart and set saile, staying for nothing else but the comming of the Generall and the payment of the furniture. And because Monsieur Roberval the kings lieutenant had not as yet his artillery, powder and munitions, and other things necessary come downe, which he had provided for the voyage, in the Countreys of Champaigne and Normandie; and because the said things were very necessary, and that hee was loth to depart without them, he determined to depart from S. Malo to Roan, and to prepare a ship or two at Honfleur,[5] whither he thought is things were come: And that the said Cartier should depart with the five shippes which had furnished, and should goe before. Considering also that the said Ca[r]tier had received letters from the king, whereby hee did expressly charge him to depart and set sayle immediately upon the sight and receit thereof, on payne of incurring his displeasure, and to lay all the fault on him.[6] And after the conclusion of these things, and the said Monsieur Roberval had taken muster and view of the gentlemen, souldiers, and mariners which were retained and chosen for the performance of the sayd voyage, hee gave unto Captaine Cartier full authoritie to depart and goe before, and to governe all things as if he had been there in person: and himselfe departed to Honfleur to make his farther preparation. After these things thus dispatched, the winde comming faire, the foresayd five ships set sayle

5 At the mouth of the Seine opposite Havre
6 Cartier

together well furnished and victualled for two yeare, the 23 of May 1540.[7] And we sailed so long with contrary winds and continuall torments, which fell out by reason of our late departure, that wee were on the sea with our sayd five ships full three moneths before wee could arrive at the Port and Haven of Canada, without ever having in all that time 30 houres of good wind to serve us to keepe our right course: so that our five shippes through those stormes lost company one of another, all save two that kept together, to wit that wherein the Captaine was, and the other wherein went the Vicount of Beaupré,[8] untill at length at the ende of one moneth wee met all together at the Haven of Carpont[9] in Newfoundland. But the length of time which we were in passing betweene Britayne and Newfoundland was the cause that we stood in great neede of water, because of the cattell, as well Goates, Hogges, as other beastes which we caried for breede in the Countrey, which wee were constrained to water with Sider and other drinke. Now therefore because we were the space of three moneths in sayling on the sea, and staying in Newfoundland, wayting for Monsieur Roberval, and taking in of fresh water and other things necessary, wee arrived not before the Haven of Saincte Croix in Canada[10] (where in the former voyage we had remayned eight moneths) untill the 23 day of August. In which place the people of the Countrey came to our shippes, making shew of joy for our arrivall, and namely he came thither which had the rule and government of the Countrey of Canada, named Agona, which was appointed king there by Donacona, when in the former voyage we carried him [Donnacona] into France: And hee came to the Captaines ship with 6 or 7 boates and with many women and children. And after the sayd Agona had inquired of the Captaine where Donacona and the rest were, the Captaine answered him, That Donacona was dead in France, and that his body rested in the earth, and that the rest stayed there as great Lords, and were maried, and would not returne backe into their Countrey: the said Agona made no shewe of anger at all these speeches: and I thinke he tooke it so well because he remained Lord and Governour of the countrey

7 The real date is 1541. The mistake doubtless arose from the year being reckoned from Easter to Easter.

8 Probably Guyon des Granches, sieur de Beauprest or Beaupré and brother of Cartier's wife Catherine des Granches

9 Grand-Kirpon between Kirpon Island and Newfoundland

10 The river St Charles

by the death of the said Donacona. After which conference the said Agona tooke a piece of tanned leather of a yellow skin edged about with *Esnoguy* (which is their riches and the thing which they esteeme most precious, as wee esteeme gold) which was upon his head in stead of a crowne, and he put the same on the head of our Captaine, and tooke from his wrists two bracelets of *Esnoguy*, and put them upon the Captaines armes, colling[11] him about the necke and shewing unto him great signes of joy: which was all dissimulation, as afterward it wel appeared. The captaine [Cartier] tooke his [Agona's] said crowne of leather and put it againe upon his [Agona's] head, and gave him and his wives certaine smal presents, signifying unto him that he had brought certaine new things, which afterward he would bestow upon him: for which the sayd Agona thanked the Captaine. And after that he [Cartier] had made him [Agona] and his company eat and drinke, they departed and returned to the shore with their boates. After which things the sayd Captaine [Cartier] went with two of his boates up the river, beyond Canada and the Port of Saincte Croix,[12] to view a Haven and a small river, which is about 4 leagues higher,[13] which he found better and more commoditous to ride in and lay his ships then the former.[14] And therefore he returned and caused all his ships to be brought before the sayd river, and at a lowe water he caused his Ordinance to bee planted to place his ships in more saftie, which he meant to keepe and stay in the Countrey which were three: which hee did the day following and the rest[15] remayned in the roade in the middest of the river[16] (In which place[17] the victuals and other furniture were discharged, which they had brought) from the 26 of August untill the second of September, what time they departed to returne for S. Malo, in which ships he sent backe Mace Jolloberte, his brother in lawe, and Steven Noel, his Nephew, skilfull and excellent pilots, with letters unto the king, and to advertise

11 Hugging
12 The river St Charles
13 The river of Cape Rouge which enters the St Lawrence from the north at a point nine miles above Quebec
14 The river St Charles, where they had passed the winter of 1535–6
15 The sense of this passage seems to be that at low water he had the cannon taken out of three vessels and planted on shore while the vessels were moved into the Cape Rouge River. The other two vessels, which subsequently returned to France, were called the *Saint-Brieuc* and the *Georges*.
16 St Lawrence
17 At the river of Cape Rouge

him what had bene done and found: and how Monsieur de Roberval was not yet come, and that hee feared that by occasion of contrary winds and tempests he was driven backe againe into France.[18]

The Description of the Aforesaid River and Haven

The sayd River[19] is small, not past 50 pases broad, and shippes drawing three fathoms water may enter in at a full sea: and at a low water there is nothing but a chanell of a foote deepe or thereabout. On both sides of the said River there are very good and faire grounds, full of as faire and mightie trees as any be in the world, and divers sorts, which are above tenne fathoms higher then the rest, and there is one kind of tree above three fathoms about, which they in the Countrey call *Hanneda*, which hath the most excellent vertue of all the trees of the world, whereof I will make mention hereafter.[20] More[o]ver there are great store of Okes the most excellent that ever I saw in my life, which were so laden with Mast[21] that they cracked againe: besides this there are fairer Arables,[22] Cedars, Beeches, and other trees, then grow in France: and hard unto this wood on the South side the ground is all covered with Vines, which we found laden with grapes as blacke as Mulberies, but they be not so kind[23] as those of France because the Vines bee not tilled, and because they grow of their owne accord. More[o]ver there are many white Thornes, which beare leaves as bigge as oken leaves, and fruit like unto Medlers.[24] To bee short, it is as good a Countrey to plow and mannure as a man should find or desire. We sowed seedes here of our Countrey, as cabages, Naveaus,[25] Lettises, and others, which grew and sprong up out of the ground in eight dayes. The mouth of the river[26] is toward the

18 Cartier himself had encountered such exceedingly bad weather that he supposed Roberval, being nearer home, had turned back. These two vessels reached St Malo on 3 October. Jalobert at once set off to inform Francis I of Cartier's safe arrival in the river and to learn what were the king's wishes about taking reinforcements to Cartier early in the year 1542.

19 The river of Cape Rouge

20 If the author did so, that portion of his narrative has not been preserved.

21 Acorns

22 Maples, in French *érables*

23 Mild or sweet

24 Medlar, the fruit of the *mespilus*, a genus of large, ornamental fruit trees

25 'Or small Turneps'

26 Of Cape Rouge

South, and it windeth Northward like unto a snake: and at the mouth of it toward the East there is a high and steepe cliff,[27] where we made a way in maner of a payre of staires, and aloft we made a Fort to keepe[28] the nether Fort and the ships, and all things that might passe as well by the great[29] as by this small river.[30] Moreover, a man may behold a great extension of ground apt for tillage, straite and handsome and somewhat enclining toward the South, as easie to be brought to tillage as I would desire, and very well replenished with faire Okes and other trees of great beauty, no thicker then the Forrests of France. Here wee set twenty men to worke, which in one day had laboured about an acre and an halfe to the said ground, and sowed it part with Naveaus or small Turneps, which at the ende of eight dayes, as I said before, sprang out of the earth. And upon that high cliffe wee found a faire fountaine very neere the sayd Fort: adioyning whereunto we found good store of stones, which we esteemed to be Diamants.[31] On the other side of the said mountaine and at the foote thereof, which is towards the great River,[32] is all along a goodly Myne of the best yron in the world,[33] and it reacheth even hard unto our Fort, and the sand which we tread on is perfect refined Myne, ready to be put into the fornace. And on the waters side we found certaine leaves of fine gold as thicke as a mans nayle. And Westward of the said River[34] there are, as hath bene sayd, many faire trees; and toward the water a goodly Medow full of as faire and goodly grasse as ever I sawe in any Medowe in France; and betweene the sayd Medow and the Wood are great stores of Vines: and beyond the said Vines the land groweth full of Hempe which groweth of it selfe, which is as good as possibly may be seene, and as strong. And at the ende of the sayd Medow within an hundred pases there is a rising ground, which is of a kind of slate stone blacke and thicke, wherein are veines of mynerall matter, which shewe like gold and silver: and throughout all that stone there are great graines

27 This high promontory is Cape Rouge, so called from the reddish argillaceous limestone of which it is almost wholly composed.
28 Defend
29 The St Lawrence
30 Of Cape Rouge
31 Doubtless the limestone of Cape Rouge
32 St Lawrence
33 Some bits of the limestone of Cape Rouge look slightly like iron-ore when first broken off.
34 Of Cape Rouge

of the sayd Myne. And in some places we have found stones like Diamants, the most faire, pollished, and excellently cut that it is possible for a man to see. When the Sunne shineth upon them, they glisten as it were sparkles of fire.

How after the Departure of the Two Shippes Which Were Sent Backe into Brittaine,[35] *and That the Fort Was Begun to Be Builded, the Captaine Prepared Two Boates to Goe up the Great River to Discover the Passage of the Three Saults or Falles of the River*

The sayd Captaine having dispatched two ships to returne to carry newes, according as hee had in charge from the king,[36] and that the Fort was begun to be builded, for preservation of their victuals and other things, determined with the Vicount of Beaupré, and other Gentlemen, Masters, and Pilots chosen for counsayle, to make a voyage with two boates furnished with men and victuals to goe as farre as Hochelaga, of purpose to view and understand the fashion of the *Saults* of water, which are to be passed to goe to Saguenay,[37] that hee [Cartier] might be the readier in the spring to passe farther, and in the Winter time to make all things needefull in a readinesse for their businesse. The foresaid boates being made ready, the Captaine and Martine de Painpont,[38] with other Gentlemen and the remnant of the Mariners, departed from the sayd place of Charlesburg Royal[39] the seventh day of September in the yeere aforesayd 1540.[40] And the Vicount of Beaupré stayed behind for the garding and governement of all things in the Fort. And as they went up the river,[41] the Captaine went to see the Lord of Hochelay,[42] which dwelleth betweene Canada[43] and Hochelaga:

35 Brittany

36 Francis I

37 The mysterious kingdom of the Saguenay

38 Paimpont, a village in the forest of the same name not far from Rennes in the Department of Ille-et-Vilaine

39 The fort was doubtless so called after Charles Duke of Orleans, the second surviving son of Francis I.

40 1541

41 St Lawrence

42 An Indian village in the neighbourhood of the present Portneuf, thirty-two miles from Quebec.

43 The region about the mouth of the St Charles

which in the former voyage had given unto the said Captaine a little girle, and had oftentimes enformed him of the treasons which Taignoagny and Domagaya (whom the Captaine in his former voyage had caried into France) would have wrought against him. In regard of which his curtesie the said Captaine would not passe by without visiting him, and to let him understand that the Captaine thought himselfe beholding unto him, hee gave unto him two yong boyes, and left them with him to learne their language, and bestowed upon him a cloake of Paris red, which cloake was set with yealow and white buttons of Tinne, and small belles. And withall hee gave him two Basins of Laton,[44] and certaine hatchets and knives: whereat the sayde Lord seemed highly to reioyce, and thanked the Captaine. This done, the Captaine and his company departed from that place: And we sailed with so prosperous a wind, that we arrived the eleventh day of the moneth [of September 1541] at the first *Sault* of water,[45] which is two leagues distant from the Towne of Tutonaguy.[46] And after wee were arrived there, wee determined to goe and passe as farre up as it was possible with one of the boates, and that the other should stay there till it returned: and wee double manner her to rowe up against the course or streame of the said *Sault*. And after wee had passed some part of the way from our other boate, wee found badde ground and great rockes, and so great a current, that wee could not possible passe any further with our Boate.[47] And the Captain resolved to goe by land to see the nature and fashion of the *Sault*. And after that we were come on shore, wee founde hard by the water side a way and beaten path going toward the sayde *Saultes*, by which wee tooke our way. And on the sayd way, and soone after, we found an habitation of people which made us great cheere and entertained us very friendly. And after that he [Cartier] had signified unto them that wee were going toward the *Saults*, and that wee desired to goe to Saguenay,[48] foure yong men went along with

44 Latten, a kind of bronze used in the Middle Ages for making basins, candlesticks, etc.

45 The rapid of St Mary

46 This is the first appearance of this name, which resembles the Huron word *Tionontaté*, 'people beyond the mountains.' It seems to have been a new Huron-Iroquois village somewhere near the site of the old Hochelaga.

47 The Lachine rapid

48 The kingdom of the Saguenay

us to shewe us the way, and they brought us so farre that wee came to another village or habitation of good people, which dwell over against the second *Sault*,[49] which came and brought us of their victuals, as Pottage and Fish, and offered us of the same. After that the Captaine had enquired of them as well by signes as wordes, how many more *Saults* wee had to passe to goe to Saguenay, and what distance and way it was thither, this people shewed us and gave us to understand that wee were at the second *Sault*, and that there was but one more to passe,[50] that the River[51] was not navigable to goe to Saguenay, and that the sayd *Sault*[52] was but a third part farther than we had travailed, shewing us the same with certaine little stickes, which they layd upon the ground in a certaine distance, and afterwarde layde other small branches betweene both, representing the *Saults*. And by the sayde marke, if their saying be true, it can be but sixe leagues by land to passe the sayd *Saults*.

Here after Followeth the Figure of the Three Saults

After that we had bene advertised by the sayde people of the things abovementioned, both because the day was farre spent and we had neither drunke nor eaten the same day, we concluded to returne unto our boats and we came thither,[53] where we found great store of people to the number of 400 persons or thereabout, which seemed to give us very good entertainment and to reioyce of our comming: And therefore our Captaine gave eche of them certaine small trifles, as combs, brooches of tynne and copper, and other smal toyes, and unto the chiefe men every one his litle hatchet & hooke,[54] whereat they made certaine cries and ceremonies of ioy. But a man must not trust them for all their faire ceremonies and signes of ioy, for if they had thought they had bene too strong for us, then would they have done their best to have killed us, as we understood afterward. This being done, we returned with our boats and passed

49 The Lachine rapid
50 Since according to the second Relation the best route to the kingdom of the Saguenay was up the Ottawa River, this would be the Long Sault with the Carillon.
51 Ottawa
52 The Long Sault
53 Back to the foot of the St Mary rapid where the boats had been left
54 A kind of sickle

by the dwelling of the Lord of Hochelay, with whom the Captaine had left the two youths as hee came up the river, thinking to have found him: But hee coulde find no body save one of his sonnes, who tolde the Captaine that hee was gone to Maisouna,[55] as our boyes[56] also told us, saying that it was two dayes since he departed. But in truth hee was gone to Canada[57] to conclude with Agona what they should doe against us. And when we were arrived at our Fort,[58] wee understoode by our people that the Savages of the Countrey came not any more about our Fort as they were accustomed, to bring us fish, and that they were in a wonderful doubt and feare of us. Wherefore our Captain [Cartier], having bene advertised by some of our men which had bene at Stadacona to visite them that there were a wonderful number of the Countrey people assembled together, caused all things in our fortresse to bee set in good order: etc.

THE REST IS WANTING.

Underneath the Aforesaid Unperfite Relation That Which Followeth Is Written in a Letter Sent to M. John Growte,[59] Student in Paris, from Jaques Noel of S. Malo, the Grand Nephew of Jaques Cartier[60]

I can write nothing else unto you of any thing that I can recover of the writings of Captaine Jaques Cartier my uncle disceased,[61] although I have made search in all places that I could possibly in this Towne:[62] saving of a certaine booke made in maner of a sea Chart, which was drawne by the hand of my said uncle, which is in the possession of master Cremeur:[63] which booke is passing well marked and drawne for all the River of Canada, whereof I

55 This name does not occur elsewhere.
56 The French boys left by Cartier on the way up.
57 The region about the mouth of the St Charles
58 Charlesbourg Royal, at the mouth of the river of Cape Rouge
59 Probably Jean Grout, sieur de La Ruaudaye, a well-known St Malo family
60 He was the son of Estienne Nouel mentioned above and was born 5 February 1551.
61 Cartier died on 1 September 1557. The statement in the text would lead one to infer that Cartier looked upon himself as the author of these Relations.
62 St Malo
63 Jan Jocet, sieur de Cremeur, then Constable of St Malo

am well assured, because I my selfe have knowledge thereof as farre as to the *Saults*, where I have bene: The height of which *Saults* is in 44 degrees. I found in the sayd Chart beyond the place where the River is divided in twaine in the midst of both the branches of the said river somewhat neerest that arme which runneth toward the Northwest,[64] these words following written in the hand of Jaques Cartier: 'By the people of Canada and Hochelaga it was said, That here is the land of Saguenay, which is rich and wealthy in precious stone.'

And about an hundred leagues under the same I found written these two lines following in the said Carde enclining toward the Southwest. 'Here in this Countrey are Cinamon and Cloves, which they call in their language Canodeta.'

Touching the effect of my booke whereof I spake unto you, it is made after the maner of a sea Chart, which I have delivered to my two sonnes Michael and John, which at this present are in Canada. If at their returne, which will be God willing about Magdalene tyde,[65] they have learned any new thing worthy the writing, I will not faile to advertise you thereof.

Your loving Friend,

Jaques Noel

64 The Ottawa, which enters the St Lawrence just above the Lachine rapid

65 22 July; but the year in which the letter was written is not given.

Roberval's Voyage, 1542–1543

The Voyage of John Francis de la Roche,[1] *Knight, Lord of Roberval, to the Countries of Canada, Saguenai, and Hochelaga, with Three Tall Ships and Two Hundred Persons, Both Men, Women, and Children, Begun in April 1542. In Which Parts He Remayned the Same Summer and All the Next Winter*

Sir John Francis de la Roche, knight, lord of Roberval, appoynted by the king[2] as his lieutenant general in the countreis of Canada, Saguenay, and Hochelaga, furnished three tall Ships, chiefly at the kings cost: And having in his fleete 200 persons, aswel men as women, accompanied with divers gentlemen of qualitie, as namely with Monsieur Saine-terre his lieutenant,[3] l'Espiney his Ensigne,[4] captain Guinecourt, Monsieur Noirefontaine,[5] Dieu lamont, Froté,[6] la Brosse[7] Francis de Mire, la Salle,[8] and Roieze and John

The text here given is that first published in *The Third and Last Volume of the Voyages, Navigations, Traffiques and Discoveries of the English Nation*, etc., collected by Richard Hakluyt (London 1600), 240–2.

1 Jean François de La Roque
2 Francis I
3 Paul d'Aussillon, seigneur de Sauveterre in the Department of Tarn, near Castres
4 Perhaps Nicolas de Lespinay, seigneur de Neufville sur le Wault. There was another branch at La Fraye not far from Roberval.
5 Probably one of the children of Jean de Noirefontaine, seigneur du Buisson et du Vouciennes, two places near Châlons-sur-Marne
6 Probably a son of Jacques de Frotté, President of the Parliament of Paris, whose wife's mother was a La Brosse
7 Perhaps a son of Pierre de La Brosse
8 Probably Jean de La Salle, 'homme d'armes de la compagnie dont avoit

Alfonse of Xanctoigne,[9] an excellent pilot, set sayle from Rochel the 16 of April 1542.[10] The same day about noone we came athwart of Chefe de boys,[11] where we were enforced to stay the night following. On Munday the seventeenth of the sayde Moneth wee departed from Chefe de boys. The winde served us notably for a time: but within fewe days it came quite contrary, which hindered our journey for a long space: For wee were suddenly enforced to turne backe, and to seeke Harborough in Belle Isle, on the coast of Bretaigne,[12] where wee stayed so long, and had such contrary weather by the way, that wee could not reach Newfound lande untill the seventh of June. The eight of this Moneth wee entred into the Rode of Saint John, where wee founde seventeene Shippes of fishers. While wee made somewhat long abode heere, Jaques Cartier and his company returning from Canada, whither hee was sent with five sayles the yeere before, arrived in the very same Harbour. Who, after hee had done his duetie to our Generall, tolde him that hee had brought certaine Diamonts, and a quantite of Golde ore, which was found in the Countrey. Which ore the Sunday next ensuing[13] was tryed in a Furnace, and found to be good.

Furthermore, hee[14] enformed the Generall[15] that hee could not with his small company withstand the Savages, which went about dayly to annoy him: and that this was the cause of his returne into France. Neverthelesse, hee and his company commended the Countrey to bee very rich and fruitfull. But when our Generall, being furnished with sufficient forces, commaunded him to goe backe againe with him, hee [Cartier] and his company, mooved as

---

charge et conduite Monsieur le Baron de Curton,' and who by a commission dated 16 February 1542 (N. St.) was ordered to muster this company at Tréguier not far from St Malo.

9 Jean Alfonse of Saintonge

10 La Rochelle on the west coast of France. The date of 1542 shows that the year 1540 given in Cartier's third Relation should be 1541, since they met in the next year 1542 in the harbour of St John's. They left on a Sunday.

11 *Chef de Baie*, the point of the mainland at the northwest corner of the bay of La Rochelle

12 Belle Isle, on the coast of Brittany off the mouth of the Loire, is nine miles and a quarter long by five miles wide at its broadest part. The two main harbours lying on the west coast are Port Sauzons and Le Palais.

13 Probably Sunday, 18 June

14 Cartier

15 Roberval, who was his superior. Cartier had merely been appointed the Master-pilot of the expedition.

it seemeth with ambition, because they would have all the glory of the discoverie of those partes themselves, stole privily away the next night from us, and, without taking their leaves, departed home for Bretaigne.[16]

We spent the greatest part of June in this Harbour of Saint John, partly in furnishing our selves with fresh water, whereof wee stoode in very great neede by the way, and partly in composing and taking up of a quarell betweene some of our Countreymen and certaine Portugals. At length, about the last of the aforesayde Moneth,[17] wee departed hence and entred into the Grand Baye,[18] and passed by the Isle of Ascension:[19] and finally arrived foure leagues Westward of the Isle of Orleans. In this place wee found a convenient Harbour for our shipping, where wee cast anchor, went a shoare with our people, and chose out a convenient place to fortifie our selves in, fitte to commaund the mayne River, and of strong situation against all invasion of enemies. Thus towarde the ende of July, wee brought our victuals and other munitions and provisions on shore, and began to travaile in fortifying of our selves.

Of the Fort of France-Roy, and That Which Was Done There

Having described the beginning, the middest, and the ende of the Voyage made by Monsieur Roberval in the Countreyes of Canada, Hochelaga, Saguenay, and other Countreyes in the West partes: He sayled so farre (as it is declared in other bookes) that hee arrived in the sayde Countrey, accompanyed with two hundred persons, souldiers, mariners, and common people, with all furniture[20] necessary for a Fleete. The sayde Generall at his first arrivall built a fayre Fort, neere and somewhat Westward above Canada[21] which is very beautifull to beholde, and of great force, situated upon an high mountaine,[22] wherein there were two courtes of buyldings, a great Towre, and another of fortie or fiftie foote long: wherein

16 Brittany. This dukedom had only been formally annexed to France in 1532.
17 June 1542
18 The Gulf of St Lawrence inside the Strait of Belle Isle
19 Anticosti, which Cartier had named the 'Island of Assumption.' Alfonse, who was with Roberval, also calls it Ascension.
20 Stores
21 Quebec and the mouth of the St Charles
22 Cape Rouge

there were divers Chambers, an Hall, a Kitchine, houses of office, Sellers high and lowe, and neere unto it were an Oven and Milles, and a stoove to warme men in, and a Well before the house. And the buylding was situated upon the great River of Canada, called *France prime* by Monsieur Roberval. There was also at the foote of the mountaine another lodging, part whereof was a great Towre of two stories high, two courtes of good buylding, where at the first all our victuals, and whatsoever was brought with us was sent to be kept: and neere unto that Towre there is another small river.[23] In these two places above and beneath, all the meaner sort was lodged.

And in the Moneth of August, and in the beginning of September every man was occupied in such woorke as eche one was able to doe. But the fourteenth of September, our aforesayde Generall sent backe into France two Shippes which had brought his furniture, and he appoynted for Admirall Monsieur de Saineterre, and the other captaine was Monsieur Guine-court, to carie newes unto the King, and to come backe againe unto him the yeere next ensuing, furnished with victuals and other things, as it should please the King: and also to bring newes out of France how the King accepted certaine Diamants which were sent him, and were found in this countrey.

After these two Shippes were departed, consideration was had how they should doe, and how they might passe out the Winter in this place. First they tooke a view of the victuals, and it was found that they fell out short: and they were scantled[24] so that in eche messe they had but two loaves weighing a pound a piece, and halfe a pound of biefe. They ate Bacon at dinner with halfe a pound of butter: and Biefe at supper, and about two handfuls of Beanes without butter.

On the Wednesday, Friday, and Saturday they did eate dry Cod, and sometimes they did eate it greene[25] at dinner with butter, and they ate of Porposes and beanes at supper.

About that time the Savages brought us great store of Aloses,[26] which is a fish somewhat redde like a Salmon, to get knives and other small trifles for them.

23 The river of Cape Rouge
24 Broken up into small portions
25 That is, uncured
26 The common shad

In the ende many of our people fell sicke of a certaine disease in their legges, reynes,[27] and stomacke, so that they seemed to bee deprived of all their lymmes, and there dyed thereof about fiftie.

Note that the yce began to breake up in April [1543].

Monsieur Roberval used very good justice, and punished every man according to his offence. One whose name was Michael Gaillon was hanged for his theft. John of Nantes was layde in yrons, and kept prisoner for his offence, and others also were put in yrons, and divers were whipped, as well men as women: by which meanes they lived in quiet.

The Maners of the Savages

To declare unto you the state of the Savages, they are people of a goodly stature, and well made, they are very white, but they are all naked: and if they were apparelled as the French are, they would bee as white and as fayre: but they paynt themselves for feare of heat and sunne burning.

In stead of apparell, they weare skinnes upon them like mantle; and they have a small payre of breeches, wherewith they cover their privities, as well men as women. They have hosen and shooes of lether excellently made. And they have no shirts: neither cover they their heads, but their hayre is trussed up above the crowne of their heads, and playted or broyded. Touching their victuals, they eate good meate, but all unsalted, but they drye it, and afterward they broyle it, aswell fish as flesh. They have no certaine dwelling place, and they goe from place to place, as they thinke they may best finde foode, as Aloses in one place, and other fish, Salmons, Sturgions, Mullets, Surmullets,[28] Barz,[29] Carpes, Eeles, Pinperneaux,[30] and other fresh water fish, and store of Porposes. They feede also of Stagges, wilde Bores, Bugles,[31] Porkespynes,[32] and store of other wilde beastes. And there is as great store of Fowle as they can desire.

Touching their bread, they make very good: and it is of great myll: and they live very well; for they take care for nothing else.

27 The loins
28 The red mullet
29 The maigre
30 Perhaps water pimpernel, a species of water plant
31 This was no doubt the moose.
32 Porcupines

They drinke Seale oyle, but this is at their great feasts.

They have a King in every Countrey, and are wonderfull obedient unto him: and they doe him honour according unto their maner and fashion. And when they travayle from place to place, they cary all their goods with them in their boates.

The weomen nurse their children with the breast, and they sit continually, and are wrapped about the bellies with skinnes of furre.

The Voyage of Monsieur Roberval from His Fort in Canada unto Saguenay, the Fifth of June 1543

Monsieur Roberval the kings Lieutenant generall in the Countries of Canada, Saguenay, and Hochelaga, departed toward the said province of Saguenay on the Tuesday the 5 day of June 1543, after supper: and he with all his furniture[33] was imbarked to make the sayd voyage. But upon a certaine occasion they lay in the Rode over against the place before mentioned:[34] but on the Wednesday[35] about sixe of the clocke in the morning they set sayle, and sayled against the streame: in which voyage their whole furniture was of eight barks,[36] aswell great as small, and to the number of threescore and ten persons, with the aforesayd Generall.

The Generall left behinde him in the aforesayde place and Fort thirtie persons to remayne there untill his returne from Saguenay, which hee appoynted to bee the first of July[37] or else they should returne into France. And hee left there behinde him but two Barkes to cary the sayde thirtie persons, and the furniture which was there, while hee stayed still in the Countrey.[38]

And for effectuating hereof, he left as his Lieutenant a gentleman named Monsieur de Royeze, to whom he gave commission, and charged all men to obey him, and be at the commandement of the sayd lieutenant.

The victuals which were left for their mayntenance untill the sayd first day of July were received by the sayd Lieutenant Royeze.

33 Stores
34 The fort of France-Roy at the mouth of the river of Cape Rouge
35 6 June, the following day
36 Longboats which could be worked with oars or sails
37 This shows that the kingdom of Saguenay was thought to lie not far from the mouth of the Ottawa, since Roberval expected to reach it, to affect its conquest, and to return all in the short space of three weeks.
38 That is, passed the winter in the kingdom of Saguenay

On Thursday the 14 of June Monsieur de l'Espiney, la Brosse, Monsieur Frete, Monsieur Longeval,[39] and others returned from the Generall, from the voyage of Saguenay.

And note that eight men and one Barke were drowned and lost, among whom was Monsieur de Noirefontaine, and one named la Vasseur of Constance.

On Tuesday, the 19 of June aforesayd, there came from the Generall, Monsieur de Villeneufve, Talebot, and three others, which brought sixescore pounds weight of their corne, and letters to stay yet untill Magdalentyde, which is the 22 day of July.

THE REST OF THIS VOYAGE IS WANTING.

39 In 1519 a Robert de Longueval, sieur de Thenelles in the Oise, married the daughter of a Catherine de La Roque, wife of Robert de Hangard.

Documents relating to Jacques Cartier and the Sieur de Roberval

1 GRANT OF MONEY TO CARTIER FOR HIS FIRST VOYAGE

18 March 1533/4

To Jean de Vimond, treasurer of the Marine, the sum of six thousand *livres tournois* ordered to be delivered to him from the moneys coming from the funds of the general receiver's office for Outre-Seine for the year ended on the last day of December 1532 by the King and his letters patent issued in Paris on the 12th day of March 1533, signed François Bochetel and sealed with the seal of the said seigneur, to change and use in the exercise of his said office, and also for the payment of the expenses that will have to be incurred for the provisioning, fitting out, and equipping of certain ships which the said seigneur has ordered to be fitted out forthwith in the country of Brittany, and for the pay and maintenance of the sailors and other persons who in the company and under the leadership of Jacques Cartier are to make the voyage from this kingdom to Newfoundland to discover certain islands and countries where it is said that a great abundance of gold and other precious things is to be found. Which sum has been paid him in ready money by the said officer of the Crown from the moneys taken and withdrawn from the said funds, in particular from those that came from the said remainder from the said year, in the presence of the presidents, in twelve-, ten-, and three-*denier* pieces as is shown by his receipt signed in his hand the 13th day of March 1533, registered by me the 23rd day of the said month and year.

For this 6000 *livres.*

2 COMMISSION FROM ADMIRAL CHABOT TO CARTIER

30 October 1534

Philippe Chabot, knight of the Order, Comte de Buzançais et de Charny, Baron d'Aspremont, de Paigny, et de Mirebeau, seigneur of Beaumont and Fontaine-Française, admiral of France, Brittany, and Guienne, governor and lieutenant general for the King in Burgundy, also lieutenant governor for Monseigneur the Dauphin in the government of Normandy, to the captain and pilot Maître Jacques Cartier of Saint-Malo, greetings. We have commissioned and appointed, commission and appoint you as our deputy, at the wish and command of the King, to conduct, guide, and employ three ships, each equipped and provisioned for fifteen months, to complete the navigation already begun by you of the lands to be discovered beyond Newfoundland, and during this voyage to endeavour to carry out and fulfil what it has pleased the said seigneur to command and order you, for the equipment of which you will buy or charter at a price that you, on the advice of honest persons who are well informed on the matter, will consider to be reasonable, and according as you will see and recognize to be suitable for the success of the said navigation, which said three ships you will take, and will hire the number of pilots, masters, journeymen, and mariners as will seem to you to be required and necessary for the accomplishment of that navigation, for the supplying, delivery, and embarking of which things we have given and give you power, commission, and especial command with the entire charge and superintendence of those ships, the voyage, and the navigation, on the outwardbound and homewardbound passages. We order and command all the said pilots, masters, journeymen, mariners, and others who will be on the said ships to obey and follow you for the service of the King as indicated above, as they would obey ourself without any contradiction or refusal, and this on the penalties usual in such a case for those who will disobey and act against others. Given under our mark and armorial seal the second-last day of October in the year one thousand [five] hundred and thirty-four. As given under the hand of Philippe Chabot and sealed unfolded with red wax.

3 CHOICE OF VESSELS FOR THE SECOND VOYAGE

3 March 1534/5

On Wednesday the third day of March in the year 1534 at the abbey of Saint-Jean in the presence of my said seigneur the Captain, being present Maître Pierre Le Gobien, Monsieur the agent of the court of the said Saint-Malo, Maître Regné Le Maire, Sieur de Tormie, Constable of Saint-Malo, Monsieur de Baudetz, senior chaplain of Monseigneur the bishop of Saint-Malo; also present Maîtres Georges Bastard, Jean Du Liscouet, canons; Jacques Cartier, Julien Cronier for Jean Billard, attorney of the bourgeois, etc., Jacques Chenu, Bertrand Beaulbois, Gilles Aran, Robin Gaultier senior, Robin Boulain, Etienne Richomme, Guillaume Boulain the son of Jean, Guillaume Launay, Pierre Durant, Etienne Chevallier, Guyon Serainet, Jean Boulain *vif argent*, Hamon Gaultier, Colas Gaultier, Jean Hacoul, Colas Philippe, Georges Baulain, Josselin Eberard, Pierre Jolif, Pierre Dauphin, Jean Eon, Etienne Odièvre, Thomas de La Bouille, and several others of the said bourgeois, etc.

To begin with mention was made by my said seigneur the Captain concerning the epidemic and plague which is beginning and is now beginning to be prevalent in this said town, which it is necessary to guard against and those who will be stricken by this malady must remain in their homes without going out and they will be provided with food and drink by the persons ordered to do this, and to do this it is necessary to engage a barber-surgeon and at a good salary.

Up till now there has been a delay of three or four days, yet the said Du Bois, present, was ordered to attend to this, if not, it will be provided for otherwise.

A statement was made by the said Cronier for the said bourgeois that the said Cartier has had the ships of this said town held up, asking that he be allowed to choose ships publicly as he pleases because the season is arriving to go to Newfoundland.

It was stated by the said Cartier that it was not necessary to debate whether they should go on the spot & off the town to look at the said ships in order to seek the advice of competent persons about them. Which Robin Boullain agreed to for this galleon & several others likewise, etc.

The said Boullain's said galleon was left by the said Cartier & he said that he did not want to have it & that he wanted to have the said Etienne Richomme's ship, etc.

4 PAYMENT OF THREE THOUSAND *LIVRES* TO CARTIER FOR HIS SECOND VOYAGE

30 March 1535

To Jean de Vimond, treasurer of the Marine of Normandy, the sum of three thousand *livres tournois* ordered to be paid him out of the monies held for the King's personal use by the said seigneur and his letters patent issued at Le Bec-Hellouin on the 25th day of March before Easter 1534, signed François Bochetel and sealed with the seal of the said seigneur, to change and employ for the fitting-out, equipping, provisioning, and other expenses that will have to be paid for the conduct of the voyage that Jacques Cartier, master pilot from the country of Brittany, has undertaken to make to go to discover certain distant lands in accordance with the charge which the said seigneur has given him. Which sum has been paid to him in ready money by the said officer of the Crown in 1534 gold *écus soleil* and 15 *sous* in 12-*denier* pieces as is shown by his receipt signed in his hand on the second-last day of March 1535 and registered by me on the 22nd day of May of the said year.

For this 3000 *livres.*

5 ROLL OF THE CREWS FOR CARTIER'S SECOND VOYAGE

31 March 1535

On Wednesday the last day of March before Easter 1535 at the abbey of Saint-Jean, in the presence of my said seigneur the Captain, being present Maître Jean Le Juif, lieutenant of the court of Saint-Malo, the constable, Jean Billard, attorney of the said bourgeois, Jn Cronier, Jac. Chenu, Jean Grout junior, Bertrand Beaubois, Pierre May, François Gaillard, Jean Maingard Huperie, Jacques Martinet, Robin Boullain, Etienne Richomme, Guillaume Boulain Villauroux, Pierre Hancelin, Guillaume Maingard, Guillaume Pepin, Jean Brisard senior, Jean Boulain Belestre, Thomas de La Bouille, Robin Gaultier junior, Thomas Maingard, François Martin, Guillaume Grout, Roullet Souchart, Yrlet Morel, Guillaume Le Breton Bastille, Georges Boulain, Guillaume Saint Mains, Pierre Gosselin, Jean Grout senior, Charles Cheville, Guillaume Gaillard, Pierre Jouchée, Pierre Gaillard, Jean de May, Pierre Colin.

And several others of the said bourgeois assembled, etc.

After what was stated by the said attorney concerning a proclamation that was made yesterday by Pierre Gautier, sergeant, the said sergeant was present, who admitted to having made the said proclamation, which he showed; and said that a certain Jean Poulet, present, had him do it, and no one else, which proclamation was ordered to be inserted in this document; and the said Bastille, present, who denied having had the said proclamation made; and the said Poulet, present, who said that by virtue of the charge that had been given him the said Cartier had had the said proclamation made.

And the said La Bouille and Maingard, present, who, the charge that Jacques Cartier gave the said Jean Poulet having been heard, took entire responsibility for the said proclamation.

And this Poulet presented the roll and number of the journeymen whom the said Cartier has taken for the said navigation & it was handed over to me to insert it hereunder, & this Poulet protested that the number be reduced by 25 to 30 & that others be taken at his choice.

The insertion of the said masters, journeymen, mariners & pilots follows:

Jacques Cartier, captain
Thomas Fourmont, master of the ship
Guillaume Le Breton Bastille, captain and pilot of the galleon
Jacques Maingard, master of the galleon
Macé Jalobert, captain and pilot of the *Courlieu*
Guillaume Le Marié, master of the *Courlieu*
Laurent Boulain
Etienne Noël
Pierre Emery, *dit* Talbot
Michel Hervé
Etienne Pommerel
Michel Odièvre
Brand Sauboscq
Richard Cobaz
Lucas Saumur
François Guitault, apothecary
Georges Mabille
Guillaume Sequart, carpenter
Robin Le Tort
Samson Ripault, barber
François Guillot
Guillaume Esnault, carpenter
Jean Dabin, carpenter
Jean du Nort, carpenter
Julien Golet
Thomas Boulain
Michel Philipot
Jean Hamel
Jean Fleury
Guillaume Guilbert
Colas Barbé
Laurent Gaillot
Guillaume Bochier
Michel Eon
Jean Anthoine
Michel Maingard
Jean Maryen
Bertrand Avril
Gilles Ruffin
Geoffroy Olivier
Guillaume De Guernesey
Eustache Grossin
Guillaume Alliecte
Jean Raby
Pierre Marquier, trumpeter
Guillaume Le Gentilhomme
Raoulet Maingard
François Duault
Hervé Henry
Yvon Le Gal
Antoine Aliecte
Jean Colas
Jacques Prinsault
Dom Guillaume Le Breton
Dom Antoine
Philippe Thomas, carpenter
Jacques Du Bog
Julien Plancouët
Jean Go
Jean Le Gentilhomme
Michel Donquan, carpenter
Jean Aismery, carpenter
Pierre Maingard
Lucas Clavier
Goulhet Riou
Jean Jac, du Morbihan
Pierre Niel
Le Gendre Étienne Le Blanc
Jean Pierres
Jean Coumin
Antoine Des Granges

Louis Douayran
Pierre Coupeaulx
Pierre Jonchée, etc.

6 ORDER FROM KING FRANCIS THE FIRST FOR THE PAYMENT TO CARTIER OF FIFTY CROWNS

22 September 1538

Francis by the grace of God King of France to our beloved and faithful counsellor, treasurer and receiver general of our extraordinary finances and perquisites Maître Jean Laguette, Greetings and affection. We wish and order that out of the first and most certain funds of your said general revenue that have come or will come from the sale and creation of offices and other perquisites you pay, give, and deliver in ready money to our dear and beloved Jacques Cartier, our pilot in the Western fleet, residing at Saint-Malo in Brittany, the sum of fifty *écus soleil* worth at 45 *sous* each 111 *livres* 10 *sous*, for whom we have ordered and order it by these presents, on what may be owing him for his wages and fees and for the food and upkeep of a certain number of savage people whom he has fed and kept at our order for two years now. And referring to these presents signed in our hand and a receipt from the said Jacques Cartier covering this only, We wish that the said sum of fifty *écus soleil* at the rate as above be passed and allowed on the outlay of your accounts and deducted from your said general revenue by our beloved and faithful servants of our accounts whom we order to carry this out without question. For such is our pleasure, notwithstanding the ordinances issued by Us concerning the establishment of our Treasury at the Louvre in Paris and distribution of our finances, and whatever other ordinances, restrictions, orders, or prohibitions to the contrary. Issued at Saint-Germain-en-Laye the 22nd day of September in the year of grace 1538 and the twenty-fourth of our reign.

FRANÇOIS By order of the King Bocherel

7 LIST OF MEN AND EFFECTS FOR CANADA

September 1538

Statement of the men and supplies needed for the vessels that the King wished to send to Canada.

Through this statement can be seen the piety, magnanimity, and open-heartedness of the great King Francis, & how, notwithstanding that wars had exhausted his finances and even involved His Majesty in enormous debts, nevertheless, finding himself in a state of peace, he is not afraid to engage in new expense, to establish the Christian Religion in a country of Savages at the other end of the world from France, and where he was well aware that there were no gold or silver mines nor any other gain to be hoped for, other than the winning over of an infinite number of souls to God and their liberation from the domination and tyranny of the infernal Demon, to whom they used to sacrifice even their own Children.

To make the voyage which the King our Sovereign Seigneur wishes to be made to Canada, it is necessary to be ready by mid-March at the latest & to have the number of persons and Ships listed hereafter, to be increased or reduced at the discretion of the said Seigneur and of Monseigneur the Constable.

And first, six score mariners are required to guard the ships that will remain there and to equip several boats that will have to be equipped to sail on several Rivers & Streams, for this 120 men

Item, forty soldiers Arquebusiers are required, for this	40 men
Item, thirty Carpenters, both ships' and house Carpenters, and pit-sawyers, for this	30 men
Item, ten Master Masons, & they will use the help of the people of the country, to serve them, for this	10 men
Item, three men who can make lime, for this	3 men
Item, three tilemakers, for this	3 men
Item, two charcoal-burners to make charcoal for this	2 men
Item, two Master blacksmiths, each with a smithy provided with two servitors, for this	4 men
Item, two Ironsmiths, a fully equipped smithy and two servitors, for this	4 men

Item, four smiths, to look for and determine whether there is an iron mine, & to set up ironworks and make iron, for this — 4 men
Item, it is requisite to take along six Vine growers and six farm Labourers at least, for this — 12 men
Item, three Barbers, each with an assistant, for this — 6 men
Item, two Apothecaries, each with an assistant, to identify plants and determine their uses, for this — 4 men
Item, it would be very much requisite to take along a Doctor with an assistant, for this — 2 men
Item, two Gold-and-silver Smiths who are Lapidaries, provided with all the items they need, and each with an assistant, for this — 4 men
Item, two Master Tailors, two Master Hosiers, each with an assistant, for this — 8 men
Item, two Joiners and two assistants, provided with their tools, for this — 4 men
Item, two Master Rope-makers and two assistants, because there is hemp for making rope, for this — 4 men
Item, four Gunners at least are needed, and the soldiers will serve as Gunners if need by, for this — 4 men
Item, six members of the clergy, having the things requisite for divine service, are needed, for this — 6 men

And as far as all other sorts of craftsmen are concerned, they can be done without for this initial voyage, therefore the number of men included here would amount to two hundred and seventy-six, for this — 276 men

Which men must be provided with provisions for at least two years, so that if the Ships that will be sent to take them provisions next year were to met with some accident, they would not lack provisions.

Item, it is also requisite that the said victuals be well prepared and suitable to last for so long a time, & there must be dry Spanish wines, & the said victuals may cost one hundred *sous* per month for each man, which would be, for the said two hundred and seventy-six men for twenty-four months, the sum of thirty-three thousand one hundred and twenty *livres*.

It is also necessary that those who will remain there for the said time be supplied with clothes, beds, covers & all other effects for two or three years, & that they leave their wives and children some money to live on, & they will need to be paid in ready money for fifteen or sixteen months, & they will cost at the least one hundred *sous* per month on an average.

Item, it is requisite that ten iron barrels be taken, which will cost fifty *livres.*

Item, eight or ten barrels of salt, for the people in the Country, who regard it highly, and for those on the Ships, which will cost, bought in Brittany, sixty *sous* each.

Item, four thousand bolts of ordinary canvas, for the people of the Country as well as for those on the ships, to be taken from their pay.

Item, three hundred lengths of serge, for the people of the said Country as well as those of the Ships, against their said pay.

Item, several sorts of small-wares must be taken which will be bought and paid for by order for payment of the Commissioner.

Item, all sorts of house utensils and appointments, for the use of those who will remain there, must be taken, also millstones to make watermills, windmills, and handmills.

Item, it is requisite that all sorts and species of domestic animals and fowl, as many as possible, be taken there, for tilling the soil and settling the country, and all sorts of cereals and seeds.

Item, to make which crossing, at least six Ships, the smallest of one hundred tons burden, are requisite, along with two Barks of forty-five or fifty tons each, which will remain there with the smallest of the six Ships, & the other five will return immediately upon landing the people and provisions; for the return of which five Ships, twenty men will be needed over and above the number stated earlier, who may spend five or six months for the voyage there and back and for the stay there, for which time they will have to be supplied, & paid for two months on their departure and the remainder when they return.

Item, munitions of war must be taken to be landed and installed in the Forts, including Artillery and Arquebuses with forked rests, Pikes, Halberds, Lead, Cannon-balls, Shot & and other munitions at your discretion.

Item, three Longboats must be carried on the Ships ready to be assembled upon arrival, to navigate the said Rivers & Streams.

Item, all sorts of Nails, Pitch, and Tar must be taken for the said Ships.

The six Ships must be of seven to eight hundred tons which will cost one *écu* per ton per month for affreightment, which at nine hundred *écus* per month will amount for six months to the sum of 4900 *écus.*

The King's Galleon which is at Saint-Malo may serve as one of the two Barks. As for the other Bark, it will have to be bought.

In addition, the pay and supplies are needed for a hundred men to bring the Ships back this year, who with the stay there and the voyage there and back may be absent for a period of six months, which would be 6000 *livres* for six months. Prepared ... September 1538.

8 LETTER FROM LAGARTO TO JOHN THE THIRD, KING OF PORTUGAL

22 January 1539?

Item. On the same day I spoke with the King and, as Latin is commonly used in France, I spoke Latin, and he said he did not know it, and the grandees who were round him said: 'Speak in Spanish to his Majesty, he will understand you,' and he said: 'I know it well, but I may not be able to remember it.' I then spoke in Spanish and told him who I was, and how I had come from far away to serve him; and I gave him the letter given me by the grandee, who by his order had summoned me to the Court. And I showed him two sea charts containing all the discovered parts left by my brother-in-law, and an astrolabe, which charts and astrolabe I carried, and always carry with me, and would never give a copy of them to anyone, nor sell them; and the King was much pleased to see them and was conversing more than an hour with me with understanding and intelligence; and at the close of our conversation the Constable came and, feigning ignorance, and speaking much, and passing in front of others, said to the King, 'Who is that there?' and the King replied: 'It is a man who is very learned in matters of navigation of the ocean, and he has very fine sea charts, and an astrolabe, and he has come to serve me, and I am very pleased with him.' To which the Constable replied: 'It is well that this should be considered and debated in council,' and the King was a little abashed and turning said: 'If so, let it be at dessert after supper.' And the following night the King again examined the charts, and conversed more than an hour with me, and showed me two other charts belonging to him, well painted and illuminated, but not very accurate; and he showed me a river in the land of Cod marked out and set down at his request; and he has sent there twice, and he has in this matter a great desire and longing, as was clearly shown, and what he says and wishes to do in the matter would make men marvel. And he spoke of this to me many times until I seemed to see it with his eyes; and he has despatched thither a Breton pilot named Jacques Cartier, who lives in Brittany, in a town called St Malo; and in the two voyages he made thither, on the first he lost two ships out of three, and on the second one out of two, but always brought one home; and on the last voyage he brought back three Indians, two of whom are dead, the one who is left being King of three or four towns, according to what the King said, for all that I say here I heard from his own lips. And thus he told me that the river he sent to discover he has heard is eight hundred leagues long, and well up the river there are two falls, and he wishes to send two brigantines with the ships, and when the falls are reached the brigantines can be taken overland; and beyond the falls the King of France says the Indian King told him there is a large city called Sagana, where there are many mines of gold and silver in great abundance, and men who dress and wear shoes like we do; and that there is abundance of clove, nutmeg, and pepper. And thus I believe he will again decide to send there a third time seeing his great desire; and thus he told me that he wished to build a fort well up the river, on the north side, and that commencing it in the summer, in the following year the brigantines may go there to pass the falls, for in that land the summer is short, and winter long and exceedingly cold; and it is said that down the river are snow-clad mountains; and the river contains an abundance of good fish, and at its mouth there are oranges and pomegranates. And that there are certain animals whose hides as leather are worth ten cruzados each, and for this sum they are sold in France, and that ten thousand of these skins being brought they are worth 100,000 cruzados. Greatly praising the rich novelty of the land and telling these and other tales; and that there are men who fly, having wings on their arms like bats, although they fly but little, from the ground to a tree, and from tree to tree to the ground. And the said Jacques brought to the King a sample of gold, ten or twelve stones shaped like small goose quills, and he says it is fine gold and comes from the said city of Sagana. And he believed that by this river would be found a passage to the other southern ocean, but he now knows that there is none. And he asked me what I thought, to which I replied that spices had never yet been found anywhere but below the line or close to it, and that this river of his is in the tropic of Cancer, but further north than the distance from the tropic of Cancer to the line; and that it seemed to me impossible that spices or gold could be found there, though there might well be silver. He then said that in Hungary there was a mine, or mines, of very fine gold, and that that country was just as cold and more so, for it lies farther north of the line, which is a fact. I replied that it was a rare thing and a great marvel, and not the general rule, and that what I had said was the rule in all parts of the world. All these and other things he spoke of on various occasions, and it would become tedious to relate all; and thus he told me that this Indian King spoke strict truth, because he was questioned on coming on board, and the Notary took it down, and the Captain again questioned him at times, and the King also after his arrival, and he always said the same, and he had never been found in error. And the Indian King says that he with all his people, friends, and relatives will help to pass the falls and to reach the great city of Sagana in the brigantines, and he will show them the clove, nutmeg, and pepper plants. I said to the King, may he not be like him who tempted Christ who said *'haec omnia tibi dabo,'* so as to return to his own land, and it seems to me that this is what will happen. The King laughed and said that the Indian King was an honest man, and would not act other than he had said.

Item. In Bourges a fine town on the road to Paris two pilots came to me, one named Jacques Cartier, of whom I spoke before, resident of Brittany, and the other named Michel who lives in the town of Rochelle, being those whom the King wished to send to the afore-mentioned river, and they only know the Land of Cod, and the Islands. And by order of the admiral, I not knowing, nor whither I was going, they took me to his house; and entering we found him at table beginning his dinner; and he made us sit down to table, which I did and dined with him, not knowing, and I afterwards learnt, that he had done your Highness certain disservice. And having finished eating he rose and taking me by the hand led me to a garden, and we walked about for a time; and he told me that he had certain very big ships of heavy tonnage, and he would give me those I most wished for, and I should make a good prosperous voyage to India and rejoice to have him for a friend, and I should not repent it. But as he was going to a property of his at some distance, and would not be seeing me soon, the Viscount of Dieppe would speak to me of this more fully, and that the terms would be all that I could desire. I replied that I held it a great favour, and offered myself for his service, the others having told me that he was a personage of great importance in the kingdom.

...

... I heard here of a captain named Joam Cabeça de Vaca who was commissioned by Christoval de Haro of Burgos to go to explore the Codfish River, which is called of the King of France, and that he has licence from the Council of the Indies, and he told me that he would not go, it being a very doubtful business, and he left here about eight days ago for River Plate. ...

9 THE BAPTISM OF THE SAVAGES FROM CANADA

25 March 1538/9

On this day of Our Lady the 25th of March in the year 1538 [1539 N.S.] were baptized three male savages from the parts of Canada, taken in the said country by the worthy man Jacques Cartier, Captain for the King our Liege Lord to discover the said lands. The first was named Charles by the venerable and judicious Dom Charles de Champ-Girault, dean and canon of the said place, and principal godfather, and the second godfather Monsieur the Lieutenant, seigneur of La Verderye, and the godmother, Catherine des Granges. And the second was named Francis, the name of the King our Liege Lord, by the worthy man Jacques Cartier, the principal godfather, and the second godfather Maître P. Le Gobien, [the godmother] Madame ... La Verderye, wife of the Lieutenant ... The third was named ... by Maître Servan May ... of the said place, and the second [godfather] ... Noël ... and the godmother ... [Mai]ngart ...

10 CARTIER'S COMMISSION FOR HIS THIRD VOYAGE

17 October 1540

Commission as Captain and Pilot General of the Ships that the King is Sending to the Saguenay

Francis by the grace of God King of France, to all to whom these presents may come, Greetings. Since, desiring to learn of and be informed about several countries that are said to be uninhabited, and others to be possessed by savage peoples living without knowledge of God and without the use of reason, We had some time ago sent at great expense and outlay of money for discovery to be made in the said countries by several good pilots and others of our subjects of good judgment, knowledge, and experience, who had brought to Us from those countries various men whom We have kept for a long time in our kingdom, having them instructed in the love and fear of God and of His holy law and Christian doctrine in the intention of having them taken back to the said countries in the company of a number of our willing subjects, in order more easily to lead the other peoples of those countries to believe in our holy faith. And among them we had sent there our dear and beloved Jacques Cartier, who had discovered a great country in the lands of Canada and Hochelaga, forming one extremity of Asia on the West, which countries he found, as he related to Us, provided with several valuable commodities and the peoples of those countries well formed of body and limb and well endowed in mind and understanding, of whom he brought back at the same time a certain number whom We have had kept for a long time and instructed in our said holy faith with our said subjects. In consideration of which, and of their favourable disposition, We have considered and deliberated sending the said Cartier back to the said countries of Canada and Hochelaga and as far as the land of Saguenay, if he is able to touch land there, with a number of ships and of our said willing subjects and possessing all the qualities, arts, and industry to go farther into the said countries, to frequent the said peoples of those countries and live with them, if necessary, in order better to arrive at our said intention and to do something that is pleasing to God our creator and redeemer and that will be to the exaltation of His holy and sacred name and of our mother the holy Catholic Church, of which We are called the eldest son. Whereas it is necessary for the better command and execution of the said enterprise to appoint and establish a captain general and master pilot of the said ships who will have control of their guidance and over the persons, officers, and soldiers commissioned to and established upon them, know all men, that, having entire confidence in the person of the said Jacques Cartier and his judgment, competence, loyalty, prudence, daring, great diligence, and good experience, for these reasons and others prompting Us to this, We have made and constituted, commissioned and established, make, constitute, commission, and establish him by these presents captain general and master pilot of all the ships and other seagoing vessels commissioned by Us to be conducted on the said enterprise and expedition, for the said state and charge of captain general and master pilot of those ships and vessels to be had, held, and exercised by the said Jacques Cartier with the honours, prerogatives, pre-eminences, franchises, liberties, rewards, and benefits, as they will be decreed for him by Us for this, so long as it will be our pleasure, and We have given and give him power and authority to place, establish, and appoint on the said ships such lieutenants, masters, pilots, and other ministers necessary for the functioning and conducting of the same, and in such number as he will see and recognize to be needed and necessary for the good of the said expedition. And We give as commission by these presents to our admiral or vice admiral that, the required and customary oath for this having been taken and received from the said Jacques Cartier, they put and install him or have him put and installed in our name in possession and seisin of the said state of captain general and master pilot, and of that state together with all the honours, authorities, prerogatives, pre-eminences, franchises, liberties, rewards, and benefits such as will be decreed for him by Us, they have, suffer, and allow him to enjoy and use fully and in peace and to obey and heed him in all those and as it will be fitting in the things affecting and concerning the said state and charge. And furthermore that they have, suffer, and allow him to take the little galleon called the *Emérillon*, which he has now received from Us, which is already old and worn out, to serve for the refitting of those of the ships that have need of it, and which We wish to be taken and used by the said Cartier for the purpose mentioned above, without him being held to render any other account or remainder thereof, and of which account and remainder We have discharged and discharge him by these presents. By the same We also instruct our provosts of Paris, bailiffs of Rouen, Caen, Orléans, Blois, and Tours, seneschals of Maine, Anjou, and Guienne, and all our other bailiffs, seneschals, provosts, and agents and our other justiciaries and officers, both of our said kingdom and of our country of Brittany united with it, before whom there are any prisoners accused of or charged with any crimes whatsoever, except the crimes of heresy and lese-majesty against God and Us, and counterfeiters, that they are forthwith to deliver, surrender, and give into the hands of the said Cartier or his agents and deputies bearing these presents, or the duplicate of them, for our service in the said enterprise and expedition, those of the said prisoners whom he will judge to be fit, suitable, and capable to serve in that expedition to the number of fifty persons and according to the choice that the said Cartier will make of them, those first judged and sentenced according to their faults and the seriousness of their misdeeds, if they are not judged and sentenced, and satisfaction also previously ordered for the civil and interested parties, if it had not been done, for which, however, We do not wish the delivery of their persons into the hands of the said Cartier if he finds them fit to serve, to be delayed or held up, but the said satisfaction will be taken only on their goods and chattels, and which delivery of the said prisoners, accused or charged, We wish to be made into the hands of the said Cartier for the purpose mentioned above by our said judiciaries and officers respectively, and by each of them in their survey, power, and jurisdiction, notwithstanding any oppositions or appeals whatsoever made or to be made, registered or to be registered, and without that delivery in the manner stated above being deferred in any manner through them. And in order that a greater number of them beyond the said fifty not be taken, We desire that the delivery that each of our said officers will make of them to the said Cartier be written down and certified in the margin of these presents, and that nevertheless a register of them be made by them and sent forthwith to our beloved and loyal Chancellor to be informed of the number and condition of those who will have been given up and delivered thus. For such is our pleasure. In witness thereof We have had our seal affixed to these presents. Delivered at Saint-Prix on the seventeenth day of October in the year of grace one thousand five hundred and forty, and the twenty-sixth of our reign. As signed on the fold under the hand of the King, you, Monseigneur the Chancellor, and others present, de La Chesnaye. And sealed on the said fold with yellow wax on a single ribbon.

11 LETTERS PATENT FROM THE DUKE OF BRITTANY EMPOWERING CARTIER TO TAKE PRISONERS FROM THE GAOLS

20 October 1540

Henry, eldest son of the King, Dauphin du Viennois, Duc de Bretagne, Comte du Valentinois et du Diois, to our beloved and faithful members of our council and chancellery, seneschals, agents, lieutenants, and all our other justiciaries and officers in our said country and duchy, Greetings. We instruct you that in accordance with the contents of the Letters Patent of the King our highly respected seigneur and father, delivered at this place of Saint-Prix on the seventeenth day of the present month, to which these presents are attached under the counter-seal of our chancellery, you are forthwith to deliver, surrender, and give into the hands of our dear and beloved Jacques Cartier, captain general and pilot of all the ships and other sea-going vessels that the King our said seigneur and father is sending to the countries of Canada and Hochelaga and as far as the land of the Saguenay for the reasons fully revealed in the said letters, or to his agents and deputies bearing the said letters and these said presents, the prisoners accused or charged before you of any crimes, whatever they be, except the crime[s] of heresy and lese-majesty, divine and human, and counterfeiter, whom the said Jacques Cartier will judge to be fit, suitable, and capable to serve on the said voyage and enterprise up to completion of the number of fifty persons and according to the choice that the said Cartier will make of them, they first having been judged and sentenced according to their faults and the seriousness of their misdeeds, if they are not judged and sentenced, satisfaction also previously having been given to the civil and interested parties if it has not been done, without however delaying for the said satisfaction the delivery of their persons into the hands of the said Cartier, if he finds them fit for service as is stated, but to order that satisfaction to be taken on their goods and chattels only, and in order that a number greater than fifty not be taken, each of you respectively will pay attention to the margin of the said letters, how many of them will have been delivered to the said Cartier, and you will have written and certified in that margin those whom you will have delivered to him, and you will nevertheless keep a register of them which you will send to our very dear and faithful chancellor of France and ours, to be informed of the number and condition that will have been delivered thus, all according to and as it is contained at greater length and explained in the said letters of the King our said seigneur and father, and as the said seigneur desires and orders by these letters. Delivered at Saint-Prix on the twentieth day of October one thousand five hundred and forty. As given under the hand of Monseigneur the Dauphin and Duke, Clausse, and sealed with red wax on a single ribbon.

12 THE EMPEROR TO THE CARDINAL OF TOLEDO

11–13 November 1540?

I have received today letters from my ambassador in France, in which he advises me that in spite of the efforts of the ambassador of the most Serene King of Portugal, there residing, and what he, himself, has told the Council of the King of France respecting the licence that the said King gave to his subjects to proceed to the Indies, a certain Jacques Cartier has received a commission to equip a fleet of ships to go to the New Lands. And it is said he will sail with, some say twelve, others eighteen, others twenty vessels; and my ambassador speaking of this to the Constable of France, that it might be remedied, was given to understand that the said Cartier has gone to make discoveries in parts not belonging to us nor to the most Serene King of Portugal; saying that to uninhabited lands, although discovered, anyone may go. And that the said Cartier had given him to understand that he hoped to obtain licence to go wheresoever he desired; therefore the efforts of our said ambassador and those of the ambassador of Portugal have up to the present not borne fruit. And although I have ordered a reply to be sent to him to the effect that he do continue to insist and make fitting instance that the said licence be not proceeded with, being, as it is, in direct contravention of the treaty between us and the said King of France, and contrary to the grace and concession granted by the Apostolic See to the Kings of Castile and Portugal for the said conquest, it has appeared to me fitting to advise you thereof that you may consider and confer in Spain respecting such further measures it may now be desirable to take besides those already taken; providing for intelligence to be had through the merchants, or in other ways, to learn whether the said Jacques is employed in equipping the said vessels, their number and order, and the season in which they will set sail. And whether any other Frenchman is engaged in fitting out other ships, and their nature; so that the necessary fleet may be speedily formed in Spain to resist and destroy them. And it would be as well for you to send full information thereof to Luis Sarmiento that the King of Portugal may be advised thereof, that in the same way he may on his part take such measures as are required; and let the person who is in command of the said fleet (should it be necessary for such to be fitted and sail) carry orders to unite with the fleet of the said King of Portugal and let each fleet give help and support to the other. And should they meet with the ships of the said Jacques or any other Frenchman sailing with a fleet bound to the said Indies, let them engage and destroy them, since the intention of these Frenchmen is known; and let all the men taken from their ships be thrown into the sea, not saving any one person, for this is necessary as a warning against the undertaking of similar expeditions. Advising me at all times of what you have provided, and learnt of the doings of the said Frenchmen, and we will give order that you be advised of all that we learn here, as we at present advise you.

13 AN ORDER FROM KING FRANCIS TO INQUIRE INTO THE HINDRANCES PLACED BEFORE CARTIER

12 December 1540

Francis, by the grace of God, King of France, to the seneschal of Rennes his lieutenant and agent of the said place, Greetings and affection. Our dear and beloved Jacques Cartier, captain general and master pilot of all the ships and other sea-going vessels that We desire to send to the lands of Canada, Hochelaga, as far as Saguenay, forming one of the extremities of Asia on the North, has had it told and pointed out to Us that for the expedition of the said enterprise it is necessary for him to obtain a large number of pilots, sailors, and other masters properly experienced in navigation for the conducting of the said ships, to which end he has wanted to meet and reach an agreement with several experts of the said state and marine, who have been perniciously and maliciously diverted and dissuaded by some of our subjects, in the town of Saint-Malo and other towns, ports, and harbours of the duchy of Brittany, and by this means the said voyage in danger of being greatly delayed and put off against our wish and intention, the said Cartier requesting on this matter our decision to provide for this. Therefore, this having been considered, We order and instruct you by these said presents and each one of you called upon in this matter that you investigate this diligently, secretly, and thoroughly concerning the said hindrances, malicious and pernicious dissensions and warnings, their circumstances and consequences, which will be given to you more fully in writing and under oath, if necessary, by the said Cartier for the said investigation conducted and recorded in the presence of the members of our privy council, once they have been seen, to be enacted upon as may be thought proper: We give you by these said presents power and authority to do this, We order and command all our justiciers, officers, and subjects that you be obeyed in so doing. Delivered at Fontainebleau the twelfth day of December in the year of grace 1540 and the twenty-sixth of our reign. As given under the hand of the King in his counsel, de La Chesnaye, and sealed in yellow wax.

14 ROBERVAL'S COMMISSION

15 January 1540/1

Francis, by the grace of God, King of France, to all to whom these presents may come, greetings. Since, desiring to hear and learn about several countries, parts of which are said to be uninhabited and others possessed by savage and foreign peoples, living without knowledge of God and without good use of reason, We had some time ago, at great expense and outlay of money, sent to be discovered in several of the said countries by some good pilots and other subjects of ours of good judgment, knowledge, and experience, who had brought back to Us various men from some of the said countries; and in like manner We had had discovered among others a great part of the lands of Canada and Hochelaga and other places circumjacent, which have been found, as has been reported to Us, endowed with several valuable commodities, and the peoples of those places well formed of body and limb and well endowed in mind and understanding, from which also have been brought to Us other men apparently of good disposition. In consideration of which We have taken counsel and deliberated sending back to the said countries of Canada and Hochelaga and others circumjacent, moreover to all transmarine and maritime countries, uninhabited or not possessed and ruled by any Christian princes, a certain number of gentlemen our subjects and others, soldiers and commoners, of each sex and of the liberal and applied arts, to penetrate farther into the said countries and as far as the land of Saguenay and all the other countries mentioned above, to live in them with the said foreign peoples, if that is possible, and to dwell in the said lands and countries, build and create towns and forts, temples and churches for the communication of our holy Catholic faith and Christian doctrine; to constitute and establish laws in Our name, along with officers of justice, to make them live in law and order and in the fear and love of God, so as better to succeed in our intention and to do something pleasing to God, our Creator, Saviour and Redeemer, and which will be to the sanctification of His holy name and the extension of our Christian faith and growth of our mother the Holy Catholic Church, of which we are said to be and are called the eldest son. To succeed in which, and in order to give greater order and dispatch to the execution of the said enterprise and to all matters concerning it and which depend upon it and might occur, it is needed and necessary to depute and constitute some excellent personage, of great loyalty and integrity to Us and who is of good judgment, worth, and experience, to be head and leader of that enterprise, and to whom is given by Us such power and authority as such a matter requires, to use and generally dispose of in all cases and matters that arise, as will seem to him most expedient and necessary, as We might do if We were there in person. Be it known that because of the great and entire confidence that We have from long experience in the person of our beloved and faithful Jean-François de La Roque, knight, seigneur of Roberval, and in his good judgment, sufficiency, loyalty, and other good and praiseworthy qualities, for these reasons and others prompting Us to this, We have made, constituted, commissioned, and established, make, constitute, commission, and establish him by these presents our lieutenant general, head, leader, and captain of the said enterprise, and of all the ships and seagoing vessels, and likewise of all the persons, both soldiers, seamen, and others commissioned by Us and who will go on the said enterprise, expedition, and army going on the said voyage. And We have given and give him full power, puissance, and authority and special mandate to choose, take, and elect or to have chosen, taken, and elected such as will seem to him to be fit and proper for the execution of the said enterprise and its dispatch, to place and elect captains, colour bearers, ship's masters, pilots, and other soldiers and mariners, and to distribute them among the ships, and to assemble and reassemble them when he will see fit, to command and commission in our name all the said persons and to commission and dispose of the form of and of their service, and to decree, enjoin, and command in all the matters that he will see to be good, useful, and suitable yet under our authority, power, and puissance, and through imposition and proclamation of fines and penalties, corporal, civil, and pecuniary, and at sea and on land, in the places and localities that will be brought under our obedience, and also to order the payments of their salaries and pay, and to increase or decrease them, and to extend, equalize, and spread out the monies that have been distributed to so do, so that, if possible, he may increase the number of people and equipment. And We desire that all those mentioned above swear loyalty and take an oath to serve Us well and faithfully under the charge and obedience of our said lieutenant general. And likewise We desire to hear him and to be informed, by him and by his said clerks and deputies, of the diligent purchase of the munitions and provisions necessary for the said army and at the reception of the same as they put them aboard the said ships and vessels, and at the dividing up, distribution, and counting of the same, that there be no abuse committed in that. And the above-mentioned ships and vessels, fitted out, equipped and supplied with people, provisions, artillery, and other things necessary, We have given and give to our said lieutenant general by the said presents power, authority, and special commission to take, lead, and have sail from the ports and harbours of our Kingdom, countries, and seigneuries in our subjection, and to cross and recross the sea, to go to and return from the said foreign countries, to disembark and enter into them and bring them into our possession, through friendly means or amicable arrangements, if possible, and through force of arms, violence, and all other hostile means, to attack towns, fortresses, and habitations and to build and erect or have built and erected others in the said countries and to install inhabitants in them; to create, constitute, establish, dismiss, and remove from office captains, justiciaries, and in general all other officers as will seem good to him in our name and as will seem to him to be necessary for the maintenance, conquest, and defence of the said countries and to attract the peoples of them to the knowledge of love of God, and to bring them under and keep in our obedience; to make laws, edicts, statutes, and ordinances for law and order and others, to add to or reduce them in number, to have them kept, observed, and maintained by all due and reasonable ways and means; to punish and have punished those who are disobedient and rebellious and other malefactors, both those who will go on the said expedition and others from the said countries, either by death or other exemplary punishment; to pardon and remit the misdeeds of those who will request it, entirely as he will consider to be proper. Provided, however, that they not be countries held, occupied, possessed, and ruled by or being under the subjection and obedience of any princes or potentates our allies and confederates, and likewise of our very dear and beloved brothers the emperor and the King of Portugal. And in order to augment and increase the good will, courage, and affection of those who will serve Us in the execution and expedition of the said enterprise and voyage, and likewise of those who will remain in the said lands, in consideration of this We have in addition given and give by these presents full power and authority to our said lieutenant to give of those lands that he will have been able to acquire for Us on this voyage, as it will seem to him to be to our utility and profit, and therewith to give them a lease on them, to be held, possessed, and enjoyed by them, their successors and rightful claimants, in perpetuity with all rights of property, tenure, and seizin, that is to say: to the gentlemen and other persons of excellent character or industry in fief and seigneury, answering to Us and under our jurisdiction, and rendering fealty and homage to Us for them on account of the forts and fortified places in the localities that our said lieutenant will order or others our clerks or deputies in his name and absence, and with the charge of serving Us in the defence, protection, and preservation of the said countries, and with such number of people as the said fiefs and seigneuries will be held responsible for by their said leases, and to the others of lesser state and condition, on such charges of annual payments as our said lieutenant will consider that the lands of their leases can bear, payable at the places and in the way and manner that will be ordered them; of which charges and annual payments We have granted and consented, consent and grant that they be released and exempted for the first six years, if that seems fitting to our said lieutenant, or for some other lesser period that he will perceive to be necessary, with the exception, however, of the duty of service for war, defence, preservation, and enlarging of the said countries; and furthermore to give greater willingness and courage to the said gentlemen, the others, soldiers and seamen, to serve Us better, more diligently and loyally, We desire, permit, and consent that on his return our said lieutenant may give and distribute to those who will make the said voyage with him the third of all the movable gains and profits proceeding from the said voyage, army, and expedition, and to favour some as he sees fit and remunerate any services that they will have done Us there, and to deprive all the others who had not done their entire duty; also to retain for himself another third of them to meet in part, if that seems fitting to Us, the expenses and advances of money that it may be necessary to make for the continuation of the said voyage for the space of the next five years, as also to recompense him somewhat for his labours and efforts; and as for the other third, We have reserved and reserve it for Ourself, to be used, when it pleases Us, in several other navigations that We have hoped and hope to make for the extension of our holy faith or elsewhere where it will be commissioned by Us hereafter, and of which We intend and desire that our collectors or clerks make diligent receipt through good and loyal inventory in the ports and harbours of the places to which our said lieutenant or other individual of the said army may return; and because We desire the said army to be accompanied by several of our subjects whom We wish to contribute to the success of the said voyage, and in order that the said countries may be more amply discovered and that it will be possible to penetrate farther into them, to build forts, habitations, and buildings in various places in them, We have gladly given and give to our said lieutenant full power, puissance, and authority to associate with himself in the said army all the gentlemen, merchants, and others, of whatever estate, quality, or condition they may be, who will want to go on the said voyage and to the said country or send people or ships, fitted out and supplied at their expense, and to join them to the said army under our obedience and that of our said lieutenant; in doing which, there will be done by them something very pleasing to Us and which we desire greatly; and of the gain and profit resulting from the said voyage, to give them that part and portion thereof, such rights being reserved to Us and to others of the said army as will be agreed to by our said lieutenant and by them, and draw up letters, promises, on that, and concerning those rights by them or their attorneys, which letters, as of now and henceforth, We hold to be acceptable, accept, approve, and ratify their contents, as if they had been prepared by Us in person. And inasmuch as some persons under the cloak of our said army might take it upon themselves to enter the passages and straits leading into the said countries of Canada and Hochelaga, Saguenay and others circumjacent, without however joining and associating themselves under the authority of our said lieutenant and do some damage, harm, or wrong to the inhabitants of the said countries which might be a cause of alienating them and turning them away from the good will and affection that they might bear Us and our people who will have entered the said countries, We have forbidden and forbid all our subjects to take it upon themselves to navigate through the abovementioned passages and straits, unless they are associated and joined with our said army and under the authority of our said lieutenant, nevertheless permitting them the other passages and entrances to lands that are not forbidden by Us, in going to and coming from which We desire and enjoin them, in the event of a meeting on land or at sea, to give all support and aid, favour and succour, and to obey our said lieutenant or his authorized agents in the said army. And if previously We had given any letters or power to anyone that were contradictory to the terms of his said letters, We have, now and henceforth, revoked and revoke, quash and annul them by these said presents, except inasmuch and for as long as our said lieutenant would allow and put up with them. And in so far as it will be necessary for the realization of the said voyage and settlement of the said countries to conclude several letters and contracts, We have herein approved and approve, authenticated and authenticate the marks and seals of our said lieutenant and of the other officers appointed and deputed by him in this respect. And considering that some great misfortune of malady and perchance death might happen to our said lieutenant, also that upon his return it will be necessary to leave one or several, our lieutenant or lieutenants, We desire and intend that he may name, create, constitute, and establish, by testament or otherwise, as he will see fit, one or several of them having equal and similar power, authority, and special commission or a part of that which We have given him and give by these presents. And because We cannot have sufficient knowledge of the said foreign countries and peoples to specify further the power that We should desire to give our said lieutenant general in this matter, to attract them to the knowledge of God and to bring them into our obedience, if that can be done, and to rule and govern them according to our desire and intention and others of our said army and associated with it, for this reason We desire, intend, and choose that the specifications that We have declared above may in no way derogate from the general power that We have given and give by these presents to our said lieutenant, which is in general to dispose of, execute, and command in all matters whatsoever, foreseen and unforeseen, concerning the said voyage, army, and its expedition, as the matters and necessities will seem to him to require, and as We ourself would and might do if We were there in person. And everything that will be done, said, constituted, ordered, established, contracted, accomplished, and arranged by our said lieutenant, by force of arms, through friendship, confederation, or otherwise, in whatever way and manner that it be or may be, because of the said enterprise and its expedition, by sea and by land, We have approved, accepted, and ratified, approve, accept, and ratify by these presents, and We hold and desire it to be held good and valid as if done by Us; and We give in commission by these same presents to our beloved and faithful chancellor and to all our beloved and faithful judges and counsellors of our sovereign courts, lieutenants general, governors of our countries, admirals and vice-admirals, provosts, bailiffs, seneschals, and others our justiciers, officers and subjects, both ordinary and extraordinary, or their lieutenants, and to each one of them with respect to himself, as it will concern him, that they have, suffer, and permit our said lieutenant, to whom We have today administered the oath for the said charge of our lieutenant general that is customary in such a case, to enjoy and exercise that charge fully and peaceably, and to make this obeyed and understood by all those persons and as it shall be deemed advisable in matters concerning our said lieutenant, and to give him in everything and everywhere all counsel, support, succour, aid, and shelter, if need be. For such is our pleasure; and because our lieutenant may have to make use of these presents in several and different places, We desire that the duplicate or the *vidimus* of them made under royal seal be credited as is the present original, and in order that this be firmly and permanently established, We have had our seal put on these said presents. Delivered at Fontainebleau on the fifteenth day of January in the year of grace one thousand five hundred and forty and the twenty-seventh of our reign. Signed on the fold of the said letters: under the hand of the King, the Cardinal de Tournon, and You, present, Bayard; a paraph. And on the fold near the bottom is written the following: Jean François de La Roque, knight, seigneur of Roberval, took before Monseigneur the Chancellor the oath due and required for the state of lieutenant governor, head, leader, and captain for the affairs contained in these presents, and was received into the said state and charge by my said seigneur and chancellor on this day, the sixth of February, in the year one thousand five hundred and forty, I being present; signed: Sanson; a paraph; and sealed with yellow wax on a double ribbon.

Collated

From the Registers of the court of the *parlement* of Rouen in which, in accordance with the decree granted by the said court on the ninth day of March one thousand five hundred and forty concerning the ratification of a request and letters patent from the King presented to it by Jean François de La Roque, seigneur of Roberval, for the voyage commissioned by the said seigneur to be made to various transmarine and maritime countries such as Canada, Hochelaga, Saguenay, and others, have been registered the letters of the power given to the said La Roque and other letters mentioned above that were presented by him for the purpose of executing the said commission. The letters of commission of the said La Roque have been extracted in the form and terms transcribed above.

Surreau

15 SECRET REPORT ON CARTIER'S EXPEDITION: REPORT BY A SPANISH SPY ON JACQUES CARTIER'S PREPARATIONS [SAINT-MALO, APRIL 1541]

April 1541

From Saint-Malo there are seven hundred and sixty leagues and from the said Newfoundland to Canada, where it is intended to take the said army, another six hundred. And one must necessarily go by Newfoundland. The said Canada faces the emperor's Indies, and certainly it is a cape of the latter. For where the ships of his Most Christian Majesty wish to put into port there falls a great river of fresh water coming from the said Indies. And Jacques Cartier is quite sure of that, according to Rolet Morin.

The order that they intend to keep to discover the land is that, when they arrive at the port that Jacques Cartier has already discovered, they will leave their ships there and will make XVIII or XX small rowboats, smaller than brigantines, each of which will be capable of carrying six light pieces of iron artillery, which they have had made expressly, in order to charge the vessels less heavily.

The soldiers and mariners will carry arquebuses, crossbows, and bucklers, because the savages, who are the people of the country, shoot with bows and can swim a good two leagues underwater.

When the members of the said army have arrived on land, they will search for gold and silver mines. And Jacques Cartier is certainly informed by the same savages that there is a great quantity of them.

As far as the navigation and discovering land is concerned, Roberval and all the others will obey the said Jacques Cartier. And when the land has been conquered, the said Roberval will remain general for the king and will be in command of the buildings, fortifications, supplies, and other things necessary.

The vessels for this navigation are ten in number, all of them at the cost and charge of the king, who has not been willing that any private individuals whatsoever outfit ships with him. Among those vessels is a port galleon of seventy tons; two ships, one of six score, the other of one hundred and ten tons, and these three belong to the king. There are two ships belonging to Jacques Cartier, each of ninety tons, and one belonging to another merchant of Saint-Malo of four score tons. These six vessels are at the said Saint-Malo; the three near the Tour de Polidor, which are already loaded with everything except the artillery. The other three are close to the town and had not yet begun to take on cargo on the 29th of last month. For the complement of the ten ships mentioned above, four more ships are required, which Roberval is bringing from Rouen and Honfleur, carrying three hundred soldiers, and were to arrive on the VIIIth of the present month of April. The said ships are each of ninety to a hundred tons burden. And those ten vessels have been completely refitted in the last two years.

The king pays six score francs a month to each ship that he borrows, and four months are paid them in advance, and Jacques Cartier binds himself towards them to pay for them at the same price if they remain for a longer period on this voyage.

The said Jacques Cartier is taking four hundred mariners and twenty master pilots with him, the best that he has been able to find in Brittany, and he may take them as he wishes. For the king commands all those that he will select to go there on pain of banishment from this kingdom and of seizing all their property,

He is also taking twenty workmen to build boats and is paying them according to what they are; to the least important he gives five francs a month, to the others eight, ten, twelve, fifteen, and as much as twenty. He is paying four months in advance to each of two hundred of his mariners, a whole year to the others, and is giving all of them a black and white livery, and all manner of provisions necessary for going, staying, and returning at the expense of the said seigneur the king.

Roberval is in charge of the three hundred soldiers, sixty masons and carpenters, ten churchmen, three doctors, and ten barbers.

It is not known whether any gentlemen are going on the voyage other than Savonnières and two unfortunates from Brittany who have committed some killing, for which they will do penance on this voyage. The said Savonnières is the man who challenged the brother of Échenay, his first cousin, in Paris, and has been sentenced to go on this voyage because, it is said, he insulted in Monseigneur d'Orléans's great hall a major-domo of Monseigneur the Dauphin and another of the said d'Orléans, two brothers, called de Pierrevive. He is taking twenty or XXV companions with him, who he says are gentlemen. But from what I have been told of them, they do not much seem to be so, except for two or three. He says that there will be one hundred and sixty gentlemen in the company. But the other opinions do not correspond to his, including those of Monsieur de Corvel and the said Rolet Morin, who know and hear all the talk about this enterprise and say that the total number, soldiers, mariners, workmen, and others, will be from eight to nine hundred persons.

The galleon and three of the ships are sailing less heavily laden than the others, except for artillery and the best soldiers, to sustain the weight if they meet a ship to speak on the way. The others are sailing as heavily laden as they can support, and are carrying provisions for three years, bread, wine, fat pork, salted meat, oil and butter.

They are carrying fifteen hundred sides of fat pork, eight hundred oxen and cows, salted and air-cured, a hundred barrels of wheat, part of which will be for sowing, two hundred pipes of flour, twenty pipes of mustard, twenty of oil, and as many of butter. All the rest is made up of ship's biscuit, two hundred casks of wine and a hundred of cider. They are also taking twenty live cows, four bulls, a hundred ewes and wethers, a hundred goats, and ten pigs, for breeding them in the country where they are going, and also twenty horses and mares to transport the things necessary for putting up buildings and fortifications. Similarly they are carrying carts already made and all their equipment and also implements for ploughing the land and twenty ploughmen; furthermore, they are taking a great deal of good artillery, which the said Roberval is bringing in the four ships mentioned above, with in addition four hundred arquebuses, two hundred bucklers, two hundred crossbows, and more than a thousand pikes and halberds.

Furthermore they are carrying fifty barrels full of iron and all the tools and instruments needed for ten ironworkers and smiths whom they are taking.

In each ship there are two handmills, to use them if necessary.

After deliberation they have decided to send seven of the abovementioned ships back when they have reached Canada, in order to give the king more ample information about the land and so that the said ships may return, if necessary, laden with provisions and people. For that reason, only four months will be paid in advance to part of the vessels and mariners and a year to the others who will stay.

The departure of the army is set for a week after Easter and they count on reaching Canada in four weeks if the weather is favourable to them, or at the latest in seven weeks. Jacques Cartier wanted to detain the merchant ships that are going to Newfoundland and load them with some things necessary for the said army. But they were excused from it, because they are already as full as possible with barrels to put the barrelfuls of salt needed for salting the fish which they are going to take on and with other items for their use. Finally they were allowed to leave and already this year more than twenty-four ships have gone to the said Newfoundland.

16 CARTIER'S WILL

15 May 1541

Here in our presence, notaries sworn & admitted to the court of Saint-Malo signing below & in the name of the court, were today present and their identity established in person Jacques Cartier, captain & master pilot of the King in Newfoundland, & Catherine Des Granges his partner and wife, Sieur and Dame of Limoilou, & bourgeois in this town & city of Saint-Malo, on both sides. This said Catherine having been authorized at her request adequately and who has promised to agree to, respect, & carry out what follows, both by her said husband and Jacques Des Granges, Sieur de la Ville-ès-Gards, her father, present at this, who in effect decrees to her his paternal authorities, with all that is contained in these presents, has promised & sworn on her oath &, on a blanket mortgage of all her present & future property, never to make revocation of that authority; and Jeanne Cartier, sister of the said Cartier, also present, not to oppose on any manner. Which persons, [&] each one named above, respectively submitting & have submitted themselves each with their chattels & real estate present & future, to the power, distraint, jurisdiction, seigneury, & obedience of our said court, and to give it power of judgment and to obey it as to the contents of these presents, results, & consequences; which persons & each one, without any inducement or coercion, but of their true & generous wishes & as best pleased them, made & make a contract together one with the other as a true, mutual, & equal gift, in the form & manner that follow: by which they have given to each other, accepting reciprocally the entirety of the usufruct, enjoyment, and revenue of the houses, lands, appurtenances, heritages, & heritable items whatsoever belonging to them either by acquest or otherwise in any manner & without any reservation in the village of Limoilou, commonly called *La maison de Lymouellou*, situated & standing in the parishes of Paramé & Saint-Ydeux, and for the survivor to enjoy each of them for his lifetime only after the death of the first to die, to pay the duties and to maintain the latter in proper & good repair during the time that the survivor will have enjoyment of it, and without making alienation or diminution of it in any manner. In addition the said married couple have given to each other, for themselves, their heirs & successors, at the death of the first, the sum of one hundred *livres* in ready money to be taken first and raised on the most valuable & important rings & gold chains of their communal estate at the choice of the survivor up to the value of that sum. Said & consented between them, in the presence of the said Jacques Des Granges, Jeanne Cartier, each for themselves, their heirs & successors, that if & in the case that the said death of the said Jacques Cartier should occur before that of his said wife, in that case during the lifetime of the said Catherine she will have enjoyment of the said place & lands of Limoilou, that Jeanne Cartier or her heirs will have & enjoy, during the said time, the usufruct, possession, & revenue of a small house & rear garden situated and standing in the said town of Saint-Malo beside its wall in the neighbourhood of Buhen, adjoining on one side the street of the said Buhen, at another place and end another garden belonging to Jeanne Éberard & on one side the manorhouse of Buhen. And if the death of the said Catherine occurred during the lifetime of the said Cartier, that he would have the enjoyment of the said place & heritage of Limoilou, that Jacques Des Granges will have for himself or his family the enjoyment, usufruct, & revenue of the small house & garden standing in the said town, as is stated, until the time of death of the said Cartier. And upon the death of the said survivor, all their said heritages will be apportioned & divided among the heirs & successors of the said married couple, each as shall seem proper according to customary law. And, as of now and as the time of death of the first to die, they have desired & consented to each other that the survivor shall take and hold the real, physical, & actual possession & enjoyment of them, without other ground or office of justice, by constituting the survivor between them the true possessor to the said title for life only, as above. And by this they have promised to each other a firm & due guarantee on their said property, notwithstanding law & custom which state to the contrary: giver not to be held to guarantee the thing given by him. And the said parties & each of those named above, & each party present insofar as he is concerned, have recognized each & all of the things above to be true, similarly they have promised & sworn to keep & to execute, without having power to oppose or act to the contrary, to have or to seek in any manner whatsoever any delays, which they have renounced. And therefore we have laid &

lay upon them the obligation to act thus with respect to their agreements & requests; delivered in witness thereof the seals prescribed for the contracts of our said court. And this was done & approved in the said town of Saint-Malo in the house & domicile of the said man and wife, on the nineteenth day of May 1541. As given under the hand of Jac. Cartier, G. Rehauld, and F. Le Bret.

17 EXAMINATION OF NEWFOUNDLAND SAILORS REGARDING CARTIER

23 September 1542

In the town of Fuenterrabia[1] on the twenty-third day of the month of September of the year of Our Lord Jesus Christ 1542, I, Antonio de Ubilla, notary public of their Majesties, one of the notaries of the said town, did, by order of his Excellency Don Sancho Martins de Leybra, Captain General of this province of Guipúzcoa, alcalde of the said town, in presence of the undersigned witnesses, administer to and receive oath from Robert Lefant, a Frenchman resident of Bayonne,[2] upon the sign of the Cross, as by law directed, and confronting him with the anathemas due to a false oath, he replied Amen, and promised to speak the truth. Witnesses present, Pedro de Moya and Sancho de Tolosa, gunner.

After which in the said town on the 25th day of the said month of the said year, by order of the aforesaid General, I, the said notary, did administer to and receive oaths from Martin de Actalecu and Clemente de Odelica, residents of the said town, and from Miguel de Liçaçon and Martin de San Vicente and Juan de Arsu, residents of Pasajes, near Fuenterrabia, and Juan de Urnieta, resident of Urnieta, on the sign of the Cross, as by law directed: and confronting them with the anathemas due to a false oath, they each one replied Amen: they did swear and promised to speak truth. In presence of the witnesses, the said Pedro de Moya and Juan de Cespedes and Juan de Yguiniz, residing at present in the said town.

The which said witnesses, being questioned in accordance with certain articles of a memorandum, stated, deposed and declared as follows:

The said Robert Lefant, resident of the town of Bayonne, fifty years of age, a little more or less, was asked in what ship did he go fishing, and whose it is; replied that this witness is master of a vessel of sixty tons, which belonged to Garcia de Soto, resident

1 On the French frontier near San Sebastian
2 Bayonne in France, near Biarritz

of Bayonne.[3] Asked from whence it set sail, and its destination: said that this witness set sail from Bayonne and went to La Rochelle to take in provisions for his journey, that they were going to Terra Nova to fish for cod. Asked how long it is since they went in the said ship: said that he left Bayonne in the middle of April and reached La Rochelle within three days, and having obtained his provisions he set sail within eight days, and was driven by foul weather into the port of Blavet[4] in Brittany, where he remained till 1 May, and on that day he left Blavet and set out on his voyage. Asked what other vessels he had in convoy: said, One small vessel of St Pol de Leon,[5] from Blavet, into which port he had been driven by a tempest. Asked what crew he carried: said he took thirteen men, who with himself made fourteen, and four boys. Asked what arms he carried: said, Only three swords, and knives for cutting. Asked what course he followed: said that he followed the direct course to Terra Nova, for the fishing; and the said ship of St Pol de Leon sailed in his company. Asked what other French ships he met on the way, which sailed in company with him: said he met none on the journey, but when he reached Terra Nova there was a vessel there from St Jean de Luz,[6] which belonged to Urdina, and a ship from St Malo. That the ship of Urdina was of 180 tons, that of St Malo of 100 tons, and there was another vessel of 100 tons from Lormanto, a town just above Calais[?] Asked the name of the port where he found the said ships: said, It is called Caprouge.[7]

Asked whether there is a town there: said, No, only a harbour and beach. Asked whether he saw Jacques Cartier or Roberval, French captains, who sailed armed, or whether he knows when they set sail, and their destination, and what ships they had, and what men and provisions: said that this witness heard from a Breton master of a ship who was fishing in a port with witness for the men from Llanes,[8] that Jacques left Honfleur over a year ago with three ships bound for Terra Nova, and afterwards when he was with his ship in a harbour of Terra Nova, known as the island of Spear,[9] the said Jacques came there and he had eleven barrels

3 It is not clear whether this was Bayona in Spain or Bayonne in France.
4 Blavet, now Port Louis, opposite Lorient, in Brittany
5 St Pol de Leon in Finistère, thirteen miles northwest of Morlaix
6 St Jean de Luz, near Biarritz
7 Possibly Cape Rouge Harbour near Kirpon Island
8 A port near Santander
9 Probably St John's, near Cape Spear

of gold ore and close on a fanega[10] of precious stones, rubies, and diamonds. And he came along with one vessel, and the other two he left in a port called Canada, with 300 men; and this is what the said Breton told him; and he also told him that the said Robert[val] went on to the said port and came up with the said Jacques on the way, and they spoke together, and Jacques told him that because Robert[val] told him to come back with him, he would not, but wished to go over to France; and so the said Jacques went to France, and Robert[val] continued his course. And that the said Robert[val] had four ships with many articles for women, and cows and oxen and sheep, and all things; and that it is a very good land, flat and fertile for much grain; and that it is a very healthy land, and the said Breton told him all this, and that he even carried horses and workmen to build houses, and all things necessary to found a settlement and people it. Asked the whereabouts of this Breton who told him this: said that this witness was ill on the road, and the Breton went on to France. Asked when he left: said that as far as he remembered, more than eight days ago. Asked whether he knows the direction he followed: said that all he can say is that he believes he passed through this town of Fuenterrabia or by the Bilboa[11] Pass; further said that from La Rochelle to the port where witness took his cargo is a distance of 660 leagues, and to the port where the said Jacques went, called Canada, 800 leagues; and before reaching Canada, about half-way, that is 400 leagues, he went up a river and found fresh water for drinking; and the entrance is called Grand Bay,[12] and its width from one shore to the other is twelve leagues, and entering the river they went two leagues inland; and he further stated that the said Breton told him that there is wine, millet, herbs, and all kinds of animals for meat in that land, which is very healthy, and the people very well clothed in skins of deer, sheep, and cows. Asked what wind is favourable to entering the river: said he was told the entrance could be made in all winds, but wind from the east and east to west is more favourable than any. And that five years ago this witness was at the said harbour called Grand Bay, and fifty leagues farther on at a port called Brest,[13] where he loaded his ship with a cargo of cod, and there are no houses but only huts made of the bark of trees;

10 About a bushel
11 Bilbao, capital of the Province of Vizcaya
12 The western end of the Strait of Belle Isle
13 Probably Bonne Esperance Harbour, inside the Strait of Belle Isle

and there is an abundance of cattle and birds of all kinds, and skins, and the people trade in marten skins and other skins, and those who go there take all kinds of ironware. And that the Indians understand any language, French, English, and Gascon, and their own tongue. Asked whether he knows, or has heard, that any Spanish ships had been to those ports: said, No. Asked whether he knows that any Spaniards have settled in those parts: said that all he knows or has heard is that five ships from Spain, seven from Portugal, and one from England were in Terra Nova at the same time engaged in the fishery, and have returned, that two were from Corio,[14] and three from San Sebastian;[15] and this is the truth under seal of the oath he had sworn, and he did not sign, as he said he could not write.

The said Martin de Actalecu, resident of the town of Fuenterrabia, forty years of age, or thereabouts, having taken the customary oath, being questioned, answered as follows:

Was asked to declare all he knows or has heard concerning the journey to the Indies made by Jacques Cartier and Roberval, the time of their leaving, their destination, the number of ships, the ports they entered and why, and what they did, and all that he knows of this matter, what he has seen, or had heard say: said that in the month of April of last year, that is 1541, this witness was with his ship at La Rochelle, taking in provisions to proceed to Terra Nova for the cod fishery; and in the said month, having victualled and procured the salt he required, he set sail; and according to what he heard in La Rochelle, Jacques Cartier was in St Malo and Roberval with him making preparations, and that he was told that Roberval remained behind with three vessels, which were not ready, and Jacques Cartier, by order of the King of France, set out with seven vessels for the Indies during the said month of April of last year. And this witness was in Terra Nova in the month of June, and being employed in fishing he heard from certain sailors from French ships who were also engaged in the fishery in the ports of Terra Nova, that the said Jacques passed them and took from them wine and bread, and some shallops which they were taking for fishing; and that he went on and reached a port called Grand Bay. And from thence, so the French sailors told him, he

14 Corunna (?)

15 The capital of Guipúzcoa

proceeded in a northerly direction to a port they have discovered called Canada which is more than 250 leagues from Grand Bay, as they told him; and they further told him that his ships were in the form of an armada, and carried men and workmen to build houses and to form a settlement. And that later in Canada the carpenters working there were killed; for they found the Indians there fierce and valiant, and their arms were lances and bows and arrows; but that in the port of Grand Bay and several leagues farther on they found a more kindly people. Asked whether he heard that the said Jacques had touched at the Islands of the Azores, or other parts: said, No. Asked whether he had heard what kind of a land is that of Grand Bay and Canada: said that it is a very cold country, producing very little food. Asked whether he has heard what river they went up to reach Canada: said that the said French told him that the said Jacques said that he was going up a river, and that he took away their fishing shallops for the purpose, because the ships could not go up it; and that about four months ago, when witness was fishing in a port of Terra Nova called the Spear Islands[16] in the month of June, the said Jacques came there with three ships, for he had sent back the other four the previous year to victual for this year, and he came with the other three. A shallop with some of his men came to witness's ship and came aboard, the said Jacques being himself in another port, and the companions of the said Jacques told witness and other masters that the said Jacques had wintered with the three ships in Canada, which is situated on the river which is entered through Grand Bay, and that he had put on shore some carpenters to build houses, whom the Indians had murdered. And that being in that district they had discovered mines of gold, silver, and precious stones, and found pearls, and that they carried ten barrels of gold ore and seven of silver, and seven quintals[17] of pearls and precious stones; and the gold mine was of good quality, and they returned very rich. And the said Jacques, passing seven leagues from where this witness was, met with Roberval,[18] who had two ships, and Lartigue had another, which made three ships; and that Lartigue went round by England, and was captured by the English with his ship, and

16 Perhaps the Bay of Bulls near the Spear Islands, a few miles south of St John's

17 About 700 lb.

18 In St John's Harbour

the King of England held him prisoner. And that the said Roberval wanted the said Jacques to come back with his ships and return to the said port of Canada with him; and the said Jacques would not; and the said Robert[val] went on with his two ships and the said Jacques returned to France. Asked what was the intention of the said Robert[val], was it to found settlements there, or to return forthwith: said that this witness saw the said two ships and their crews, and is of opinion that he had not the means of founding a settlement, for the men were discontented and unwilling; and if he winters there this year, he believes he will have few men left; and that they took a barrel of cider and a cask of biscuit, even from this witness. Asked if he knows whether Jacques Cartier left any men in Canada: said that he heard that he had left none but the murdered men, and others who died.

Asked if he has heard what manner of trade existed between the French and the Indians: said that he heard that they received them well, and showed them the mines, and told them that there were other mines farther inland; and that they found the pearls at the edge of the river bank, and that they shone from a distance; and he heard further that the land is very cold with much snow and ice, and when a pot of anything was put on a fire, the side to the fire was cooked, and the part not touching the fire remained uncooked; and the people are dressed in skins.

Asked whether he knows that any fleet has set sail from France for the route followed by the ships from the Spanish Indies, for the purpose of intercepting the Spanish ships: said that in returning from Terra Nova he heard that a fleet of many French ships had set sail, and that in a port of Galicia, called Artedo,[19] there were three or four of them, and this is what he knows under the seal of the oath he has sworn, and he signed his name, Martin de Actalecu.

The said Clemente de Odelica, resident of the town of Fuenterrabia, thirty-eight years of age, or thereabouts, was sworn in the customary fashion, and deposed as follows:

Asked how long ago it is since he went to Terra Nova: said that on 8 May of this year he set sail from St Jean de Luz in a vessel belonging to that place, in company with men of the said town of St Jean de Luz. Asked their destination: said they were bound for

19 A few miles northwest of Oviedo, on the north coast of Spain

Terra Nova to the Cod Fisheries. Asked what vessels had he in convoy: said there was only the ship in which witness sailed in company with Miguel de Licarca and Juan de Arsu and Juan de Urnieta and Martin de San Vicente, residents of Pasajes[20] and of Urnieta. Asked whether he knows or has heard when Jacques Cartier sailed from Britanny, whither he was bound, the number of ships and how equipped: said, No.

Asked whether he knows or has heard any news of the said Jacques Cartier or Roberval, who sailed with a fleet: said that when witness and his aforesaid companions with the said ships of St Jean de Luz were at the port called Grand Bay fishing for their cargo, during the month of July of this year, there came there three French ships, one of three masts and the other two of two masts, and the sailors of witness's ship who were from St Jean de Luz spoke to the crews of the said ships, who told them that their ships were bound for Canada, 300 leagues distant from the spot where witness was with his ship, to the west-southwest; and some of Jacques Cartier's companions who were in the said ships told the men from St Jean de Luz that Jacques Cartier, returning from Canada, had met with these three ships, and that he carried nine barrels of gold ore and seven barrels of silver, and a certain quantity of pearls and precious stones of great value. And that they were going to join their said companions, in accordance with a promise given by the captain to return at the end of August with two ships to bring necessary supplies; and that the said captain was determined to stay three years, and to subjugate the land of the Indians.

Asked whether he knows who the captain of the three ships was: said that he does not know, nor has he heard his name, and knows no more than that the men of St Jean de Luz said that he was a person of noble rank, nor did witness dare to speak to the sailors of the said Jacques [Cartier], nor to his own companions, nor to ask any questions whatever.

Asked whether he knows or has heard what wind is favourable for entering the river which goes from Grand Bay to Canada, and what is the distance: said that he heard from the men of St Jean de Luz that from Grand Bay, which is at the mouth of the river, to Canada, is 300 leagues, and that the coast runs west-southwest, and the river is seven to eight leagues wide from shore to shore, and sometimes more, sometimes less; and that there are walnut;

20 Bay of Pasajes, near Fuenterrabia

and chestnut trees on the banks, and that farther up the land juts out. And that outside in Grand Bay which is at the entrance, and in Terra Nova, the country is very cold, so much so that not until June is it possible to navigate or to enter by Grand Bay because of the cold and snow and ice, and the mountains of ice which touch the bottom of the sea, though 100 fathoms deep. Asked who are the inhabitants of this land of Grand Bay, and farther up the river: said that many savages came to his ship in Grand Bay, and they ate and drank together, and were very friendly, and the savages gave them dear and wolf skins in exchange for axes and knives and other trifles; and for people dressed in skins they are men of skill, and he believes that farther up the river the inhabitants are much the same, for they gave them to understand that one of their number was the leader in Canada. And that they killed more than thirty-five of Jacques's men, and their arms are bows and arrows and pinewood shields; and they have many boats; and there are many springs and rivers, and the country is very healthy.

Asked whether he knows or has heard that the said Jacques and his companions had found or discovered gold and silver mines, or whether the Indians told them where these were: said that he knows no more than that he heard that the said Jacques brought back the barrels and other things, as previously stated. Asked whether he knows or has heard that any Spaniards had put into those ports, or had founded any settlement there: said that he does not know, nor has he heard anything beyond that the said French from St Jean de Luz and others had said that from the port of Canada one could reach the land of Peru. Asked whether he knows or has heard that Jacques Cartier had left men behind in Canada, when he returned: said that he heard that the said Jacques had left no men behind, but had brought back all he had. Asked whether he knows or has heard that the said Jacques or Roberval had done any injury to certain Spaniards: said that he knows no more than that the captain of the three ships took a shallop and a barrel of lard from the ship where witness was, and gave them a shallop in exchange; and that they took another shallop from another French ship, and he knows no more than this. Asked whether on the outward or homeward journey they had met with any Spanish ship: said neither in going nor returning. Asked whether he knows or has heard that the said Jacques or anyone else had sailed with a fleet against the ships from the Spanish Indies: said he does not know, and has not heard; and this is the truth under seal of the oath he has sworn, and he knows nothing further; and he signed his name, Clemente de Odelica.

The said Miguel de Liçarça, resident of Pasajas near Fuenterrabia, about thirty years of age, little more or less, being sworn, was questioned concerning the deposition made by the said Clemente; and said that this witness was aboard a vessel from St Jean de Luz with the said Clemente, and witness asked that the latter's deposition be read to him; and upon its being read to him, witness said that he had heard the same things as declared by the said Clemente, and neither knows nor has heard anything further than what is contained in the deposition, and it is the truth, by the oath he has sworn; and he signed his name, Miguel de Liçarça.

The said Juan de Arsu, resident of Pasajes near Fuenterrabia, twenty-eight years of age, or thereabouts, being questioned concerning the deposition made by the said Clemente, asked that it be read to him, since he knew neither more nor less than the said Clemente, as they were together when anything relating to this matter took place; and upon its being read to him, he said that he declared the same, and it was the truth, and he neither knew nor had heard anything further; under seal of the oath he had taken, and he did not sign, as he could not write. Antonio de Ubilla.

The said Martin de San Vicente, resident of Fuenterrabia, forty years of age, or thereabouts, being questioned concerning the said Clemente's disposition: said that they were all together aboard the said ship of St Jean de Luz, and that the declaration made by the said Clemente, which had been read to him, is the truth, and he heard the same; under seal of the oath he had sworn, and he neither knew nor has heard anything further; and he did not sign, as he said he could not write. Antonio de Ubilla.

The said Juan de Urnieta, resident of Urnieta, thirty years of age, or thereabouts, was questioned concerning the said Clemente's deposition, and said, under seal of the oath he had taken, that he had been in the company of the said Clemente and the other three companions, and they had all seen and heard the same thing: and the deposition of the said Clemente being read to him, he said that it was the truth, and witness declared the same, and he had not heard and knew nothing further, under seal of the oath he had taken; and he did not sign, as he could not write.

And I, the said Antonio de Ubilla, notary public, signed all the aforesaid declarations with the said witnesses, and by order of the said Captain General I caused these seven pages to be copied from the original, which remains in my possession, and in witness of the truth thereof I have affixed my customary signature, etc. ANTONIO DE UBILLA, Notary.

18 CARTIER TAKES PART IN A 'NOISE'

20 May 1541

On the said day of Friday [20 May 1541].

Etienne Mur *dit* Alexandre, manufacturer of missile weapons, dwelling in this town, aged XXXIIII or thereabouts, a witness sworn to tell the truth, & interrogated by court order about the complaint by Jean Brillault, deposes that last Wednesday in the afternoon of the said day, as the speaker was in his shop working at his craft, he heard quarrelsome language which was coming from a certain Pierre, he does not know his surname, who is a trumpeter & is married to one of the daughters of Marie Cochon, on one hand; & Jean Brillault, a shoemaker and neighbour of the person speaking, this Brillault being in his workshop, on the other; concerning some shoe-making work that the said Brillault had done for the said trumpeter for which he was offering the said Brillault seven *sous* two *deniers* and the said Brillault was saying that he owed him & had promised seven *sous* and a half; & that in addition he had since done other work for him. Upon which the said Pierre said to the said Brillault that he had lied like a wretch; to which the said Brillault said that he was a wretch like him; & straightway the speaker heard the scraping of a sword, because of which he suspected that it was the said Pierre who had drawn his sword. And the speaker went outside & saw the said Pierre, that he was slashing about with his naked sword in the shop of the said Brillault, and then he saw a last that was thrown from the said shop that struck the said Pierre in the face. And thereupon arrived Maître Jacques Cartier, who blamed the said Pierre & put an end to the quarrel. And then came out Jamette Hobes, wife of the said Brillault, who complained to the said Cartier, showing a hand all covered with blood, saying that it had been the said Pierre who had wounded her in this way. And as the said Brillault came out of his said shop complaining to the said Cartier about the said Pierre, Jean Verger, a carpenter, arrived, who without more ado took hold of the said Brillault & in the presence of the said Cartier & several others threw him by the hair to the ground & punched him several times & would have given him more if it had not been for the said Cartier. And that is how he deposes.

Louise Mur, wife of Jean Galliot, aged XXVIII, witness sworn to tell the truth & interrogated the said day & year, deposes that she being last Wednesday in the afternoon of the said day near the house of Villedieu, opposite the shop of Jean Brillault, shoemaker, there arrived Pierre, son-in-law of Marie Cochon, a trumpeter, who asked for his shoes from the said Jean Brillault who was in the said shop and offered him VII *sous* IIII *deniers*; and the said Brillault said that in the morning he had offered him VII *sous* VI *deniers* & that moreover he had since done some other work for him. Whereupon a quarrel broke out, & the said Pierre drew his sword & slashed about with it several times in the said shop, she did not see that he struck anyone, nor did she see the said Brillault's wife there. And thereupon arrived Maître Jacques Cartier, who put an end to the quarrel, & as the said Brillault & his wife, which woman came to complain to the said Cartier & show him her hand all covered with blood, saying that it had been the said Pierre who had wounded her in this way, this Brillault and his wife standing outside the said shop, there arrived Jean Verger, a carpenter, brother-in-law of the said trumpeter, who without doing or saying anything else took the said Brillault by the hair & threw him to the ground and struck him several blows, & the said Cartier separated them. And that is how she deposes.

Having seen the attestations of the two witnesses here above & the complaint of a party, the prosecutor of the said court demands personal writ of summons & by arrest against a certain Pierre, trumpeter, son-in-law of Marie Cochon, & Jean du Verger. Executed the XXth of May VCXLI (541 sic). N. Jocet prosecutor.

19 STATEMENT OF CARTIER'S ACCOUNT

21 June 1544

(Collation done by us Etienne Gravé and Julien Lesieu, royal notaries of the court of Rennes established at Saint-Malo and Châteauneuf, respectively, on the originals presented to us by Jacques Odièvre, a merchant living in the said Saint-Malo, one of the successors of the said late Jacques Cartier, and in addition the said Odièvre has presented to us an account written on paper and signed Jac. Cartier, containing seventy sheets of writing, the commencement of which to as far as the third sheet verso only, with the conclusion that appears on the last sheet of the said account, we have inserted word for word, as follows, and no more because of the length of the said account.)

In order that by you, Maître Robert Legoupil, counsellor of the King our Liege and lieutenant in the Admiralty Court in the courtroom of the *Table de Marbre* in Rouen, commissioner appointed by the said seigneur to see and hear the accounts of the receipt, advances, and expenditure that Jacques Cartier, captain and pilot by royal authority on the voyage made recently by him to the land of Canada and other places, the item and ground of the said accounts be examined fully and completely, at the same time to hear and examine the differences between the Sieur de Roberval and the said Cartier, four commissioners having been commissioned in association with you according to and at the wish of the said commission, this Cartier is ready to give an account and offers to do as this commission desires, and according as the said seigneur desires. And firstly, this Cartier says and recognizes that forty-five thousand *livres tournois* had been ordered by the said seigneur for the execution of the said voyage to be given to Jean François de La Roque, Sieur de Roberval, and to the said Cartier to use and change for the things needed for such an expedition, mentioned more fully by verbal arrangement, set forth and itemized in writing on behalf of the said seigneur by Maître Guillaume Preudhomme, M. the [receiver] general of Normandy, and the said La Roque and Cartier, and attached to these presents, of which forty-five thousand *livres* there remain fifteen thousand in the hands of the said La Roque, of which he took responsibility, as is shown by instruments signed by the said La Roque and Charles de Kermarec, Sieur of the said place, and the said Cartier, dated the seventh day of May of the year one thousand five hundred and forty-one, drawn up at Saint-Malo, which instruments, together with other documents, in the event of denial by the said La Roque, you are requested to look at and to allow the said Cartier, his supporting documents and defending arguments, to use, as you will see rightly to concern the remainder of the said sum which is thirty thousand *livres*, constituting two-thirds of the forty-five thousand *livres*, which thirty thousand *livres* being delivered to the said Cartier by the agency of Maître Jean Duval, treasurer of the said seigneur's privy purse, for which sum the said Cartier makes himself entirely responsible and offers at this time to demonstrate by sections and items if the distribution of those moneys had been carried out by him honestly, this said Cartier requesting an inspection and to be heard beforehand to reply to what might prove to be ambiguous and uncertain to be found, and to prove after the viva voce by means of documents and authentic supplementary instruments, and requesting, as to this, that they be seen, heard, and received according as to whether right and reason presume in favour of the said Cartier, even in those matters that cannot otherwise be heard, for which the said Cartier assumes the responsibility for proof, recognizance, and probation, if more ample information is required. The said Cartier further recognizes having received from the said Sieur de Roberval the sum of thirteen hundred and fifty *livres tournois* in six hundred *écus soleil*, which the said Sieur de Roberval borrowed from François Corsnier, bourgeois of Saint-Malo, which were employed separately from the payments and investments of the said Cartier and for which sum the said Sieur de Roberval has since given surety to the said Crosnier, Alloncze de Civille, Sieur de Saint-Martin, and consequently the said Cartier remains accountable for thirty-one thousand three hundred and fifty *livres*.

Which responsibility being acknowledged, it remains to hear the calculation of what is at his charge and when that is known, to compare it to the said charge and see who will lose.

But before proceeding, it remains to ascertain and fully foresee the King's intention [?] the expedition of the said voyage, five ships are to be supplied by the said Roberval and Cartier, in part by outright purchase and on charter for the others, all of four hundred tons burden, for which taken all round eight thousand five hundred *livres* are ordered for all of the said ships for carrying out the said voyage, as is fully contained in the said verbal transaction agreed upon in the name of the said seigneur and by Maître Guillaume Preudhomme, and reiterated again and specified by the said Duval's receipt, when he took it, that he handed over the said thirty thousand *livres* to the said Cartier, and for more ample specification of what the said Cartier had done and employed for the execution of the entire said voyage, and this by the express command of the Sieur de Roberval, lieutenant for the King on the said voyage, which will be shown to suffice, the said Cartier states, maintains, and affirms that he employed honestly and better than for his own affairs eight thousand five hundred *livres* for the payment and repair in outright purchase of part of the said ships and in the settlement of the freight and chartering for the others, which five ships he supplied and paid by himself out of the said sum of thirty-one thousand three hundred and fifty *livres* that he had, being of more than fifty tons burden beyond what was in the contents of the said verbal transaction, and what was commanded by the said seigneur for the execution of the said voyage as far as the five ships were concerned, all by order of the said Roberval, as will be shown by explicit letters and instructions from him, wherefore the said Cartier requests that the said sum of eight thousand five hundred *livres* be adjudged to him in deduction and allowance from the said sum of thirty thousand *livres* and for which he is responsible, in consideration of the debt that he assumed, also that when the said money from the King was not at hand, he had put in his own at great risk for the service of the said seigneur, as will be shown you when it will be the moment to speak of the third ship, which could not be paid for as was the intention of the said seigneur, but in the absence of the money that the said Roberval had and was supposed to produce from one day to the next to do what would remain for that voyage, Cartier was compelled by him to take the other two, at great risk to himself, at the chartering fee, as is fully contained in the said article that the said Cartier puts at your option, Messieurs, as representatives of the said seigneur in this present accounting, to deduct in his favour the said sum adjudged him by the said verbal transaction, for the said five ships, which is eight thousand five hundred *livres*, to which he adds what the said Cartier spent for the *Emér-*

illon, which belonged to the King, and for repairing it, proof of which will be presented to you by an inquiry made upon it by persons worthy of belief in the matter, which amounts to the sum of one thousand *livres*, of which the said Cartier offers to give ample certification, and takes upon himself as to this to present sufficient proof or else accept that the cost of the said two ships the *Hermine* and the *Emérillon* is four thousand five hundred *livres*, and as far as the third ship is concerned, you will set for seventeen months that it was on the said Cartier's said voyage, and for eight months that it took returning to seek the said Roberval in the said Canada, at the chartering risk; that the other two will be two thousand five hundred *livres*, and, for the two others that were on the said voyage, six months at one hundred *livres* per month, that is to say twelve hundred *livres*, thus finally it would be eight thousand two hundred *livres*, the said third ship remaining the property of the said Cartier and receiving it from the King, the return done at his rate with the repairs to the said *Emérillon*, it will be found that eight thousand seven hundred *livres* were employed by the said Cartier, which the said Cartier requests be attributed to him in deduction from the charge for which he is accountable, which is thirty-one thousand three hundred and fifty *livres*, and thus, deducting eight thousand seven hundred *livres*, there will remain only twenty-two thousand six hundred and fifty *livres*, for which the said Cartier is accountable, and this deducted from it and put on account against it.

This present account has been seen, heard, and examined by us, Robert Legoupil, esquire, bachelor of Laws, lieutenant general in the jurisdiction of the Admiralty at the *Table de Marbre* in the law courts in Rouen of the high and mighty seigneur Monseigneur the Admiral of France and King's commissioner in these parts, in the presence of Maîtres Robert Lelarge, Pierre Caradas lawyer and King's attorney, Jean Loue, clerk of the court of my said seigneur the Admiral, Thomas Saldaigne, Alvara de La Tour, François Maillard, and Jean Noury, summoned by us in accordance with the commission addressed and sent to us by the King, the hearing, reckoning, and calculation of the same juxtaposed with the laws and written in the margin of this said account and the report on it prepared and signed by us, and of the above-mentioned officers and commissioners, in the opinion and judgment of the said commissioners, from the reckoning and calculation that they have done of it, it appears that the said Cartier used and expended for the ships, provisions, settlement of accounts, merchandise, interest on loans, advances, and other expenses met by the said Cartier up to the rendering of this said account for the preparation and expedition of the said voyage, the sum of thirty-nine thousand nine hundred and eighty-eight *livres* four *sous* six *deniers tournois.*

The said Cartier recognizes having received from the King our Liege for the expedition and undertaking of the said voyage the sum of thirty thousand *livres tournois*, through the agency of Jean Duval, treasurer of the King's purse.

In addition he recognizes having received through the agency of the said La Roque, Sieur de Roberval, six hundred *écus soleil* worth thirteen hundred *livres.*

Thus it appears that in awarding the said expenses and moneys advanced, there would be owing to the said Cartier over and above his said account for the undertaking of the said voyage for having advanced and promised to pay more than was received, the sum of eight thousand six hundred and thirty-eight *livres* four *sous* six *deniers tournois*, according to the reservations and conditions contained in the said laws and said report. In witness thereof, we, the above-named lieutenant, officers, and commissioners, have signed the present and had it sealed with the great seal of the said Admiralty court on a cord passed through the said account, which contains seventy sheets, on the twenty-first day of June in the year of grace one thousand five hundred and forty-four. As given under the hand of: R. Legoupil, R. Lebarge, P. Carada, Thomas de Saldaigne, Alvaro de La Tour, F. Maillard, Jean Noury, J. Loue, and sealed with a seal of red wax attached to a silk ribbon passed through the said account.

(Which insertion here above, consisting of the commencement of the said account and its conclusion, we the said notaries have also faithfully collated on the original, and they contain the résumés of the letters and insertions here above, fourteen sheets of writing, not including the one immediately following, on which we will set our marks, and the said fourteen sheets are the writings of Sébastien Odièvre, brother of the said Jacques. And the originals of the said letters and account have remained with the said Jacques Odièvre and with his consent the present résumé delivered to the captain Jacques Noël, of the said Saint-Malo and one of the successors of the said late Cartier, requesting it for his use and that of the said Jacques Odièvre and their jointly interested parties as may be deemed proper. Drawn up at the said Saint-Malo in the office of the said Etienne Gravé on the twenty-sixth day of November in the year one thousand five hundred and eighty-seven in the forenoon. And the said Jacques Odièvre and Jacques Noël have signed, witness the royal seal here appended. As given under the hand of: Jacques Nouel, Jac. Odièvre, E. Gravé, royal notary, Jn. Lesieu, royal notary, and sealed.)

20 DEATH OF CARTIER

1 September 1557

Wednesday, the first day of September 1557, the agent and Le Gobien, attorney.

Guillaume Aoustin is ordered, in the presence of Chaton, his attorney, to appear in person on the days & at the sittings of the court.

On this said Wednesday at about five o'clock in the morning died Jacques Cartier.